The PREACHER and the PRELATE

For Zoë and Josh

Patricia Byrne is captivated by Achill Island. Her book *The Veiled Woman of Achill: Island Outrage and a Playboy Drama* was published by The Collins Press in 2012. Her memoir essay 'Milk Bottles in Limerick' was named one of the Notable Essays of the Year in *Best American Essays* 2017. Her work has featured in *New Hibernia Review*, *The Irish Times* (Irishwoman's Diary), RTÉ's *Sunday Miscellany* and *The Irish Story* among other outlets. A graduate of the NUI Galway writer programme, she lives in Limerick, Ireland. www.patriciabyrneauthor.com

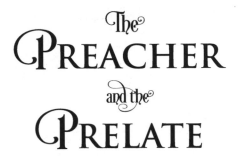

The PREACHER and the PRELATE

THE ACHILL MISSION COLONY AND
THE BATTLE FOR SOULS IN FAMINE IRELAND

PATRICIA BYRNE

MERRION
PRESS

First published in 2018 by
Merrion Press
An Imprint of Irish Academic Press
10 George's Street
Newbridge
Co. Kildare
Ireland
www.merrionpress.ie

9781785371721 (Paper)
9781785371691 (Kindle)
9781785371707 (Epub)
9781785371714 (PDF)

British Library Cataloguing in Publication Data
An entry can be found on request

Library of Congress Cataloging in Publication Data
An entry can be found on request

Interior design by www.jminfotechindia.com
Typeset in Minion Pro 11/14 pt

Cover design by www.phoenix-graphicdesign.com
Front cover: The Achill Mission Colony (National Library of Ireland).
Back cover right: Edward Nangle, St Thomas's Church, Dugort
(P. Byrne); Back cover left: the Right Rev. Dr. M'Hale, Archbishop Of
Tuam (The New York Public Library Digital Collections); Back cover
background: Slievemore, Achill (National Library of Ireland).

This is a work of nonfiction.
Research sources are cited in Endnotes.

'Achill, wind-swept and bare, heavily peat-covered, with great gaunt brown mountains rising here and there, and a wild coast hammered by the Atlantic waves on all sides but the east, has a strange charm which everyone feels, but none can fully explain.'

Robert Lloyd Praeger, *The Way That I Went*

CONTENTS

Map   ix

Acknowledgements   x

Prologue   xii

PART 1

1. Shaking the Dry Bones   3
2. The Most Destitute Spot in Ireland   12
3. Bonfires in the West   22
4. Scriptural Education   30
5. Fractured   42
6. Is it a Wafer or is it a God?   51
7. Murder   61
8. Public Scrutiny   72
9. Tenth Year   82
10. The Finger of God   91

PART 2

11. Quicksilver Illness   103
12. Death is Now Loose   107
13. Buyer of Souls   116
14. Vicious and Rotten   126

15. Feed the Children   135

16. Workhouse War   142

17. Three Women   149

18. Battle of Stones   155

19. Root and Branch Change   164

PART 3

20. Clearances   173

21. Achill Transformed   184

22. Implosion   193

23. Weapons of His Own Forging   201

Epilogue   208

Endnotes   211

Bibliography   226

Index   235

Achill Island, Ireland

Belfast

Ballina
Cavan
Newport
Westport
Croagh Patrick
Maynooth
Dublin
Galway

Limerick

Cork

Blacksod Bay
Ridge Point

Slievemore
Dugort
Bullsmouth
Inishbiggle

Croaghaun
Dooagh
Keel
Bunacurry

Achill
Head
Keem
Cashel
Keel Bay

Mweelin

ATLANTIC
OCEAN
Dooega
Achill Sound

Corraun Peninsula

Kildownet/Ailt

Darby's Point
Achillbeg

Scale (km)
0   5   10

Clew Bay

Acknowledgements

Researching and writing this book has been a long journey and I am grateful for the support of many along the way.

Achill is a place that never ceases to astound me with its beauty and excite me with its richness of history and folklore. I have made numerous trips to the island in all seasons and in all weathers, and left with journals bursting with anecdotes and musings. Writing this book has filled me with a deep admiration for the people of Achill through the generations.

It was while on a residency at the Heinrich Böll cottage in Dugort that I first walked on to the site that was the Achill Mission colony, and where my appetite was whetted for this story. I am indebted for the support of the Heinrich Böll committee, particularly Sheila McHugh and John McHugh, over almost a decade, and for the opportunity to present on the topic of this book at the Heinrich Böll Weekend in May 2015.

On my frequent visits to the island I have enjoyed hospitality and sustenance at Gray's Guesthouse in Dugort, Bervie Guesthouse and The Beehive in Keel and numerous other hostelries around the island.

I am grateful for the inputs received from Dollie Darlington, Pat Gallagher, John 'Twin' McNamara, Anne O'Dowd, Mary Jo O'Keefe, John O'Shea and Tim Stevenson. Brian Thompson generously allowed me to use certain Achill photographs.

For me, one of the gratifying things in researching and writing this book has been the opportunity to spend hours on end in wonderful libraries and I wish to thank the staff of the following: Castlebar County Library, Cavan Johnston County Library, Dublin Diocesan Archives, Irish Church Missions Archives,

National Archives of Ireland, National Folklore Collection UCD, National Library of Ireland, NUI Maynooth Library, Representative Church Body Library, RIA Library and Trinity College Library. It was encouraging to have material for the book published and broadcast in a number of outlets and I am grateful to *The Irish Times* (An Irishwoman's Diary), *The Irish Story*, *New Hibernia Review*, the *Western People*, and RTÉ *Sunday Miscellany*.

Hilary Tulloch has been an immense support throughout this writing journey. She welcomed me into her home, generously shared family archival material, pointed out sources that I missed, occasionally challenged my views and, always, encouraged me when the task of finishing the book seemed daunting.

Patrick Comerford cast a forensic eye over my draft manuscript and I value and appreciate his insightful and gracious comments.

It has been good to take a break from the writing work through walks and rambles on Irish and Camino trails. I am grateful for the friendship and encouragement of those in the Duck walkers and the Gawbata walking group who regularly enquired about my writing progress and wondered why the project was taking so long.

Kathleen Thorne and David Rice, Killaloe, have been constant in their encouragement as they have been to numerous writers from all over Ireland over many years.

Thanks to IAP/Merrion Press for accepting my manuscript for publication and for the professional inputs in getting the story to print.

Finally, thanks to my family, Mick, Breon, Jill, Michael and Gemma, for all the days filled with love and fun.

Patricia Byrne
Limerick
March 2018

Prologue

A chill Island: I am sitting in a pub on a western island off Ireland's Atlantic coast in a crowded, damp room after an island outing as part of an arts weekend programme. Coats steam across the backs of chairs, wellington boots squeak and black Guinness overflows on white formica table-tops. Cold hands reach greedily for sandwich triangles piled high on plates and cups rise to receive the flow of steaming tea from large stainless-steel teapots.

We are within shouting distance of the Atlantic Ocean across which the rain has surged through the morning. Behind us are the hill slopes where we stood a half-hour ago among the stone ruins of what was once an outpost of an island mountain colony: the Achill Mission – a nineteenth-century settlement that sought to evangelise and civilise an isolated west-of-Ireland island community.

People settle, grateful for the warmth of a glowing fire and sustenance. It is 180 years since Edward Nangle landed on the northern shores of this island to establish his enterprise on the mountain slopes of Slievemore. A spectacle soon appeared, one never before witnessed by the island people. A village of neat slated houses sprang up and land was reclaimed on the barren mountain. In a place where education was entirely absent, schools buzzed with children learning the Bible in their native tongue. There was a hospital and a dispensary, and a hotel soon followed bringing visitors in droves to view the island's awesome natural beauty. Hundreds received employment and food during the Great Famine years, saving many from certain calamity.

There is a visceral pull to this story, as if I am being lured back to an ancestral space. My birthplace is less than an hour's drive from this island in a series of townlands where all of my great-grandparents were born in the middle decades of the nineteenth century when the Achill Mission thrived and food famine swept the country. I have a sense that I can delve deeper into my own story by following the twists and turns of this island's narrative.

The speaker is forceful. The time has come to reclaim the Achill Mission and its founder, Edward Nangle, whose achievement was impressive given the remoteness and barrenness of the place and the destitution of the people he came to save. His legacy is one of modernisation, enterprise, education, tourism development and advancement – civilisation. The time is surely right to look upon the Achill Mission and its founder in a new light.

The room appears to quieten, the rattle of crockery and cutlery no longer deafening. It is an uneasy quiet, like the calm before a storm, or an intake of breath. There is a disquiet in the audience and a sense that not all present agree with the speaker's assessment. Within minutes there is an outburst of charged, passionate exchanges as the legacy of Edward Nangle and his colony are fiercely contested.

'We are talking about the Achill Mission, a sectarian, ugly and obnoxious episode in our history.'

'That's not the whole story,' came the retort. 'Did the Achill Mission not save the lives of hundreds of islanders during the Great Famine, by giving the people employment and feeding the children in the schools? That can't be forgotten.'

'Nangle detested our people, their religion, their culture, their laughter and drunkenness. For him, they were savage, uneducated and degenerate barbarians.'

'What about the mission women and their hardship?,' asked another. 'Eliza Nangle was a broken woman, and her remains and those of her children were laid to rest here in Achill on the slopes of Slievemore.'

These are sharp, angry words. Watching on, I vacillate, swayed in turn by the urgings of both sides, transfixed by the inflamed passions in the room.

'Edward Nangle was a vicious, vile, vindictive man. He robbed us of our most precious possessions, offering our ancestors food in return for their faith in their hour of greatest need.'

'Those are unfair charges,' a man objected loudly. The Achill Mission initiated development and modernisation on the island and took the place out of the dark ages. Open your eyes and you can see the signs of that work all around to this very day.

There is no let-up in the rancorous din, disagreement and discord, arguments for and against. It feels like a hot house. I hear a tumbling rush of waters in the pub gutters and the misted windows run with drips, obliterating the Achill heath outdoors.

What are the rights and the wrongs of the Achill Mission, and how can these distant nineteenth-century events excite such passions?

I realise that, beneath the emotive exchanges, large and weighty issues loom. What happens when an outside force with a vigorous agenda descends upon an isolated community, when the forces of religion, imperialism, famine and landlordism coalesce like a whirlpool on a remote Atlantic island? What brought a stream of nineteenth-century commentators to Achill to observe with fascination this island settlement?

Is this, when all is said and done, a narrative about the fusion of good and bad and the seduction of idealism by other forces?

I am hooked by the story. I decide to retrace these events, walk the places where they were played out, search the archives, and listen to the stories handed down by the people.

PART 1

On a winter's night, 6 January 1839, a woman listens in the darkness of her mountainside home. The wind strengthens by the hour; it is more terrifying than any island gales Eliza Nangle has experienced in five gruelling Achill winters. Her husband is absent, away on important engagements, for he must travel to raise funds for the Achill Mission's work and for the family's survival. Perhaps her three small daughters rush to her for comfort as successive squalls roll up the mountain, Slievemore, to a screaming crescendo. It is the 'Night of the Big Wind' – the most devastating storm ever recorded in Ireland, which will leave hundreds dead in its wake. What goes through her mind? Perhaps she looks out into the darkness where, less than a hundred paces away, the remains of her three infant sons rest: one for each of her first three years on this island. Slievemore will become her resting place too – her body, blood and bones forever sunk into the island mountain where Atlantic winds furiously pound.

– Patricia Byrne

CHAPTER ONE

Shaking the Dry Bones

At precisely midday on Friday, 26 January 1827, a stern man in his sixties, known for his mild manner in private and his obstinate views in public rose to address a gathering in a packed courthouse in the mid-northern Irish town of Cavan. John Maxwell-Barry, 5th Baron Farnham and head of an expansive 30,000-acre estate, ought to have been wintering in England with his wife, Lady Lucy, to escape the winter dampness that seeped into his bones. But he could not leave, for he was swept up in developments which could well drag pathetic Ireland out of its stupor.

The town crackled with religious commotion, the agitation reported in the *Freeman's Journal* with a suggestion – in something of an overstatement – that 'recent events have directed all eyes towards Cavan', and that those events could have implications far beyond the town.[1] For months, Roman Catholics in Cavan had been renouncing their faith and converting to Protestantism in a wave of evangelical fervour.[2] Bulletins on the town's walls carried daily updates, and hired men walked the streets with placards announcing the latest conversions. Lord Farnham himself claimed that 453 people had defected from Catholicism since October: evidence, surely, that the conversion of thousands of Ireland's inhabitants to Protestantism was no longer 'a matter of Utopian speculation'.[3] He believed that Cavan was at the nerve centre of nothing less than a new moral order in Ireland. It was the clever coincidence of a system that both improved the moral and practical conditions of the tenants while boosting the efficiency of the landlord's estate.

Public notices announced the purpose of the Cavan courthouse assembly that winter day. There were plans afoot to establish a new society, one that would promote the progress of the Reformation and Protestantism across the whole of Ireland. Many of those gathering to listen to Lord Farnham believed that the spirit of evangelical revival would sweep out from Cavan like wildfire, delivering Ireland from the forces of the antichrist in the shape of Roman Catholicism and its priests. Cavan had to seize the moment. This was the point in time when a number of factors coalesced to germinate a remarkable narrative: the historical phenomenon of the second reformation as the evangelical movement swept across the midlands region and the southern belt of Ulster; the fusion of this movement with economics and landlordism as exemplified in the figure of Lord Farnham and the innovative management of his estate; and a young, volatile clergyman who became caught up in the Cavan turbulence with life-changing repercussions. Out of this maelstrom emerged an astonishing series of events that reached across Ireland into an isolated island community.

On a winter's morning, the sun splashes light on the high grey walls of Farnham House, flinging thick shadows across the green pastures. Nowadays, the demesne – a modern golf and spa hotel resort – boasts several nature trails across what the hotel promotion literature describes as 'the three-hundred-year-old footprints of landed gentry'. Grazing cattle move out of the shadows into the warmth of the morning sunshine while hotel guests stroll nearby. The only embellishment on the plain building façade is the Farnham coat of arms incorporating the family motto: *Je suis prêt* (I am ready).

It is a brisk twenty-minute walk along the old estate road pathway to the secluded Farnham Lough where decaying leaves of beech, oak and sycamore are soft underfoot. Perhaps Lord Farnham strolled here before heading out through the arch of the stone perimeter estate wall on the short journey into Cavan town. He was a landlord on whom the wellbeing of many tenants rested; he was also a man imbued with the sureties of his faith and a conviction that the religious reformation of the people was good not just for his estate and tenants, but for the progress of the whole of Ireland.

Sectarian tension seethed through 1820s Ireland as agitation for full Catholic emancipation grew. Among the landed classes across the southern stretch of the province of Ulster, including Cavan, a counter force was at work: it was the Protestant evangelical movement known as the 'second reformation'.[4] Evangelicalism and landlordism combined in reacting to the growing assertiveness of Irish Roman Catholicism as evangelical Protestantism and economic progress became inextricably linked. The evangelical crusade aimed at nothing less than the moral reformation of the minds and hearts of the Irish peasantry and Cavan was leading the campaign. The movement was underlined by a belief that the Protestant Irish had the moral character and enterprise essential to economic progress, while Catholicism and its priests were held responsible for the wretched state of the country and its peasantry.

It was five years since John Maxwell-Barry had inherited the Farnham estate on his uncle's death and he had wasted no time. Believing that there was nothing more injurious to good estate management than idle, slothful tenants and the influence of the Catholic Church and its priests, he immediately set about the transformation of his estate with a neat formula: break the hold of Catholicism on the tenants, promote evangelical education with good moral living, and improved estate efficiency would follow. It was a win-win for landlord and tenant and the landlord quickly circulated his plans in a pamphlet to over 100 of his tenants.[5] He told them that he wanted them to prosper, to be virtuous and happy, and to live good moral lives. If they did so, they would receive his praise, his support and his practical help; but all evildoers would be punished, without favour or leniency. They, his tenants, must use their own industry and exertions to improve their lot, remove all evil from their lives and grow in prosperity.

Education and religion were at the heart of Lord Farnham's system. He encouraged parents to send their children to the estate schools, to train them in virtue and sobriety, and withdraw them from 'dances, ball-alleys, cock-fights and all other scenes of dissipation'.[6] The schools were strictly scriptural: classes opened and closed with the singing of a hymn, a reading from the Bible and a prayer.

Soon, change was visible across the Farnham estate. In place of run-down shebeens there were neat slated dwellings, whitewashed inside and out, with perimeter fences, painted gates and a kitchen garden for fruit and vegetables – an attractive vista, like in a contemporary glossy property brochure. Tenants could purchase building materials, shrubs and implements from the estate depot at reduced prices. On no account were pigs or cattle permitted indoors, and an area of six feet in width had to be kept clear and clean around each dwelling. As to the moral improvement of his tenants, Lord Farnham did not leave this to chance, but introduced the most innovative part of his new management system: a special moral agent took charge of the moral and religious development of the tenants to the exclusion of any commercial duties. The role was central to the new order of converting the native Catholic population to the reformed religion.

Cavan town everywhere bears the stamp of the Farnham family, including the wide elegant Farnham Street built by the 5th Baron's predecessors to cater for the burgeoning coach trade of the early nineteenth century. Here is the Farnham Centre and the Johnston County Library with a statue of a grim-looking 7th Baron Farnham at the entrance. Inside the library are the faded pages of Lord Farnham's courthouse speech with its powerful message: convert the people to the reformed faith and prosperity and civilised living will follow. It was an address that brimmed with confidence and assurance.

Up until very recently, he told his audience, he was of the opinion that the superstitious attachment of the people to their priests was so strong, and the sway of the clergy over the minds of their flocks so absolute, that the idea of them adopting the reformed faith seemed far-fetched. But all that had changed in recent months, ever since 8 October when seventeen people had arrived at his home and read their recantations, rejecting Catholicism in favour of the reformed faith. Since then, the recantations had continued unabated on each successive Sunday and he was now convinced that the demeaning grip of Catholicism on the people could finally be broken forever.

It was no surprise, he said, that a fierce backlash against their work was underway. Had not four Catholic prelates – including the firebrand John MacHale from the County Mayo diocese of Killala – arrived in the town just a couple of weeks earlier, and made totally unfounded allegations that money, jobs and other briberies were used to bring about the Cavan conversions. They had even falsely claimed that ignorant and starving people had been carried in carts to Farnham House to revoke their faith.

'There is,' said Lord Farnham, 'no thinking man who does not perceive in the preponderance of the Roman Catholic religion in this country, the fruitful source of most of the calamities and agitations with which it is afflicted.'[7] Together, they must emancipate the Irish people from these chains and rescue them from their degrading bondage. It was their duty to advance the Reformation in Ireland.

The meeting overwhelmingly agreed to establish 'The Cavan Association for Promoting the Reformation' and nominated Lord Farnham as president. It was, for him, an unforgettable day and he returned, satisfied, to the comforts of his fine home where he and Lady Lucy planned to dine as usual with their new moral agent, appointed to his post a mere nine months earlier. The young man and his daughter had become as family to the childless Farnham couple.

***

On 19 February, three weeks after the Cavan courthouse meeting, William Krause sat at his desk in his cottage home on the Farnham estate, overlooking a delightful parkland vista, as he wrote a letter to his sister. It was two and a half years since his wife's death and the cottage was a tranquil refuge for him and his small daughter who, he wrote, was delighting him with her infant prattle.[8]

A reserved young man, described by some as aloof and cold, he was born in the West Indies and served as an officer of the British army at Waterloo. Well-educated and fashionable in his early years, a personal illness and his wife's death brought about a change in character and a conversion experience now reflected in an exaggerated religious tone. Lord Farnham had selected him personally for the linchpin position of moral agent and he relished the work. It had been a hectic few months, leaving the cottage early in the morning and seldom returning until nine or ten at night; at times he was absent for two to three days at a time, calling to schools throughout the estate and visiting as many tenants as possible to improve their habits and moral living.

He was buoyed up by his new responsibilities, somewhat awed by what he perceived as the importance of what was happening on the estate: 'Farnham's system is altogether new in this country and the eyes of all Ireland are upon him.' By improving the lot of his tenants, he was certain that his employer was inducing Catholics to free themselves from the bondage of their priests; if only other gentry across Ireland would likewise exert themselves, he believed that the Irish people would desert Catholicism and flock in their thousands to the reformed church. He knew beyond doubt that, in Cavan, he was at the centre of seismic and historic events: 'In Ireland there is a shaking of the dry bones, and a stir throughout the country, such as never was known in the land.'[9]

Not far from William Krause's peaceful cottage, another young man was feverishly absorbing the intense evangelical fervour in the Cavan district. He was witnessing first hand an exceptional moment in Irish history, the fervour of which permeated his being to bring about a psychological and spiritual tipping point. An accidental conversation with William Krause affected Edward Nangle profoundly.

***

A dozen miles to the south-west of Cavan is the townland of Arva, on the shores of Garty Lough beneath Bruse Mountain, at the meeting point of three of Ireland's four provinces: Connaught, Leinster and Ulster. The road winds and bends among the curving drumlin hills through a landscape of lake, woodland and hillock – a place where a person might find tranquillity and peace. A small, plain church sits on an elevation that slopes down to the lake at its rear, while a tower and porch added some years after the church's construction relieve the building's starkness.[10]

This inconspicuous place of worship was the focal point of the parish where the Trinity-educated curate, Edward Nangle, had already served for two years prior to Lord Farnham's famous Cavan address. He was absorbing the fever of evangelical excitement in the area and the exciting model of Lord Farnham's estate with its moral agency. A tall, thin, pale young man, Edward spoke in gentle tones, came across as serious and intense, and seldom appeared to smile or laugh. Yet, he could also display a surprising passion, according to a contemporary: 'when animated, the most extraordinary fire lights up his eyes'.

His father, Walter, was of a staunchly Catholic family from Kildalkey, near Athboy, County Meath. Walter Nangle's first and third wives were Catholic, his second – Edward's mother – was Protestant and died when her son was just nine years old, a loss which appears to have left him with an emotional vulnerability that manifested itself in bouts of depression and mania.[11]

Overworked in his busy Arva ministry, Edward neglected his physical wellbeing. Frequently his breakfast consisted only of a crust of oaten bread and a glass of water; and after a hard day's work, when mind and body had been taxed to their utmost strength, 'the remnant of the oaten cake and another draught of water served for a dinner in his lonely lodging'.[12] The elation of the Cavan evangelical explosion and his own psychological fragilities and poor physical wellbeing combined to bring about his personal collapse. A delicate, sensitive and overwrought personality had become strained to breaking point. He had to resign his Arva ministry, losing his only means of a livelihood and returning to his home place in Athboy.

Dr James Adams, a retired army surgeon in Athboy and a Nangle family friend, was worried about his guest who lay prostrate on his drawing room sofa, unable to speak, using sign language like one deaf and dumb. The young clergyman's condition was precarious, one lung was gone and the other was at risk, and the doctor held out little hope for the young man's recovery. But Edward Nangle was lucky as, throughout his life, he had the capacity to attract the goodwill of benefactors and patrons. People now entered his life who would provide a bedrock of assistance through this early illness and through his remarkable endeavours in future years.

James Adams' brother, Dr Neason Adams, ran a successful medical practice at St Stephen's Green, Dublin, and he and his wife, Isabella, took Edward under their care in their Dublin home. For the remainder of their lives, the childless Adams couple would go to exceptional lengths to support their volatile protégé and his family.

***

Recovery for Edward was slow, and he had time to read and to reflect. He travelled to recuperate in the Scottish Highlands and into his hands came the recently published *Historical Sketches of the Native Irish* by the Scottish Baptist Minister, Christopher Anderson. Over two decades, Anderson had made a detailed survey of the state of the Irish language, with a particular interest in Ireland's coastal islands, and *Historical Sketches* was the fruit of this work. Reading the book induced a conversion-style experience in the classic evangelical mode for Edward, and directed his interest towards the evangelisation of the Irish-speaking people in the west.

Christopher Anderson could not speak Irish but had developed an enthusiastic appreciation for the native Irish culture and language, and came to the view that enlightenment should be brought to the Irish people through the medium of their own native tongue. The use of the Irish language, he believed, would 'operate like the insertion of a leaven' to lead the destitute people of the west of Ireland towards the truth and towards a better life.[13] Christopher Anderson's book had a profound life-changing effect on the frail, recuperating Edward. It was like the final piece of a jigsaw that was building piece by piece in his imagination, providing the lifelong spark for his future life's work. He would credit his reading of *Historical Sketches* with the origins of the Achill Mission.

A quarter of a century afterwards, when William Krause and Christopher Anderson died within weeks of one another, Edward reflected on the profound influence of two very dissimilar men on his life: Krause, 'cold and reserved', Anderson 'affectionate, bland and open-hearted'.[14] The pair provided him with the intellectual foundations for his daunting Achill project.

A vision was taking shape in Edward Nangle's imagination, a vision that took seed among the drumlin hills of County Cavan and was motivated by a premillennial urgency and a belief in the biblical prophecy that the Lord's coming was imminent. He would build nothing less than an exemplary Christian colony in the most deprived and remote location on Ireland's west coast. It would be an oasis of civilisation in the midst of superstition and squalor. He could see it in his mind's eye: neat, orderly houses with vegetable gardens and whitewashed walls; a community conducting itself with piety, sobriety and industry; scriptural schools buzzing with the laughter of children; the people learning the Bible, the source of all truth, in their native tongue; and a people transformed beyond all recognition.

It was a daring and ambitious concept. Could Edward Nangle's ambition possibly be realised and, if so, where?

CHAPTER TWO

The Most Destitute Spot in Ireland

'The state of society is now completely unhinged.' These were the stark words of a young Catholic bishop in a letter to the British Prime Minister, Earl Grey, on west-of-Ireland conditions in 1831. John MacHale raged about the plight of the peasantry: the weather had wreaked havoc on the potato crop – what were the people to do? If the evangelical view in Cavan blamed Catholicism, popery and the clergy for the country's ills, the Catholic prelate had a different take on the root cause of Ireland's distress: there was something rotten, he asserted, at the heart of the land system in the country.

Famine and cholera were sweeping across the western counties, the public roads were crowded with thousands toiling for a wretched pittance of six or seven pence worth of meal for an entire family, while women and children thronged into depots seeking provisions. How could hundreds in Ballina cry out for food while, at the same time, the town was busy with the bustle of corn traders, and the public road crowded with vehicles bearing away food for export? It was a scandal, fumed the cleric, 'a famine in the midst of plenty'.[1]

In the three decades since the formation of the Union, Britain had flourished: it was a time of growth, industrialisation, capitalism, free trade and urbanisation, and Irish agriculture fed this economic expansion with a remarkable increase in Irish food exports. But Ireland itself was becoming progressively more chaotic: the population swelled, potato cultivation intensified, and farm holdings fragmented into a patchwork of plots with the chronic subdivision of small holdings. In the west, the decline in living standards for many 'was both dangerous and rapid', with a large subsistence underclass virtually dependent on a single crop: the potato.[2]

The *Mayo Constitution* newspaper reported that there was a 'mass of human misery to be found throughout a vast district of the west of Ireland'. For whole communities around Clew Bay there were 'no potatoes, no oatmeal, a failure of fisheries, no price to be got for kelp, no public or private markets for goods, no means of earning daily wages, no resident gentry landlords, no food but seaweed, and the small fishes that can be picked up along the strand'.[3]

In the midst of this chaos, Edward Nangle headed west on a relief mission.

***

The Atlantic waves tossed the boat dangerously close to the cliffs.

The clergyman crept from his berth on the *Nottingham* steamer, his stomach churning, as the sea frothed all around in a sheet of white foam.[4] It was near sunset, on a Wednesday evening in July 1831, and the sky glowed red like a hot furnace. He struggled to keep his footing on deck as the storm winds gusted furiously and the gigantic cliffs on Achill Island's western coast loomed overhead on the boat's lee side – Croaghaun, where the power of the Atlantic waves had chiselled away the rock face. This was Edward Nangle's first sighting of Achill Island in its wild and terrifying magnificence.

His pregnant wife, Eliza, was sheltered below deck, perhaps regretting her decision to travel as her body convulsed with sea sickness. Her thoughts must often have turned to their one-year-old daughter, Frances, left behind in Dublin in the care of her family. She had shown a steely determination in accompanying and supporting her husband, a single-mindedness and selflessness that would be a feature of their married life. The boat carried a cargo of Indian meal to provide some relief for the communities of the west in their dire need.

The *Nottingham* creaked and groaned at every seam as she plunged into successive gullies between the waves and Croaghaun cliffs. As one fearful surge of Atlantic waters succeeded the next, it must have seemed as if the steamer would never again rise from the depths. Edward watched Captain Biddy stalking the deck, knowing he had a calculation to make: should he protect the vessel by throwing some of the cargo of meal overboard or hold tight in the hope of reaching the calmer waters of Clew Bay? The captain waited, never once leaving the steamer's deck as the red sky faded on the western horizon.

When Edward and Eliza married three years earlier, he was still in recovery after the earlier disintegration of his health in County Cavan. In hindsight, their early married years at Elm Cottage, Monkstown, must have appeared idyllic, with pleasant musical evenings and violin renditions of Haydn and Mozart by Edward at their Dublin cottage. It would be a short-lived period of tranquillity in their married life.

There is a sense that an artist's soul struggled beneath the surface of Edward's personality, with glimmers of an enthusiastic musician, an eager watercolourist, a writer of soaring lyrical prose and a man awestruck by nature's beauty. This aesthetic would reveal a deficit on his part in later years with little evident appreciation of the native culture of the people he ministered to in contrast, for instance, to Christopher Anderson's regard for the native Celtic culture.

A watercolour, possibly by Edward, of Eliza with two of their daughters a few years into their marriage shows her looking downwards in a diffident, reserved way, the image reflecting the norms for the virtuous woman of the times. Her husband described her as a woman of 'few words', a trait that contrasted with his own tendency towards extravagant verbal propensity as words poured in torrents from his mouth and pen.[5] These differing temperaments would become a factor in their diverging responses to future adverse circumstances. It was as if his verbal fluency acted as a type of therapy for Edward in times of stress, while Eliza's taciturn disposition caused her to bury accumulating suffering deep within.

Mercifully, at about ten o'clock, the tension on the *Nottingham* broke as the steamer rounded Achill's southern tip into Clew Bay with the wind at its stern and the waters finally smooth. The vessel anchored within a couple of miles of Westport where the passengers got some welcome rest. They awoke to calm waters amidst the scenic surroundings of Clew Bay with its multitude of islands. Leaning over the gunwale, Edward gazed out at the sharp-summited Croagh Patrick on the southern coast of the bay: the holy mountain, imposing and resplendent as it jutted towards the heavens. Edward reflected on his Catholic countrymen who, year after year, lacerated their limbs on the mountain in pilgrimages of self-inflicted torture. He felt only sorrow for their moral condition, reflecting the thoughts of one Christopher Anderson, 'without a vernacular literature, without books, without schools, and without the ministration of the divine work in their native language'.[6] He would bend every fibre of his being towards changing their lot.

William Baker Stoney, the rector of the nearby Newport parish, boarded the *Nottingham* in Westport and claimed some Indian meal for his parishioners. The famine distress in the area was acute, he told the visitors, and nowhere was more afflicted than Achill Island. He invited Edward and Eliza to his home as guests. Already, Edward was setting his sights on the remote place where he would implement his evangelical vision. He would travel to Achill without delay.

∗∗∗

What was wrong with Ireland? Why was the country collapsing? Why was the condition of the people so appalling and disorderly in contrast to that of the English? A thoughtful, dark-haired, delicate-looking French nobleman was determined to find the answer and his conclusions would differ from those of Edward Nangle. What he found in Ireland and the west was deep-seated and intractable.

One August day in the 1830s, the young aristocrat Alexis de Tocqueville arrived at Newport, about twenty miles from Achill, where Edward and Eliza Nangle were William Stoney's guests. The Frenchman was on a six-week visit to Ireland with his friend, Gustave de Beaumont, to examine the worrying conditions in the country about which he had read much. He was already an experienced traveller with a scholarly reputation, the first parts of his voluminous study into the American political system having been published. A central concern of his intellectual life was the manner in which societies made the transition from an aristocratic to a democratic society, and he was well placed to offer a dispassionate view on the Irish situation.

He was depressed by the state of Ireland: 'a collection of misery such as I did not imagine existed in the world', a nation 'divided in the most violent way between two parties which are altogether religious and political'. The language of the Dublin aristocracy alarmed him with their description of the common people as savages, reducing them to something less than human. As for the ordinary people, he was likewise shocked at their pervasive contempt for their aristocracy and landlords. It was a divided society at war with itself.

In Newport, Alexis and Gustave reached a one-storey house at the side of a meadow facing the town's quay. It was the home of Father James Hughes, the Catholic parish priest who would become a thorn in Edward Nangle's side. Alexis had read the cleric's powerful letters to the newspapers about the state of his parishioners, and when he decided to see the conditions of the west first-hand he made it his business to meet the priest.

De Tocqueville now stood before the stout James Hughes, aged about fifty, dressed in black, wearing riding boots and speaking with a pronounced accent. 'A little common,' was De Tocqueville's comment in his journal. The priest took the visitors into a small room where the walls were covered with garish religious engravings interspersed with political caricatures. In a short time, a crowd gathered outside the priest's front door, anticipating that the visitors might have brought some relief as few had eaten that day. 'Most of them have been forced to dig up the new harvest and feed themselves on potatoes as large as nuts, which make them ill,' said the priest.

The two local landlords were the Marquis of Sligo, based at Westport, and Sir Richard O'Donnell who lived not far from the priest at Newport House. These great landlords, complained the priest, gave nothing and did nothing to prevent the unfortunate population from dying of hunger. They let the farmers die before their eyes, or evicted them from their miserable dwellings on the slightest pretext. They had drained the energy from the people.

Three hundred paces from the priest's house, the river divided into two branches and a promontory jutted between the two streams to form a hill. There, in the middle of a meadow, was the house of the Protestant rector, William Stoney. The visitors heard that there was open warfare between priest and rector, who attacked each other bitterly in the newspapers and in the pulpit, each believing passionately in his version of the truth. Rector and priest fought for souls.

Back in Dublin, de Tocqueville took soundings from influential people in an effort to understand the relationship between the Irish landlords and their tenants. What he heard was troubling: 'There is no moral tie between the poor and the rich. The Irish landlords extract from their estates all that they can yield.'

Why was the agricultural population poor if the farm yields were so good?

Yes, the yields were immense, but none of the wealth remained in the hands of the people. The Irish were raising productive crops, carrying their harvest to the nearest port, putting it on board an English vessel, and returning home to subsist on potatoes.

By the end of his visit, Alexis de Tocqueville was convinced that the profound chasm between the aristocracy-cum-landlords and the Irish people was widening by the day and he set out his thoughts in a letter to his father before his departure: 'England and Ireland have the same language, the same laws, the same social structure, they are subject to the same government, and there are no [two] countries that present a more different appearance. Both have been for a long time, and are still in many respects, subject to a powerful aristocracy. This aristocracy had produced great wealth in England, and frightful poverty in Ireland.'[7]

It was, he concluded, as if two entirely distinct nations occupied the same Irish soil: one rich, civilised and happy, the other poor, half savage, and overwhelmed by misery. 'If you wish to know what the spirit of conquest and religious hatred, combined with all the abuses of aristocracy without any of its advantages, can produce, come to Ireland.'[8]

The aristocracy and landlords were to blame for the plight of Ireland, concluded the Frenchman. The land system was rotten, said John MacHale. Popery and the Catholic clergy were at the root of the country's misery, said Edward Nangle, and he was determined to do something about it.

***

Edward Nangle crossed the strand in Achill Sound at low tide and stood for the first time on Achill soil, having travelled with a scripture reader by horseback from Newport the previous day. Afterwards, he would describe the desolate sight: 'The deep silence of desolation was unbroken, except by the monotonous rippling of the tide as it ebbed or flowed, or the wild scream of the curlew disturbed by some casual intruder on its privacy.'[9]

A couple of years earlier, a young Anglo-Irish gentleman on a leisure trip to the west had noted: 'To look at the map of County Mayo, one could imagine that nature had designed that county for a sportsman.'[10] The gentleman had chronicled his successful hunting exploits in Achill, returning from the mountain at the end of the day to the coastguard station with bulging bags of game, having shot seven hares and thirteen brace of grouse.

Achill Island presents a landscape of contrasts: an island with the shape of an upside-down boot, the hardness of its coastline countered by the black softness of the bog land that makes up most of its centre. The incessant coastal sounds of breaking waves and screaming birds are in contrast to the melancholy loneliness of large tracts of the island's interior.

Today, the main approach route from Westport to Achill hugs the eastern and northern shores of Clew Bay via Newport and Mulranny, then swings in an arc around Corraun Hill along the edges of Blacksod Bay. It follows the route of what was once the Midland Great Western Railway line, extended to Achill at the close of the nineteenth century. Nowadays, the disused railway line forms The Great Western Greenway, a 43km stretch of cycling and walking pathways, while the adjacent roadway carries motorists who follow the ingeniously branded Wild Atlantic Way along the entire stretch of Ireland's Atlantic coast.

Measuring fifteen miles from east to west, eleven from north to south and the population distributed through several villages, it appeared to Edward that much of the Achill land had not been broken for cultivation since the deluge. He took in the crude houses with the roofs resting like domes on massive walls, giving the appearance of beehives. The worst aspect of the island to his view was the moral condition of the islanders: it was a place of 'ignorance and barbarism, of intellectual and moral degradation.'[11] This was not entirely surprising to him since, he observed, it was then a widely held view that Achill was a byword for barbarism and paganism.

The pair headed north along rugged, zigzagging pathways for, had they taken a direct route, their horses would have sunk to their knees in the marshy swamp. It took an entire day to reach the coastguard station perched on Bullsmouth channel in the north-east corner of the island, an innocuous stretch of water between Achill and the small beast-shaped Inishbiggle, where the tidal swell could make a boat passage treacherous. Clergyman, scripture reader and horses welcomed the coastguard's hospitality.

The next day, they pressed on in the direction of the purple-black mountain of Slievemore at Dugort on Achill's north coast.

Edward Nangle looked upon the slopes covered with peat and overgrown with heath and hard-stunted grass, the sheltered eastern flank sliced by chasms bringing water in its torrents into the sodden swamp below – a place so inhospitable that, according to the locals, a hare could hardly walk over it.

This was the mountain area on which Edward Nangle set his sights. He needed land and decided to return to Newport and seek a meeting with the head of the Burrishoole estate that comprised most of Achill Island. Sir Richard O'Donnell was favourably disposed to the evangelicals, having closely followed events at Lord Farnham's Cavan estate, and quickly agreed a thirty-one-year lease on a tract of land at Slievemore.

Over thirty years later, Edward reflected on the difficulties he encountered in securing occupancy on even this poor-quality land from Sir Richard O'Donnell on a lease of thirty-one years: 'This was not easily to be had, as the land was all leased to tenants, who were very tenacious of their rights. With much difficulty, they were induced to surrender 130 acres of wild mountain, without any building or a rood of cultivated ground upon it.'[12] He was certain that the Roman Catholic priest, had he known what was intended for the land, would have prevented him from getting it. Goodwill money of £90 was paid to the occupying tenants.[13] The tales of the island people would afterwards speak of the pain of those they believed were dispossessed of their Slievemore fields at that time.[14]

A few weeks after his first visit to Achill, Edward sat down in Dublin to write to Christopher Anderson whose book had fired his soul five years earlier. Not only did he have a vision for his west-of-Ireland project, but he also had the organisational skills and the financial flair to drive forward his concept. He fleshed out a plan which he presented to some supporters: five directors would oversee expenditure on erecting the Achill Mission buildings, two Irish-speaking missionaries would be recruited and an agriculturist would oversee the land reclamation. If the Achill scheme was successful, he told Christopher Anderson, 'your *Historical Sketches* will have been the instrument, or the first link in the chain of secondary causes which were used to promote it.'[15]

But some of Edward's associates were unconvinced, warning him that it was a risky and foolhardy venture, a wild speculation originating in a romantic imagination, a project that would be abandoned as soon as it ran into opposition. Moreover, was it wise to sacrifice the interests of his family and career for such an undertaking? 'What wild goose chase is this that you are going upon to that Island of Achill?' asked one evangelical-minister colleague.[16]

Edward was unwavering. He would move to Achill with his wife and children and bring about the moral regeneration of the minds and hearts of the Achill peasantry. His undertaking would face the classic missionary dilemma: to bring the Bible and a ministry of service in education, literacy, medical services and economic development to a wretched people, without trampling on the rituals and way of life which bonded a people together. Despite the obstacles, Edward Nangle was convinced that his island colony could become a model Christian development and a template to demonstrate to the world how to lift a people out of poverty, ignorance and idolatry through an evangelising crusade.

CHAPTER THREE

Bonfires in the West

It was Friday night, on the first day of August 1834, when a heavily laden sailing boat – a traditional hooker – with four passengers on board cast anchor in Dugort Bay in north Achill, where the ghostly figures of a welcome party waited on the strand next to shooting bonfire flames.[1] Edward Nangle, his sister-in-law Grace Warner, the Newport rector William Stoney and a female servant stepped ashore and helping hands unloaded the Nangle family's possessions. This was to be their new home and Eliza would shortly travel from Newport with their three small daughters: Frances, Henie and baby Tilly. Edward and his family had earlier travelled from Ballina, County Mayo, where they had lived in recent years on Home Mission Society work.

In the enveloping Dugort darkness, they could just about make out the vague outline of the work already carried out on the 'infant settlement', work that became clear in the morning light. It was a most pleasing vista for Edward: a couple of two-storey slated houses on the western end of the site next to reclaimed and cultivated fields; two more houses emerging from foundations further east; and in between, hillocks of peat marking out an area where yet more buildings would rise. His vision was already taking practical shape in a spectacular mountainside development, the like of which had never before been seen in Achill.

Edward was not the first resident at the Achill Mission colony, for a steward, a schoolmaster and a scripture reader already occupied one of the houses, and the Nangle family would share the second with Joseph Duncan, the assistant missionary. The ground-floor room served as a parlour, drawing room and study during the day, and Joseph Duncan's bedchamber at night, a situation amusingly described by Edward: 'Mr Duncan could not retire to rest until we vacated the apartment for the night, nor could we come down in the morning until he had arisen and completed his toilet.'[2]

The passengers appreciated the warmth of bonfire flames and welcoming hands after their two-day journey from Newport, through Clew Bay, then northward along the eastern edges of Achill and through the treacherous straight at Bullsmouth. Edward was now the full-time permanent head of the Achill Mission, with a growing physical infrastructure and an emerging organisation to drive forward his evangelical mission. He retired to bed in his new home on the flanks of Slievemore with the sounds of the ocean ringing in his ears.

Grace Warner, Eliza Nangle's sister, is an intermittent and shadowy presence in this story. She landed at Dugort with her brother-in-law before Eliza and her daughters had yet set foot on Achill soil. A young unmarried woman, it appears that she may have divided her time between the home of her widowed mother, Patience, at Marvelstown House, Kilbeg, County Meath, and that of her sister, Eliza, with her growing family. She was in Achill from the start of the Achill Mission, and she would be there at the end of her own life, long after Edward, Eliza and their children had departed the island. In the summer of 1834, Grace made a mountainside house ready for her sister and children.

Edward plunged into his work. Slates arrived by hooker from Westport for the new colony buildings. Prayers and worship took place each morning and evening in both the Irish and English languages. Labourers worked on reclaiming the soil and planting crops, and each Sunday the congregation worshipped in the parlour of the Nangle home. Edward took to the mountain slopes to shoot rabbit for dinner and, all the while, storm clouds were gathering.

✳✳✳

In the same month that Edward alighted on Dugort strand, the Catholic pontiff, Pope Gregory XVI, then three years into his papacy, made an important announcement in Rome when he confirmed the appointment of John MacHale as Catholic archbishop of Tuam, which included Achill Island in its jurisdiction. There was consternation in Britain that John MacHale would now be among the four most powerful Catholic clerics in Ireland. 'Anybody but him', the British prime minister had implored the pontiff, for the political establishment viewed John MacHale as an agitating prelate who inflamed passions at a time when sectarian tensions in Ireland were intense.[3] Perhaps nervous of John MacHale's impetuosity, the Pope warned his new archbishop to maintain 'in every transaction of your rule singular prudence, moderation of spirit, and the greatest care for peace and beneficial quiet'.[4] The archbishop's tenure in Tuam could not have been more different in action and in tone from that recommended by his pontiff.

John MacHale was a tall, lean, athletic man fired with a colossal energy. Born a decade before Edward Nangle in the shadows of Nephin Mountain, County Mayo, he shared Edward's experience of having lost his mother as a child. He was a prominent, assertive, Irish-educated Catholic cleric, who had already made his mark as a scholar, teacher and vigorous public speaker and writer. He and Edward had crossed swords before Edward's arrival in Achill in truculent public exchanges that set the tone for their vigorous and uncompromising sparring throughout their long lives.

A year earlier, while both men were based in Ballina, County Mayo, newspapers published an open letter from John MacHale carrying a tirade against Protestantism in Ireland, contrasting its wealth and patronage with the lamentable condition of the people. The established church, he thundered, was 'the prolific womb from which all the misfortunes of Ireland teemed in fearful succession'.

Edward could not leave John MacHale's letter unchallenged and he set to work. Each week, throughout the months of August and September, he wrote a long letter of reply, defending the established church and venting a full-blooded condemnation of the evils of Irish Catholicism. The language bristled with frenzy and hysteria, conveying the sense of one teetering on the brink, such was the fierceness of emotion and hostility in the letters.

In a breathless diatribe, Edward condemned the practices of Roman Catholicism, its 'masses, and purgatory, and penances, and pilgrimages, and priestly pardons, and crucifixes, and holy ashes, clay, candles, bones, teeth, hair, nails, rings, cords, scapulars, and all other thrash and filth, which has become encrusted on it from the muddy stream of a corrupt and sinful world'.

All the religious and folk practices of the people were derided and demeaned in a vitriolic rant.

His most vehement condemnation was aimed at the most central and revered of Catholic beliefs: the mass and the Eucharist. How, he asked, could a mere wafer, 'a bit of senseless, motionless paste', be worshipped in a most odious practice? Provocatively, he queried if such a belief indicated that Catholicism condoned cannibalism.

Edward was furious that John MacHale did not take the bait by replying publicly to the letters. Is it 'beneath your dignity to reply to my statements?' he asked petulantly in his final letter in September. 'But who is Doctor MacHale? What entitles him to assume such a lofty position of self-exaltation?'[5]

The tone of the relationship between John MacHale and Edward Nangle was already set. The colony on the slopes of Slievemore would be the dramatic stage on which their raging antagonism would play out as the pair jousted, their words polished and honed with precision in support of each man's version of the truth. The pair symbolised, in a spectacular way, the social and religious fault lines that bedevilled the Ireland of their times.

Here were two driven, articulate, larger-than-life men, each with his own version of the Christian truth.

***

Edward's tenure in Achill was punctuated by bouts of poor health, depression and emotional volatility. Periods of intense activity, elevated mood, high productivity and extraordinary verbal output alternated with episodes of illness, fatigue, despondency, and occasionally total collapse: features of what nowadays could be labelled bipolar disorder. Childhood trauma, residual vulnerability from his Cavan breakdown, difficult living conditions and constant conflict in Achill may all have been contributory factors.

In the weeks immediately after his arrival in Achill, excerpts from Edward's diary reveal that his chest was causing him concern.[6]

> Monday, 18th August – Obliged, from soreness to my chest, to give up our morning meeting. Our school is greatly increased; sixty-eight children on the roll. Wrote several letters.
>
> Monday, 25th August – My chest so weak this morning that I was obliged to order Downey to assemble the people and read to them … It is a great cause for thankfulness that when I am unable to speak, in consequence of the weakness of my chest, I can still write.
>
> Tuesday 26th August – Arrived at Newport at three o'clock…my chest very poorly.
>
> Tuesday, 2nd September – Still poorly in health; our readers met with much opposition this day.
>
> Monday 8th September – My chest very sore.

Edward's spells of illness were defining life events. A contemporary writer on psychosomatic disorders has noted that, even when compared to the most aggressive multisystem disease, psychosomatic trauma-triggered illnesses are noteworthy for how little respect they have for any single part of the body.[7] Edward suffered numerous symptoms through his many and varied illnesses: headaches, stomach and joint pain as well as seizures – a possible manifestation of psychological distress. It was as if his explosions of passion and energy were sustainable only if countered by intervals of lethargy and fatigue. It was a pattern that added to the harsh conditions of life in Achill as the Nangle family faced their first winter on the island with its inhospitable storms; and Eliza was in the early weeks of pregnancy.

Hostilities broke out within weeks as the Achill Mission's programme to bring the scriptures to the people swung into action. To add to Edward's troubles, gale force winds swept across the island and he feared that the roof of one of the new colony buildings would be demolished. One squall from the north-west descended from Slievemore with such force that it threw two men off their ladders but, providentially, they escaped serious injury.

He was heartened when twenty children attended the mission's first Sunday school, but the event was not without incident when a 'Popish zealot'[8] stood near the gate with a rod and threatened to beat the attending children. One of the scripture readers was attacked, thrown to the ground and his clothes torn by two men about four miles from Dugort. When a mission steward travelled by boat to nearby Mulranny to purchase some farm implements, he was met by a hostile crowd.

Worryingly, Edward got word through an informant of a secret plan to attack the colony, kill those living there, burn the buildings and put an end to the Achill Mission. He informed Captain Reynolds, chief officer of the Achill coastguard, who made plans to have his men armed and ready on the night of the suspected attack. Eliza even took the precaution of moving the children's beds away from the positions where they might be hit by bullets. No attack took place and Edward believed that the preparations they made had deterred the assailants. Others claimed that the alleged attack was a figment of Edward's excitable imagination and that his charges were driven by a motive to attract sympathy and support for his cause.

Achill hit the headlines repeatedly in subsequent months as summonses were issued for purported assaults against the missionaries, and those charged with the offences congregated at Newport and Westport to attend court hearings. A *Connaught Telegraph* writer was infuriated at the 'outrageous proceedings', when more than forty islanders were obliged to travel, at great inconvenience and hardship, to attend the courts and answer what the paper claimed were entirely vexatious charges.[9] Prior to the arrival of Edward Nangle, said the writer, the Achill islanders had lived a life of peace, harmony and goodwill towards one another but now discord, ill will and hatred were being propagated through the island. Achill had become 'a theatre of riot and confusion.'

***

At seven o'clock on a mid-October evening in 1834, as the sun was setting in the west, 300 important guests, all men, gathered at the Mitre Hotel, Tuam, some sixty miles from Achill in a south-western direction, for a celebration dinner to honour the elevation of the new archbishop, John MacHale. Earlier in the day, at the chapel of Tuam, every available space was filled for the ceremony of installation as the *Te Deum* rang out from choir and organ. John MacHale had travelled that day from Castlebar, in an elegant Swiss carriage presented to him by the people and clergy of Killala, where he had ministered for almost a decade. A *Freeman's Journal* journalist estimated that crowds numbering up to 40,000 greeted the new prelate on the route into Tuam which was bedecked with flags, while an arch of green boughs festooned the town's north bridge.

When the dinner guests had eaten and drunk heartily, John MacHale rose to respond to the toast. He was, he said, humbled and overawed and, perhaps, a little fearful lest his future be like 'a brilliant taper which might shed a brilliant light in a narrow apartment, but would only twinkle when exposed in a broader atmosphere'. If he had been criticised for indulging in the exposure of the grievances of the poor in the past, this was an accusation to which he would freely confess, he said, without the least contrition.

Within the week, the *Freeman's Journal* was extolling the triumphal elevation of the archbishop, 'now the bright luminary of the Catholic hierarchy, fearlessly vindicated'.[10] John MacHale, asserted the writer, had vindicated his religion and cast the shield of protection around the poor at a time when besotted bigotry was at its height, and to be a Roman Catholic was considered a disgrace. The new archbishop embarked on a tour of his extensive diocese, greeted everywhere by blazing bonfires. At Newport, a large procession greeted the archbishop outside the town, those at the front of the parade on foot, followed by horseback riders, and next the carriages. Tar barrels blazed in every direction, illuminating the town. The archbishop's carriage halted at the house of the priest, James Hughes, and the people knelt to receive the episcopal benediction. One journalist claimed to have observed the rector and parish priest's neighbour, William Stoney, watching among the crowd.

More than likely, prelate and priest discussed the worrying developments in Achill as it would have been unimaginable to both men that they could allow Edward Nangle to continue with his work at Dugort uncontested. The archbishop would soon visit the troublesome island.

John MacHale and Edward Nangle had several traits in common: an ability to deliver powerful rhetoric not tempered by prudence, restless energy, combative natures and an unshakeable belief in their version of the truth. Each man excelled in the crafting of belligerent polemics and in the thrill of robust, vicious public debate. Both had outlets through pen and pulpit for their venomous words to take poisonous flight. Both exhibited also a dangerous propensity for egomania and narcissism. What a coincidence that this pair of clergymen shared the stage in nineteenth-century Ireland and played out their antagonism theatrically on a remote Atlantic island.

Their mutual hostility soon focused on education and the mission schools, for education was Edward Nangle's main bridgehead for conversions. He would combat popish error by establishing a system of scriptural education to teach the children the principles of Protestantism and civilised living. Not for the first time in the battle for the souls and hearts of a people, schools became the focal point of a religious crusade.

CHAPTER FOUR

Scriptural Education

It is hard to grasp, almost two centuries later, the phenomenon which was the Achill Mission colony and the disruptive chaos which it unleashed. What if an independent international adventurer stumbled upon the Achill scene and left behind a third-party account? As it happens, we have precisely such a report from Jane Franklin, described as the most travelled woman of her time, who visited every continent in the world except Antarctica in her lifetime.

In late summer 1835, Jane arrived at the Achill Mission colony in Dugort, just a year after the Nangles had taken up residence there. She confronted an impressive spectacle: a row of slated two-storey houses on the side of a mountain, ten acres of cultivated land producing potatoes and other crops, eight cabins under construction for colony converts – an oasis of development in the midst of the prevailing deprivation and squalor across the island. It was an impressive sight indeed to a visitor who passionately valued improvement and education.

She had spent several months the previous year separated from her husband and travelling on the Nile with a Prussian missionary, Johann Lieder, giving rise to innuendo of a romantic affair. On returning to England, she was unwell, perhaps pining for her exotic Nile travelling companion, and a trip to Ireland may have been a welcome diversion. In contrast to her middle-aged, stout, balding, explorer husband Sir John, Jane Franklin, then in her early forties, exuded the vibrant energy of youth. She was slim, graceful and elegant, amiable and charming, her expressive face framed by curly hair. But she was also sturdy and adventurous, strong and practical, one who described herself as a low-church, 'no-frills Protestant'.[1]

On their way to Achill the visitors received a favourable report about Edward Nangle's mission from an unlikely source. Father Lyons, Catholic dean of Killala, County Mayo, told them: 'He is an excellent man and he is doing a great deal of good to the poor people of Achill.' The difficult journey to the island would likely have excited the adventurous Jane: 'At Ballycroy we were detained four days by a hurricane, living all this time in the coastguard watch-house and the cottage of the chief boatman', before crossing by galley across dangerous waters to Achill's Bullsmouth.

Edward, Eliza and Grace Warner hosted Jane and her husband at their Dugort home where they dined on vegetables and potatoes from the Nangle kitchen garden. While the single decanter of wine disappeared quickly from the table at the end of the meal, Edward apologised for the deficiency and produced a bottle of whiskey for the guests. Jane could see how harsh the year had been for Eliza: her first son, the child she had carried in her womb through a harsh and difficult Achill winter, had died in April before her milk came in, surviving for just two days. Edward, she learned, had buried the infant with his own hands in the small enclosed cemetery behind the mission buildings on the mountain slope. In the years ahead, it would become a communal Nangle burial place.

What impression did Edward Nangle make? To Jane, he was a tall, thin, pale, dark man with finely formed features, wearing such a mild pensive expression 'that you would think he could not utter a harsh word, or raise his voice beyond the breathings of a prayer'. However, she could detect that he was driven by an overwhelming force, willing to persevere in his mission through fatigue, ill health, persecution and calumny in pursuit of his goals. He clearly believed that thousands of his deluded countrymen were perishing around him in their sins and errors and that it was his God-given duty to bring the true faith to these people.

'Like another Luther is Mr Nangle in Achill,' she observed, instinctively supportive of the mission's work in opposing the 'spiritual tyranny' of Catholicism. 'I have seen missionaries in many countries but never one so pure and high-minded as Mr Nangle.'

Jane sympathised with the position of Eliza and her sister: in her view, two excellent, gentle and zealous women who had renounced the luxuries to which they had been accustomed and devoted their energies to the island mission, while understandably apprehensive at the violence being directed at the colony. She heard that, during Edward's absences, the chief officer of the coastguard, Francis Reynolds, came to the colony each night 'to sit up with Mr Nangle's family and be in readiness to protect them in case of attack or insult'.[2] Grace Warner appeared to be in awe of her brother-in-law, telling Jane that, despite suffering poor health, Edward was scrupulous in economising the mission's funds, seeking few comforts for himself.

In a remarkable coincidence, Jane Franklin's group arrived in Achill just days after a triumphal visit to the island by John MacHale, his first as archbishop. What might the adventurer Lady Jane have made of the robed prelate, had they come to face-to-face, with their diametrically opposed nineteenth-century outlooks?

Dressed in episcopal robes, the archbishop had led a procession of thirteen priests, followed by an enthusiastic crowd waving banners emblazoned with 'Down the Schematics'. He officiated in a splendid spectacle at a high mass in nearby Dookinella within sight of leaping Atlantic waves in an atmosphere of near hysteria. In an impressive display in the presence of their archbishop, a succession of priests addressed the crowd and denounced the colony, calling on the people to have no interaction of any sort with the Achill Mission: 'neither borrowing nor lending, neither buying nor selling'. In a theatrical gesture that matched the striking location, a solemn curse was invoked on those who dared violate the mandate of not associating with the colony.

Soon after the episcopal visit, the *Connaught Telegraph* predicted the imminent demise of the Achill Mission: 'in six months more, within the tenantless walls of the colony will be heard only the shrill whistle of the whirlwind, or the night-screech of the owl – the buildings shall stand as a lasting record of the folly and hypocrisy of their architects'.[3] The prediction proved to be a delusion, while the archbishop's visit certainly presented an image of the fiery antagonism between John MacHale and Edward Nangle and their respective belief systems.

***

Jane Franklin believed passionately in personal improvement and in the power of education and it was this aspect of Edward Nangle's ministry that interested her most. Some months earlier, on 23 December 1834, the first Achill Mission school had opened at Slievemore village on the western flank of the mountain in a three-roomed building. Within a couple of months there were three more mission schools at Dugort, Cashel and Keel and, quickly realising the threat which these posed, the island's parish priest Michael Connolly responded by opening three competing schools in early 1835. From a situation where there was little or no education infrastructure on the island, there were now a plethora of opposing schools.

Given that the modern Irish state has struggled to deal with issues of pluralism and multi-denominational expectations in its education system to the present day, it is intriguing to reflect on how an ambitious non-denominational primary school system became embroiled in a sectarian battle for souls in 1830s Achill.

It was just a few years since the Chief Secretary of Ireland, Edward Stanley, set out the bones of his new non-denominational state-supported universal system of elementary education for Ireland in his 1831 'Stanley Letter' after decades of debate and controversy.[4] Under the new system, designed to unite children of different creeds, no religious iconography would be allowed in the schools and religious instruction would take place either before or after school hours. In practice, the demarcation between general instruction and religious instruction became blurred. The schools operated under the direction of the National Board and received financial assistance, supplemented by local resources, for school buildings, teacher salaries, school books and equipment. In a reflection of the cultural imperialist policies of the time, all teaching would be through the medium of English while school texts were centrally produced. It was a revolutionary experiment in state education and secularity.

Edward Nangle and John MacHale initially opposed the national system, both arguing that secular and religious education were inseparable and should be controlled by the respective denominations. For his part, Edward railed against a scheme which, he held, aimed to 'withhold the knowledge of God's word from the children of Ireland'.[5] He would reject the national scheme and, instead, put scripture teaching at the heart of his mission schools and operate them through privately raised funding without government support.

John MacHale was hostile to the state scheme from the beginning, opposing it on the grounds that it would be non-denominational, that the Irish language would be non-compulsory and that school texts would be British in character. However, the pragmatic archbishop, faced with the threat posed by the Achill Mission, saw an opportunity to secure state funding to establish competing island schools under the influence of his local clergy. The battle for the hearts of the Achill children was in full swing.

Jane Franklin was appalled that the national system of education, from which so much had been expected, was failing so dismally in its objectives. How could it possibly be a proper use of the national scheme to support the MacHale schools in Achill? She found it unacceptable that the National Board was providing the opportunity and means for the Catholic clergy to establish rival Achill schools which were now threatening the viability of those operated by the Achill Mission. In her view, a scheme established on a non-denominational basis had, in fact, 'widened the separation between the catholic and protestant population'.[6]

Edward Nangle was rankled at the manner in which MacHale and his priests were using the national education system and took his complaints repeatedly to the National Board, complaining that the Achill schools were adhering neither to the principles nor the regulations of the national programme. His most serious objections were made against James O'Donnell, master of Dugort national school in close proximity to the colony who, he protested, had provocatively carried a flag in a welcoming procession for John MacHale. This clearly contravened the National Board policy that school masters should refrain from any activities detrimental to carrying out a common system of education. Edward had an additional grievance: that the same teacher, James O'Donnell, had, 'with a knife in his hand threatened to take the head of one of the children attending a school under [mission] patronage'.

The National Board, through its secretary Thomas F. Kelly, took a benign view of the school master's conduct, maintaining that 'these are allegations of what passed amongst unlettered men, and amongst angry men',[7] and that the charges, while unwelcome, did not warrant the teacher's dismissal.

Sometime after this dispute, Edward was called to give evidence before a parliamentary select committee of the Lords and Commons which was examining the new Irish education system, and his testimony provides a compelling and direct account of his mission's goals and mode of operation in its early years.

Was it true, Edward was asked, that the conversion of the people of Achill was his main objective in coming to the island?

'Most decidedly. I desired to be an instrument in the hands of God. It was perfectly understood; we never made any secret of our object.'

But did he have other objectives in Achill, like improving the destitute conditions of the people?

'Certainly; we considered the reclaiming of them from the errors of Popery as the main object of the greatest importance, and the other as subservient to it.'

Were there any schools in Achill before the mission schools?

'There was no school except one; a pay school attended by very few children, I understand.'

Why did he consider that the establishment of national schools by the priests would have a negative effect on the mission schools?

'When the priest established another school then it became an act of more daring rebellion against his authority to pass by that school and to come to ours.'

Did he always address the people in the Irish language?

'Not on all occasions; I did occasionally.'

How many families were there on the Achill Mission grounds?

'There are thirty-four families altogether living on the mission grounds, twenty-seven of these families are persons who have been brought out of the Church of Rome; some of these came to the island with us; since we came into the island eighteen or nineteen families have been brought out of the Church of Rome.'

What conditions were applied to the people who were given ground at the colony?

'The manner of our proceeding is simply this: we give a cottage, and we give an acre of reclaimed ground, and for this they pay us a yearly rent of £2 5s, getting constant employment from us in reclaiming the rest of the land; they are employed as our labourers in reclaiming land.'

Was it a condition of residence at the colony that the people were Protestant?

'All the persons living on our mission ground are Protestant with the exception of one female; the place is intended as a refuge for persons wishing to be protected from the tyranny which everyone acquainted with the state of Ireland knows is practiced upon those persons who leave the Church of Rome.'

Would the colony house people who converted from Roman Catholic to Protestant?

'Yes, and are suffering persecution.'

Were the people who became converts and were admitted to the colony in a better position than the most destitute Catholics in Achill?

'They are in a better condition, certainly. But when we strive to better their temporal condition, it is insinuated that we attempt to induce them to change their religious profession by bribery.'[8]

The words were unequivocal: Edward Nangle had come to Achill to convert the Catholic people to Protestantism and all else was subsidiary to this objective. The real honey pot was the schools, for the people thirsted for education, but John MacHale and the priests sought to out manoeuvre him by setting up their own schools and the scandal for Edward was that the priests were aided and abetted by the national education system. The prizes on offer to woo the people to the colony were enticing: land and employment for any who could overcome the power of the priests and the taunts of neighbours – tantalisingly seductive if you lived a wretched life.

The explosion of new schools in 1830s Achill was remarkable. By 1837, there were almost 400 pupils, only 20 per cent of whom were female, enrolled in five national schools under the patronage of the Catholic parish priest while the Achill Mission schools, which were outside the national system, struggled to retain their earlier pupil numbers.[9] The antagonism between Edward Nangle and John MacHale at least had the merit of triggering the introduction of widespread education in Achill.

***

The contrast was astonishing between the conditions of the women associated with the Achill Mission colony on the one hand, and the common drudgery of the native Achill women on the other.[10] Eliza Nangle was a Protestant woman, reared in a comfortable, sheltered middle-class home and imbued with the evangelical values of the period. Like others of her contemporaries, she gave her whole-hearted support to a strong, evangelical figure, in her case her husband. From the early years of their marriage, as a pregnant woman and mother of a young daughter, she had accompanied Edward on the arduous famine relief journey to the west. She set up home with her young family in the most inhospitable conditions imaginable, sublimating the family needs to Edward's enterprise. For a woman imbued with the virtues of orderliness, cleanliness, temperance and domestic virtue, and attempting to inculcate these qualities in her young daughters, the relocation to Achill would have been traumatic. She could not have envisaged how the family's first year in Achill would turn out: extreme and inhospitable living conditions, her husband's poor health, the eruption of violence against the colony and a dead infant son. Most painful of all must have been the ferocity of the opposition to the mission's work for a woman who desired to do good for those less fortunate than herself.

Eliza had little in common with the island women who eked out an existence in one of the most remote and economically-deprived areas in Ireland. The Achill woman lived in 'fourth-class' houses with neither chimney nor window, had no formal schooling, could not read or write and looked after the animals and tillage when the men took on seasonal migrant work in England. The island landscape was her domain: she harvested turf and carried it home on her back; hauled seaweed from the shore to fertilise the soil; planted, weeded and harvested the potato crop; baited and gutted fish; sheaved and stacked oats and drove cattle. It was arduous physical work. The gulf between the lives of the colony women and their counterparts on the island was immense.

There was no administrative or commercial centre on the island and no middle class with the exception of the coastguard families. For over a decade, the coastguard was the most visible government agency charged with preventing smuggling, shipwreck plundering and illegal distilling. Margaret Reynolds, a Catholic woman married to the Protestant Captain Francis Reynolds of the coastguard, arrived in Achill a couple of years before the Nangles and this couple was the closest Edward and Eliza had to island friends.

Margaret's position was tense and uncomfortable as she became embroiled in a power struggle between Edward and her husband on the one hand, and the Achill Catholic clergy on the other. While rearing her large family, she stoically tried to follow her conscience, attending Catholic services and appearing bewildered by the fractious sectarian tensions around her. She listened at Sunday mass as the parish priest, Father Connolly, harangued the public about the Achill Mission and their attitude to the devotion of Catholics to the Virgin Mary. When she reported back to her husband, he, in turn, challenged the priest to a public debate on the doctrinal issues involved. Margaret was caught in an impossible situation which would, in time, turn out to be tragic.

***

Before leaving Achill, Jane Franklin set out to experience what she could of the island, used as she was to hiking, exploring, observing and note-taking. She took to the mountains, crossing the width of Slievemore behind the Achill Mission settlement on horseback, and also traversing the magnificent Minaun on the island's other coast. While disappointed not to find any Achill amethyst stone worth taking away, she appreciated the superior quality of Achill mutton grazed on Atlantic-splashed heather. While playing down her knowledge of the island plants, she noted 'the miniature fern, the abundant thrift and London pride, and the pretty little tormentilla, of which the peasants made a yellow dye for their shoe-skins'. She spied an eagle and some foxes, saw rabbits swarm the Dugort sand dunes, and witnessed the abundance of snipe, woodcock, grouse and plover, a delight for the sportsman's gun. Most delightful were the seals basking on exposed rocks in Achill Sound until they slid into the water, 'like the crocodile of the Nile'.

What, then, was her overall assessment of the Achill Mission? On this, she was in two minds. There was so much that was positive about Edward Nangle's project: 'If my good wishes are with this experiment, it is in the absence of any more effectual means of rescuing Ireland from her present state of moral and spiritual debasement.'

However, there was a hesitancy that prevented her from fully endorsing the proselytising institution. It was a reluctance that resulted from the manner in which she observed Edward Nangle deploring and castigating sincerely held Catholic doctrines such as that of the Eucharist: 'I cannot but deplore that Mr Nangle should think it right to speak as he does of a doctrine [the Eucharist] which however erroneous and, to us, incredible, is held in pious awe by many an honest Catholic.'[11]

While generally approving of the Achill Mission's programme of conversion, she was apprehensive about some of the tactics used: 'we may still regret that any weapon sharper than the voice of persuasive reasoning, any language less tender than the daily prayer which Mr Nangle fervently offers up for his deluded and deluding brethren' should have been used in achieving those conversions. While accepting the viciousness of the Catholic backlash against the mission, she feared that Edward Nangle's fierce, over zealous approach could prove detrimental in the long run. Jane Franklin's reservations would be shared by others.

On the final day of Jane's visit, Eliza Nangle and Grace Warner laid the foundation stone for a building which was to become the home of Neason Adams, the Nangles' friend who had helped nurture Edward back to health after his Cavan collapse. The Dublin physician was about to devote his resources and medical talents to the colony with his wife. Neason and Isabella Adams would bring a compassion and humanness to the work at the Achill Mission over the coming two decades.

The following year, Jane and John Franklin boarded the ship *Fairlie* with a party of twenty-three en route to Tasmania, Van Dieman's Land, where Sir John took up the post of lieutenant general while Jane swept energetically through the colony. In the coming years she would become one of the best known Victorian women of her day through her single-minded efforts in support of her husband's reputation when he disappeared in the Arctic in the 1845 North-West Passage expedition.

Jane Franklin would explore and travel to the end of her life, driven by a desire to see all parts of the habitable globe. She would be the first woman to travel overland from Melbourne to Sydney, would climb into the crater of a volcano in Hawaii, and visit Alaska when almost eighty years old. Intolerant of injustice, she had a passion for improvement, education and civilisation. Achill Island was as glorious in its natural beauty as any of the places she would journey to, the plight of its people in their poverty and ignorance as wretched as any she would witness. The opportunity and the challenge for the Achill Mission appeared great to her, but there was an ugly sting in its methods which had left her troubled and sceptical.

CHAPTER FIVE

Fractured

In following this story it has been difficult to uncover narratives of individual experiences among the Achill people through the years of the colony. It is as if the personal narratives are merged into the collective of a community struggling with day-to-day, season-to-season survival, leaving few records of individual lives. But we do have the chronicle of Bridget Lavelle, a young woman who reached out to grasp a better life and, in the process, ended up wounded and isolated.

It is not surprising that Bridget Lavelle would have longed for an existence superior to her peasant life. The Achill Mission beckoned, offering literacy, clothing, cleanliness and intellectual improvement – in short, refinement. She had the opportunity to move to a better place but wrestled with her conscience and with the conflicting dogmas presented by the priests and the proselytisers. Bridget sought out the truth but ended up a pawn in a patriarchal sectarian power play that broke her spirit and her health.

In late 1835, as the hours of winter darkness stretched, the Nangle family was seated around the fire in the parlour of their home in Dugort. They were pleased with the work of Bridget Lavelle, the children's maid who had joined them earlier in the year. Aged twenty-one, she had shown an interest in the Bible, had taken religious instruction, 'openly declared herself a Protestant' and moved to the colony, causing much unhappiness to her parents and the island's Catholic clergy.[1]

There was a knock at the parlour door and Bridget entered, clearly upset. Her mother, she reported, was in the kitchen and had brought bad news: Bridget's eldest sister had been seized with a sudden illness, was close to death and wished to see Bridget before she died. Edward was immediately suspicious since the new rabble-rouser parish priest, Father Connolly, had been in the village during the day hearing confessions and he suspected the priest's hand in the Lavelle story. Bridget was adamant that her mother would not put on such a show of grief if the story were untrue and left to accompany her mother to their home.

Afterwards, Bridget described what had happened. On reaching her parents' cabin, she found her sister by the fire in perfect health and then the tall figure of Father Connolly appeared: 'So, my lady, we have you at last.' The priest had come down heavy on the family, refusing to hear their confessions until they removed their daughter from the Achill Mission and brought her back to her own religion.

In a deposition before a magistrate some weeks later Bridget gave her story. She testified that:

> she was living peaceably and happily as a servant in the house of Rev Edward Nangle, Protestant Minister in Achill, where she enjoyed the fullest liberty of conscience, being permitted to go to whatever place of worship she pleased. That she became truly convinced that the Roman Catholic religion is false, and that the Protestant religion is the true, ancient faith. That in consequence of becoming a Protestant she was exposed to much persecution.

Bridget was caught between two worlds: two sets of competing dogmas on the one hand, the attractions of life at the colony versus the pull of her own family and community on the other. Her distress is palpable in the words of the deposition:

> that she could no longer use the prayers which she had learned in the Church of Rome, as she believed it wrong to pray to the Virgin … she never could [return to mass] with peace of conscience being persuaded that the worship

of a consecrated wafer is the great sin of idolatry against which the wrath of Almighty God is threatened in Holy Scripture.

She described how she was forcibly restrained in her parents' house and prevented from returning to service in the colony until, one day, she found an opportunity to communicate with Edward Nangle and expressed her desire to get the protection of the law to worship God in accordance with the dictates of her conscience. Edward arranged to meet her at William Stoney's house in Newport, from where she made her way to Dublin to the house of Neason and Isabella Adams who obtained employment for her in a house twenty miles outside the city.

Living in unfamiliar surroundings, away from the places and people she knew, Bridget now endured a different type of suffering – that of loneliness, home sickness and distress at the rumours that were being put around about her. Within a few months she was writing plaintively to her family: 'Dear Father and Mother, don't you know it is not the case, and why do you let it torment you.'[2] She was referring to the rumours which, she believed, were put out by the priests in Achill that Bridget had left the island because she had misconducted herself and had given birth to an illegitimate child in Dublin. She was anxious to hear from home and asked plaintively why her mother had not answered her letter when she had sent her a pound.

An unhappy marriage, poor health and an early death followed. Bridget Lavelle's was a fractured life, a microcosm of the distress caused by the collision of opposing dogmas and an innocent victim of sectarian warfare. Bridget's story is compelling in its very human desire to seek out a perceived better life which results in a rupturing of the ties of family and community and ends in isolation and tragedy. The individual and family stories of 'going over' to the Achill Mission would haunt an island people for generations to come.

***

In the depths of that same winter, a strange scene took place in Dugort when an Atlantic gale appeared as if it would drive the waves to the height of Slievemore itself. If Edward Nangle had relied largely, up to this stage, on scriptural schooling and preaching as the principal tools of his missionary work, he was now about to add another weapon to his armoury, signalled by the arrival of a novel cargo on the shores of north Achill. A printing press was safely delivered ashore, despite the lack of a local pier, and Achill witnessed the incongruous sight of children carrying parts of the equipment from shore to colony. Edward described the scenes in his journal.

Tuesday:

The hooker, with our printing press on board, came into the bay. It blew so hard that we could not land the cargo. The men on board the boat had much difficulty in mooring her: having secured her as best they could, they took to the small boat and, at the peril of their lives made for the shore, leaving the hooker to the mercy of the wind and waves. We expected that she would have broken from her moorings; however, her cable held fast, and towards evening the gale subsided, so that they were able to bring her out of the bay into harbour.

A few days after the boat again came into the bay, and her cargo was safely landed. It was an interesting sight to the children of some of the converts carrying the lighter parts of the printing press up to the Settlement, where they were to be used for the emancipation of others from the ignorance and bondage from which they had been delivered. We were indebted for this gift to some friends in London and York.[3]

The printing press enabled Edward Nangle to publish a monthly journal, the *Achill Missionary Herald and Western Witness*, which, arguably, was his most important instrument in sustaining his

Achill enterprise by promulgating the narrative around the colony and eliciting financial support from benefactors, largely in mainland Britain.[4] At a time when mass communications had not yet exploded, Edward had the technology and tools to drive a propaganda machine to propagate the message of a reforming west-of-Ireland mission. It could be compared in its impact to that of the internet, enabling the story of a bold Atlantic-island endeavour to go viral in its reach and become spectacular in its haul of financial support. The outlet of the monthly publication would whip up Edward Nangle's frenetic outpourings against Catholicism and its doctrines. Intriguingly, the acts of writing and editing in voluminous quantities may, arguably, have had a calming effect on his turbulent personality.

***

That winter saw Neason Adams and his wife, Isabella, move to Achill in December 1835, ahead of plan due to a Nangle family crisis, before their colony home was yet ready for occupation. While Neason brought crucial medical and administrative skills, Isabella brought a lightness of being and humour to their new colony home.

On their first day on the island, Isabella cast a rueful eye over her new surroundings and her husband's makeshift surgery as she sat writing a letter to a friend, close to an open window to allow the escape of smoke from a hearth filled with wet sods. It was pointless to dust as everywhere was immediately covered with a film of ashes. Dr Adams' medical supplies were gathered in a window recess on the small stairs and a little press was 'full of medicine, which was sent as a present from one of the Medical Halls in Dublin'.

A new assistant missionary, Mr Baylee, was expected to arrive shortly with his wife and children and Isabella mischievously wondered how the Baylee family could be occupied in a house which already accommodated many other needs. Two of the rooms had been converted into a printing office, two of the scripture readers used the house as their home, as did the Lendrum family. Isabella described the situation with a mix of giddiness and hilarity: 'I asked the other morning if two sorrowful-looking sheep, which I saw at the door, had been in the garden all night.' She was told that they were in Mr Baylee's parlour. 'Where were the oats threshed?' In Mr Baylee's parlour. 'Where is the old grey mare kept? And the pet eagle?' In Mr Baylee's parlour. 'Where is the Sunday-school held?' In Mr Baylee's parlour.[5] It was a far cry from their comfortable home and surgery at St Stephen's Green in Dublin and a dramatic change in their personal situation. The circumstances that caused the doctor and his wife to rush to Achill in the dead of night provides an insight into the emerging instability within the Nangle family.

It was December and a pregnant Eliza was at Dugort with their three daughters while Edward was travelling in England on preaching and fundraising work. One of the children fell ill, an illness which, Edward later condescendingly wrote, 'a mother's anxiety exaggerated into a dangerous one'. As the nearest medical services were in Castlebar, over thirty miles away, a distraught Eliza wrote to Dr Adams in Dublin describing the child's symptoms and pleading for medicine and advice by return post. A messenger was dispatched and asked to remain in Newport until the return mail car brought Dr Adams' reply. Four days elapsed before the messenger returned with the news that the doctor and his wife were travelling by mail coach from Dublin to Westport, a journey of eighteen hours, and would soon reach the colony.

'I have often heard my dear wife say that she felt ashamed for having brought her friends on so long a journey by giving expression to what proved to be a groundless apprehension', wrote Edward many years later.[6] His words reveal little sympathy or patience with his wife's anxieties and little appreciation of the difficulties for a mother and her young family experiencing winter hardship in a wild, isolated place amid a hostile community.

Edward's absence from home on speaking and fundraising engagements in the winter months, often over the Christmas period, became a regular occurrence. The reasons for this pattern of travel are unclear. Perhaps he judged it to be the optimum time for raising much-needed funds for his mission across England. Perhaps the severe Achill conditions in the dead of winter aggravated his own fragile state in a form of seasonal affective disorder. Perhaps he could not cope with Eliza's own anxiety and deepening distress and needed to escape.

Eliza's agitated message to Neason and Isabella Adams was a cry for help and the couple responded with compassion and alacrity. On seeing conditions on the island, and possibly observing Eliza's worried state and the pressures on the family, Dr Adams returned to Dublin, disposed of his house and medical practice at St Stephen's Green and settled permanently with his wife at Dugort. Neason and Isabella Adams were then in their late fifties and, for the remainder of their lives, they would dedicate themselves to supporting the Nangle family and ministering to the needs of the Achill people. Their light shone most brightly when the Great Famine hit and the islanders would speak of their charity and humanity: 'Dr Adams was a good man.'[7] Chatty, chirpy Isabella would have to give up her work at the infant school in later years when paralysis took away her powers of speech. On her death she shared, for a period, a mountain grave at Slievemore with the Nangle dead.

Eliza Nangle may well have faced into the New Year, 1836, with an improved disposition given the welcome company and support of her Adams friends. The January storms that unroofed some houses at the colony soon passed. Spring days followed with new plantings at the Dugort farm and house gardens, and she looked forward to the arrival of a new child.

On 11 July 1836, a baby boy was born. He was named Edward Neason Nangle after his father and Dr Adams. The baby was fragile and lived for just six weeks. Which was the harder? To lose a baby at birth before it uttered a cry, or to watch a delicate infant for forty days grow steadily weaker until finally it breathed its last? Was the pain lessened by holding an infant close hour after hour and day after day? Both experiences were traumatic and the latest tragedy brought a deterioration in Eliza's wellbeing. Edward Neason Nangle died on 23 August 1836 and was buried next to his infant brother in the mountain earth.

It was two years into Edward Nangle's Achill ministry and there was a growing unease about his tactics within the Protestant establishment. In the summer of 1836, an evangelical English clergyman touring Ireland raised his concerns about the Achill enterprise. Like Jane Franklin, he believed that Edward Nangle was mistaken to treat the beliefs of his Catholic fellowmen with contempt, arguing that there was nothing to be gained by outraging the feelings of Catholics through ridicule. He was unimpressed with Nangle's abusive language and terms of contempt for Catholic practices, urging that it was far better to treat one's adversaries with kindness, gravity and respect. The touring clergyman could see that Edward Nangle was grappling in a robust way with a stronghold of superstition and with an aggressive Catholic clergy led by John MacHale, but he urged that a vigorous ministry was best combined with a Christian benevolence.[8]

Sometime afterwards, another Protestant clergyman would address the issue of Edward Nangle's controversial methods, asking – on a visit to the colony – whether a gentler and less offensive approach to the superstitions and doctrines of Catholicism might be preferable.[9] The response from a member of the colony was that the Achill Mission's pugnacious approach was justified given the coarseness of the people among whom they ministered and their idolatrous practices. The mission, the argument went, would lose all claim to a religious and proselytising establishment if they treated their task with mildness. Rather, the mission could be compared to a nettle: if touched lightly, it stung the hand severely but, if grasped lustily, it could be plucked and destroyed without injury. The robust and aggressive energy which defined Edward Nangle's mission and raised concerns among commentators could be put down to a forceful personality, an impassioned hatred of everything associated with Catholicism and a lack of sympathy with the sincerely held beliefs and indigenous culture of the people. He drove his mission with gusto; he did, indeed, grasp the nettle with lust.

CHAPTER SIX

Is it a Wafer or is it a God?

The partisan battle in Achill moved beyond the island and erupted in a tumultuous public event where the Christian doctrine of the Eucharist became a lightning rod for the animosity between Edward Nangle and his followers on the one hand, and the priests on the other. Newport's rector and priest, whose relations were widely known to be acrimonious, faced one another at a gathering that rippled with hostility and division. The tension between the pair had been building for months, even years, and finally James Hughes and William Stoney confronted one another in the imposing surroundings of Castlebar Courthouse in bitter January conditions. The recent weather appeared to match the temper of the protagonists as hurricanes and snowstorms swept through the west, leaving the lakes around Castlebar frozen over and some mail cars unable to pass, such was the depth of snow. Edward Nangle was in the midst of the commotion, acting as chairman for William Stoney in the dispute about weighty theological issues.[1]

The public debate would centre on the Christian rite of the Eucharist, through which Christians remember Christ's sacrifice on the cross, but which was a rite with very different teachings in Catholicism and the reformed church. For Catholics, the bread and wine of the Eucharist were transformed through the process of transubstantiation into the body and blood of Christ, while the reformed church believed in a spiritual presence of Christ during the rite. The Eucharist became the topic around which the two rival religious groups expressed their mutual hostility.

William Stoney's association with the Achill Mission infuriated James Hughes, and he had written a lengthy letter to the Lord Lieutenant complaining that the Achill project blended everything that was 'cruel, unjust, lying and hypocritical'. He and William Stoney were neighbours: 'We live in the same town, not more than a quarter of a mile asunder.' It was Stoney, he claimed, who purchased the land for the Achill Mission colony and who conspired with Edward Nangle to induce the islanders to abandon their faith with bribes of money, cattle, houses and land.[2]

In a series of acrimonious exchanges, the pair of clergymen squabbled endlessly about the debate arrangements before finally challenging each other's debating prowess in Castlebar at an event that captured the public's interest. The rules of debate were agreed with their respective chairmen, Edward Nangle and Father Loftus of Dunmore: there would be ten points for discussion, with three hours allocated for the consideration of each point; neither debater would interrupt the other while speaking; and the chairman alone could call the speakers to order. They agreed that 300 people from each side would be admitted by ticket, but it would prove impossible to control the crowds that swelled into the courthouse despite the inclement weather. At 10am on Friday, 6 January 1837, the event got underway in Castlebar in an atmosphere of hysteria and hostility. It was an astonishing affair, akin to a prize fight between two champion boxers, each cheered to the rafters by his full-blooded supporters.

Edward Nangle had already been accused of circulating pamphlets in Achill with an image considered to be deeply wounding to Catholics: the picture of a mouse holding a Eucharistic wafer in its mouth while being pursued by a priest. It was seen in the community as a blasphemous illustration which ridiculed the most sacred aspect of Roman Catholicism and caused deep offence. To this day, an Irish Catholic generation views the Eucharistic, Holy Communion, as the most sacred element of their religion.

At one time, receiving the host required one to fast from food and drink, the unleavened bread could not be touched by hand nor bitten by teeth and it was a cause of consternation if the host fell to the ground as only the priest could handle the consecrated bread (bread transformed into the body and blood of Jesus Christ while still retaining the appearance of unleavened bread – the central Roman Catholic doctrine of transubstantiation).

The image which caused such uproar in Achill is in the crackled yellow pages of the *Protestant Penny Magazine* illustrating an Edward Nangle piece of writing entitled 'Transubstantiation disproved by a mouse'. The wood-cut illustration shows a Eucharistic wafer under the paws of a mouse while a priest and servant pursue the small animal. Edward Nangle wrote that the Catholic Council of Trent, no less, had decreed that if a consecrated host was taken accidentally by a mouse, or any such animal, 'let that animal, if he can be taken, killed and burnt, and his ashes cast into consecrated ground'. For Edward, the image represented the fanciful Council of Trent doctrine that the whole Christ is contained in every particle of the Eucharistic wafer: 'a senseless wafer-Christ in the place of a living God!' In circulating the image in his pamphlets, he claimed to be doing nothing more than presenting Roman Catholics' own idolatrous belief in a visual manner.

As for that Roman Catholic who slavishly allowed the wafer to melt on his tongue, rather than chewing it with his teeth, Edward provocatively challenged what he considered an absurd belief: 'Let him, the next time the priest places his god upon his tongue, to be dissolved in his saliva, remember that, by an imprudent movement of his teeth, he may have as many men and as many gods in his mouth, at the same time, as there are fragments of the wafer; and let him, as he values his reputation for common sense, emancipate himself from a system which gravely proposes such filthy and blasphemous absurdities to his acceptance as Divine truths.'[3]

The wafer of the Eucharist was, for Edward, the most powerful representation of the Church of Rome idolatry that contributed to the moral degradation of the people which the Achill Mission opposed. The sacred wafer had the power to explode the divisions between the two religious factions in Achill like nothing else.

The acrimonious Castlebar debate was in full swing. It was day two of proceedings and the topic for discussion was transubstantiation: 'to examine the proofs of the asserted deity of the consecrated host'.[4] The packed courthouse was uproarious and every available corner of the building was packed. Edward Nangle looked with scorn at the fat, short-necked priest, perspiration streaming from his face, as he removed his neck tie, unbuttoned his waistband, and loosened his braces. Edward disparagingly observed that, at one stage, it seemed as if, in the fervour of his arguments, the priest's trousers might even drop embarrassingly to the ground.

William Stoney pulled no punches in challenging the Eucharistic consecration ceremony in the Catholic celebration of the mass. It was ridiculous, he shouted, that the biblical references to 'eating the flesh and drinking the blood of Christ' were interpreted in a literal, rather than spiritual way. The wafer had no more resemblance to a human body after consecration than it had beforehand, and there was no carnal or corporeal presence of Christ in the consecrated wafer. All the human senses opposed such a ridiculous claim.

These statements caused uproar with many trying to shout William Stoney down: 'He is a liar. He is the devil.' Dramatically, the rector then proceeded to raise above his head a thin wafer stamped with the figure of Christ on the cross and the letters IHS. In the midst of the consternation, he roared at the crowd that he had in his possession a signed certificate from Joseph Baylee of the Achill Mission that the wafer was a host consecrated in Rome by the Pope himself. If this gesture was not sufficiently controversial, he then produced a second wafer which, he shouted, had been consecrated by none other than his opponent, Father James Hughes, parish priest of Newport. The rector raised the wafer aloft and roared: 'I ask you. Is it a wafer, or is it a God?'

William Stoney was in full flow, raising his voice another pitch above the rumpus among the crowd: 'Now gentlemen, if you were on the seas in a boat; if, with the waves running high and the storm raging, you were in danger of sinking, would you take this wafer out of your pockets and say to it, "deliver us, for thou art our God"?'

A section of the crowd stamped their feet and yelled, 'We would! We would!'

William Stoney hollered to be heard above the din. 'What is this thing that is a God to deliver? It is a small square piece of paste about three-quarters of an inch long, by five-eighths of an inch wide, of a whitish colour, and the thickness of a common wafer ... A mouse may nibble and devour what you will call upon as the great God of heaven and earth to save you from a watery grave!'

James Hughes could not contain himself and jumped onto a table bellowing: 'Who stole that host out of my ciborium? What Protestant went to my chapel and stole it? We believe that Christ is in it. Tell me the man's name that stole it. We believe it to be the Lord Jesus Christ.' He quoted Christ's words from the Bible in defence: 'I am the Living Bread which came down from Heaven – if any man eat of this Bread, he shall live forever.'[5]

The pandemonium in the courtroom during this part of the debate was so deafening that it interrupted the barrister seated in a nearby court, leading to the police being called and the gallery cleared. Before the meeting broke up, Edward Nangle complained of the behaviour of some in the crowd, suggesting that they revert to the earlier arrangement of admitting by ticket equal numbers of those supporting each side of the debate. The proposal was refused.

Because of the disturbances, permission to continue to use the courthouse for the debate was withdrawn and Sheridan's was agreed as an alternative location. Edward Nangle wanted the police to be present to prevent any further trouble but the priest's side refused and, in the absence of an agreement, the debate fizzled out. William Stoney and James Hughes returned to their respective neighbouring homes in Newport and Edward Nangle to Achill.

There was an anecdote that Edward Nangle liked to tell many years after he had departed Achill. It was the story of 'a fine boy, the son of one of the wealthiest of the neighbouring peasantry' in Dugort. The boy had attend the mission school, was withdrawn on the instructions of the priest, but again returned stating that he wished to remain at the colony. Edward recounted a conversation between the Achill Mission schoolmaster and the boy.

Asked if he and his father had a disagreement, he replied, 'No, we have not'.

Why did he come to the mission?

'Because I want to leave Popery altogether.'

Why did he want to leave that religion?

'Because it is a false religion and you have the truth.'

How did he know it was false and could he give one point where it was wrong?

'I can. The wafer. The priest says it is Christ and I know that it is not.'

How did he know that?

'Have not I the sight of my eyes?'

But did he not believe the priest as his father did?

'My father may believe him but I won't. I will not bow down to the wafer.'[6]

Edward was impressed that one so young could stand up in a popish village for what he believed when his action required no ordinary measure of moral courage. He believed that the boy could see with his own eyes that no gods were made with hands and, therefore, that the flour and water which were boiled in a saucepan and baked between two heated irons by the hands of the priest's servant, could not be God. Edward Nangle's attacks on the doctrine of transubstantiation were, for his detractors, a loathsome illustration of his abhorrence for the deeply held beliefs of the people among whom he came to minister.

***

It had to be one of Edward's most glorious days when he held in his hands the first edition of *the Achill Herald* dated 31 July 1837, and produced in Dugort with the Achill Mission's own printing press equipped with typefaces for English, Irish, Hebrew and Greek. The first edition was a print batch of 600; within two years the circulation would exceed 3,000, amounting to approximately a third of *The Times* newspaper circulation at that time. The first edition comprised of eight pages printed in small typeface and the annual subscription cost was four shillings.

On a rough calculation, producing The *Achill Herald* each month was equivalent to writing and editing two full-length books annually, without taking into account Edward's other published pamphlets, sermons, speeches and letters. It was an all-consuming task that had to have preoccupied most of his waking hours, with little time for reflection and rest for a fevered mind. Words were his weapon and month after month these words tumbled from The *Achill Herald* pages in a torrent of polemic and theological argument, anti-popery invective, and most importantly, pleas for financial support from Achill Mission friends and benefactors.

The *Achill Herald* became a formidable propaganda weapon to spread the word of the Achill Mission and to solicit donations. At the height of its success it was generating funds and attracting donations across Ireland and England, and as far away as India and Canada, of up to £6,000 annually. This extraordinary communication and fundraising effort has been compared to 'running a Christian tele-evangelical TV channel from the depths of the Amazon'.[7] Edward Nangle would continue to act as proprietor, editor and main contributor of the monthly publication for almost four decades until he resigned as editor in 1875.

There is an allure to Table 18 at the centre of the reading room in the National Library of Ireland, Dublin. It is as if there is a comfort factor in being in the middle of this elegant, horseshoe-shaped, domed reading room, rich in craftsmanship, and in switching on the soft green light. The yellow-brown pages of a bound volume of the *Achill Herald* for the years 1837–40 are brittle and fragile; they need handling with great care.

The cover page introduces the publication as 'a monthly journal exhibiting the principles and progress of Christ's kingdom'. It is a publication dedicated to 'exposing the errors and abominations of that section of the rival kingdom of antichrist commonly called the papacy'. At the top of the page is a wood cut image showing two figures, honoured as gods by pagans and, in the centre of the illustration, an image of a wafer 'boiled in a saucepan, impressed with a stamp, and clipped with a scissors': a wafer that is believed by Catholics to derive its deity and its right to divine adoration from its consecration by a priest. Transubstantiation will be a recurring theme in the *Achill Herald* pages.

One needs to carefully search the journal pages for any glimmers of information about Achill, the islanders, their way of life and indigenous culture. There are several references to the island harvests which Edward appears eager to describe: 'a small field of oats was reaped on our mission-farm . . . the grain is of the finest quality. The ground where it grew was a useless bog three years ago . . . our potato crop is remarkably productive, and we are happy to say that is generally so throughout the island.'[8]

One could easily miss important information snippets, like the tiny notice that features on the last page of the September 1837 edition:

DIED

In this Island, on the 6th Inst', of inflammation of the larynx, George Neason, aged three weeks, only son of the Rev Edward Nangle.[9]

∗∗∗

On 4 December 1837, Eliza Nangle finished a letter to her sister, Grace.[10] In contrast to the voluminous verbal outpourings of her husband, this appears to be the only record of Eliza's written words. She was grieving the death of her third son, George, less than three months earlier, and displayed the symptoms of postnatal depression.

I have so given up letter writing, that to lay a letter aside, and then forget to reply to it altogether, is quite an ordinary event. I do not, however, forget your kindness, nor the love due to all my dear friends. Your letter gave me much comfort in my trouble. I am, thank God, enabled to acknowledge His goodness and love in taking our lovely baby. I can heartily say – 'The Lord gave and the Lord hath taken away; blessed be the name of the Lord.' And yet, I often find my heart swelling with sorrow, and my eyes filling with tears that I cannot restrain. I trust I may become purified and made more [ready] for the Kingdom of Christ, with whom our three dead infants abide for ever and ever. Edward has been much spared in this owing to his absence from home. The burden rested on our affectionate friend, Dr Adams ... I am becoming very absent, much unfitted for the affairs of this life. My children often say to me – 'Now, Mamma, do you know what you are saying; and will you remember to-morrow?' I cannot write much more now than to say, that I love you with much affection.

Your very affectionate sister,

Eliza Nangle

Three years of Achill living have taken their toll: three infant deaths, sectarian attacks and islander hostility, fierce winter storms and challenging living conditions. Eliza's letter illustrates the classic symptoms of depression triggered by trauma: grief, tearfulness, lethargy, forgetfulness, inability to cope. There is, too, a hint of resentment that Edward had a means of escape from the acute suffering she experienced in Achill. Life was made tolerable only with the support of her sister, Grace, and her friends, Neason and Isabella Adams.

Writing the story of the Achill Mission three decades afterwards, Edward gave his perspective on his wife's condition: 'The absence of mind alluded to in this letter was induced by too much mental exertion and anxiety, acting on an infirm constitution.' Despite

Eliza's frail condition, Edward acknowledged his wife's tireless work on behalf of the mission while 'shrinking from notoriety under the shadow of her husband's name'.[11] She was a woman overcome by exertion, anxiety and trauma, beaten down by the hostility and notoriety that her husband's work and words attracted.

The worst was yet to come for Eliza Nangle. For now, she mourned her infant son whose body and blood were assimilated into the mountain earth.

CHAPTER SEVEN

Murder

It was only a matter of time before the Achill hostilities erupted into serious violence and tragedy. When the explosion came in a series of strange and bizarre events, it resulted in a disaster for a family that was splintered and scattered forever.

Margaret Reynolds' revulsion must have been acute as she stood on the slopes of the mountain at the rear of the Achill Mission settlement, the waters of Blacksod Bay below strangely still. She watched on as they dug up the fresh earth in the spot where they had buried her husband the previous day. Important official men crowded around: Daniel Cruise, resident magistrate in the Erris region of north Mayo who had travelled from Belmullet; George Dyer, inspecting commander of the coastguard from Westport; James Nugent, Justice of the Peace; and Fergus Ferrall, chief constable of police at Newport. Then there were the twelve jurors, six Protestants and six Catholics, who had the task of enquiring into how Captain Francis Reynolds, chief officer of the Achill coastguard, had acquired the injuries leading to his death on 2 January 1839. They all watched on as men stooped to dig and scoop up the soft earth.

The delay in arranging the inquest was an embarrassment, particularly to Fergus Ferrall who had trouble getting a coroner to travel to Achill when both the local coroner and another two magistrates declined a request. As the body of the deceased had started to decompose, George Dyer had decided to proceed with burial the previous day: 'Finding the body would not keep, I directed it to be interred.' The next day, once the magistrate Daniel

Cruise arrived from Belmullet, the inquest could proceed but they needed first to exhume the remains, to inspect the body and confirm identity.

The death of Francis Reynolds was a dramatic escalation in Achill hostilities stoked by the sectarian antagonism between the Achill Mission and the Catholic clergy. While his commanding officer would say of Captain Reynolds that the 'Crown has lost a most valuable officer',[1] all knew that the deceased had become a figure of contention in Achill. Who was this man, mourned by his pregnant widow and seven children that winter afternoon?

We get an insight into Francis Reynolds' character from his own words a couple of years earlier when questioned by the House of Lords Select Committee. He was asked what his occupation was.

'I am the civilian chief officer of the coastguard in the island of Achill.'

How long had he been in Achill?

'I have been in Achill this last six years.'

Did he ever have reason to ask his officers to provide protection to anybody?

'I have been obliged frequently to give orders to them to protect the people of the Protestant Settlement, Mr Nangle and Mr Baylee.'

Was he a Protestant or a Roman Catholic?

'I am a Protestant.'

Was his wife a Protestant or a Roman Catholic?

'She is a Roman Catholic.'

Had she heard anything from the priest in the chapel that caused him to take action?

'She told me that she heard the priest say that he would banish Mr Nangle and Mr Stoney and any man that would take their part; and it was their intention to drive the Protestants out of that island.'

Had he seen any improvements in Achill since Mr Nangle's arrival?

'I did. I saw great improvement in the cultivation of the land, and also in having schools for the instruction of the children.'

What were the feelings of the people towards Mr Nangle when he first arrived in Achill?

'They always appeared to me at the time to be very fond of Mr Nangle, and to like him very much.'

When, in his view, did the feelings of the people towards Mr Nangle change?

'When the priests gave orders to shout after the Protestants whenever they saw them. I think it was after Dr MacHale's visit that the greatest persecution was carried on.'[2]

It had to be a fraught situation for Margaret and Francis Reynolds, striving to rear their children and honour their respective faiths, while at the same time being caught up in the animosity around the Achill Mission as Francis tried to fulfil his duties on a turbulent island. Life may have been made somewhat bearable by their wild, romantic love. Family legend has it that Francis kidnapped the young Margaret Doherty from her home by the sea at Malin, County Donegal, east of the original Malin Head coastguard station.[3]

Once the magistrate from Belmullet arrived, the inquest into how Francis Reynolds received the injuries which led to his death got under way at Dugort. It was 6 January 1837 and the night ahead would become inscribed in history for what the elements would unleash on Ireland and in Achill. The first witness to be called by the inquest jury was the captain's widow, Margaret Reynolds.

Another visit by John MacHale to Achill a couple of months earlier had set in train an exceptional period of hostility between the pair of militant clergymen. Beyond the long sandy shores of Keel, home to the Reynolds family, and beneath the cliffs of Minaun, the archbishop had addressed a large crowd in what appears to have been his favoured stage for communicating with his Achill flock. Attired in vivid episcopal garments, a mitre on his head and crozier in his hand, it was a glorious amphitheatre for the archbishop as water plunged from cliff face gorges and Atlantic waves crashed all around. What made this stage even more histrionic was the fact that he could look directly across at the sprawling slopes of Slievemore, seat of the Achill Mission, and home to his bitter adversary.

The fiery priest, James Hughes of Newport, was the archbishop's warm-up act. He threw down the gauntlet to any islanders who would have dealings with the 'jumpers and preachers' of the colony, roaring out his instructions: 'Do not sell them anything, nor supply them with a particle; I expect that by these means you will make them fly out of the island.'

When it came to the archbishop's turn, John MacHale raised his arms high against the backdrop of cliffs and ocean and addressed his people: 'I call upon you to make a solemn promise this day not to have anything to do with the Achill Mission people. You must erect in this very spot a monument which, whenever you see it, will remind you of your promise to me this day. There is no place outside of hell which more enrages the Almighty than the Protestant colony ... I shall not dirty my mouth with the names of some people who are sending their children to the colony school. I hope they will give up doing so.'[4]

One of John MacHale's most effective tactics in dealing with the Achill Mission throughout his career was in his selection of Achill priests, men who appeared to mirror his own personality, who could take the fight to Edward Nangle. His new man selected as Achill parish priest was James Dwyer, whom the archbishop charged with arresting the growth of the colony and with beating Edward Nangle at his own game by wooing generous benefactors in England.

It was just a few weeks after John MacHale's visit that the series of events resulting in tragedy for Francis Reynolds got underway. Throughout the month of November gales battered the island, damaging several house roofs at the colony as gusts lashed Achill day and night. On 25 November, the brig *William & George*, having sailed from Liverpool at the start of the month, was driven on to rocks at Keel and wrecked in the south-east gale, close to the place where John MacHale had bellowed out his condemnation of the Achill Mission. Captain Reynolds and his boatmen rescued the brig's six crew and secured a portion of the cargo from destruction, but a substantial consignment of soft sugar and some crates of delph were lost. The coastguard officer then sought police assistance in protecting the surviving cargo, leading to an escalation in tension with locals who considered it their right to avail of the shipwreck bounty. It was a dangerous dispute which would end badly for the coastguard officer.

Margaret Reynolds, the forlorn widow, was sworn in before the inquest jury, signing the record of her evidence with the mark X, for she was not an educated person like her husband. She described what had happened on the night of 17 December when she saw her husband at about ten o'clock at their home at Keel before he went out; it was to do with the shipwreck and its cargo, she believed. It was between one and two o'clock the following morning when he returned home, distraught and upset, complaining that some people had tried to murder him. Francis had told her that he was attacked by Pat Lavelle and his wife, and she believed that this was a result of a confrontation her husband had with Pat Lavelle's brother, Martin, a few days earlier as locals were plundering the brig wreck.

'He was always complaining of soreness in his head,' Margaret Reynolds told the jury, 'from the morning of the 18th December until his death.' There was a great deal of ill will towards her husband, she said, and she heard the people say that they could all have collected wreck property for themselves, were it not for Francis Reynolds. After that night when he was struck, her husband had told her that, if he ever got well, he would leave the island as he was afraid the people would murder him.

Medical evidence was given by Dr Neason Adams and surgeon James Davis. When an auction of goods from the *William & George* took place on 28 December, Dr Adams, who attended the auction, noticed Francis Reynolds' poor state, ordered him to bed, prescribed medication and sought the assistance of Surgeon James Davis. On his arrival in Keel, the surgeon found the deceased man labouring 'under symptoms of compression of the brain – he had a wound or cut on the right side of his head'. When he next saw Francis Reynolds on Thursday, 3 January, the coastguard officer was dead.

Surgeon Davis made a post-mortem examination of the deceased's brain and found there an abscess, a fracture of the skull corresponding to the external wound on the head and a bone projecting inwards on the brain. 'In my opinion his death has been caused by compression of his brain in consequences of an abscess found in it which was caused by external injury from the wound received.'

The jury reached its decision and Mícheál McGreal, the jury foreman, signed off on their written verdict: 'We are of the opinion from the evidence adduced before us that the late Francis Reynolds came by his death in consequence of wounds inflicted on his head by Pat Lavelle and Nancy Lavelle his wife.'[5]

Margaret Reynolds returned to her children in Keel and jury members and officials left Dugort just hours before the seas and skies enveloping the island vented their rage.

There had been an unusual stillness in the afternoon air around the colony the day Francis Reynolds' body was exhumed for examination, the bitter cold of the previous day having given way to an unseasonal January warmth. An Atlantic warm front had brought with it a period of calm weather and a thick motionless cloud cover but, as the inquest crowd dispersed, the wind picked up and rain began to push in from the Atlantic. By ten o'clock, when the younger Reynolds' children were asleep in their beds, the intense wind and rain were causing the waves to leap and rip over the sands at Keel, the wind soon reaching a full hurricane force and the darkness shot through with lightening. Between two and four o'clock that night the hurricane was at the height of its intensity. Sleet and bursts of hail pounded the houses as the sounds of waves crashing over rocks could be heard above the roar of the storm and the island of Achill trembled with the storm's assault through to sunrise. It was the *Night of the Big Wind*, the most devastating storm experienced in Ireland in several hundred years with winds reaching 100 miles per hour – a night of trauma and disturbance to crown a day of shock and strain for Margaret Reynolds.

The people of Ireland woke next morning to scenes of devastation, with several hundred people dead across the country. *The Telegraph* reported that the oldest person in County Mayo 'cannot recall to his mind the memory of a storm so terrific as that which we were visited on the night of Sunday, 6th January'. From Sunday midnight until early light on Monday morning, 'the winds of Heaven were indeed let loose, and it seemed as though they had all united to wreak vengeance on the earth'.

Windows were smashed, doors burst open, slates shot through the air, beams and rafters smashed and roofs were blown down. Across Achill, corn stacks were flung over the landscape, boats were ripped from moorings and thatched roofs were lifted from cottages. The Achill Mission colony, perhaps benefiting from the shelter of the mountain, had, according to the *Achill Herald*, 'got off more lightly than most'.[6]

Two women, both pregnant, endured the night of the mighty storm without their husbands. Francis Reynolds lay in a fresh grave on the mountainside adjacent to the burial place of the Nangle infant sons, while nearby, Eliza Nangle comforted her three daughters in the absence of Edward, who was on speaking engagements in England.

Stories of these remarkable events have been handed down in the island folklore:

> The opening of the grave at Dugort was the cause of the storm. The wind blew down the ditches and the houses and the cornstacks. It spread over the length and breadth of Ireland.
>
> They took up his corpse for a post-mortem and had an inquest, and Lavelle and his wife and a child were arrested

and brought to Castlebar. The little infant was 5 months with them in prison, waiting for the trail.[7]

Francis Reynolds, friend to Edward Nangle, protector of Eliza and her children during Edward's frequent absences, faithful supporter of the Achill Mission, was laid to rest for a second time on the slopes of Slievemore.

***

There are times, very occasionally, when Edward Nangle engages in self-reflection and, in the process, provides a glimpse into the recesses of his character and personality. One such insight occurs in his speech to a meeting of The Protestant Association in Exeter Hall on 28 December 1838, while Edward was unaware that the life of Captain Reynolds was ebbing away in Achill. He had been invited to speak before an important audience – the Exeter Hall Association, established to promote the principles of the Reformation. In a curious diversion from his main script, Edward spent time explaining to his listeners the reasons why he was reading from a prepared text rather than speaking spontaneously, as was his practice on such occasions. It was a decision that he had taken after much reflection, given the excitable nature of the material he was dealing with and the danger that he might arouse excessive feelings of passion within himself and his audience.

He explained that he was dealing with highly charged subject matter and that he himself had experienced much oppression and injustice: 'I feared lest the galling sense of our wrongs might betray me, in the excitement of extemporaneous speaking, into the use of language inconsistent with the calm sobriety of speech which I wish to observe in laying the statement of our grievances before the British public.'[8] For these reasons he had decided to commit to paper every word of his address in order to keep his own feelings under restraint and, at the same time, provide a written record for the public press. Without the formal constraints of the written word Edward Nangle could let rip, like a man possessed, in a frenzied tirade. In later years, one supporter would recall witnessing this hyper preaching style: Edward's voice raised to a high-pitched roar, stamping his feet, Bible clasped to his chest and fierce passionate words tumbling out in uncontrolled excitement.[9]

It was a moment of self-awareness before his Exeter Hall audience when Edward appeared to accept that sober language and prudent restraint may have served the cause of the Achill Mission better on occasion than an uninhibited harangue. Perhaps the incessant writing, which was such a central feature of Edward's life, served another purpose in providing a structure and a discipline to calm his frenzied emotions, and affording a type of coping mechanism without which dark demons may have completely overwhelmed him.

John MacHale's own outbursts on his recent visit to Achill had, Edward Nangle told his audience, exposed the truth of the archbishop's intent in executing a system of 'exclusive dealing' against the colony, and forbidding any interaction between the islanders and the Achill Mission. The mission's only defence against such actions, he said, was to develop its own 'protective system', particularly for the converts who sought colony protection. He explained that when an islander came to the Achill Mission with a request to be sheltered from the Catholic priests, they were given a cottage at a fair rent with a plot of land attached. In addition, they were offered employment in reclaiming colony land and the produce of their labour sufficed to pay their wages. By this system, the people were made independent of the priests and the tenants were able to maintain themselves by their own endeavour. 'Were it not for this protective system, it would be physically impossible for us to maintain our position in Achill,' he told a receptive audience.[10]

Edward's speech was received with huge enthusiasm at Exeter Hall.

On returning to Achill, Edward had the difficult and emotional task of visiting the widow of Francis Reynolds and her children in Keel. 'Oh, Mr Nangle, if he was here today how he would rejoice to see you,' Margaret burst out, sobbing. Edward noticed a gun and a fishing rod suspended in their usual places in the house, a melancholy reminder of his departed friend. An infant slept in its cradle while another child stood close to its mother.

Edward expected that Margaret Reynolds would receive a small pension from her husband's employer, but he knew that this would be inadequate to provide the children with the level of education to which the rank of their deceased father entitled them. He did what he excelled at by issuing an appeal to the Protestants of England and Ireland for assistance for the Reynolds family. The appeal was issued on the understanding that the children would be educated in the Protestant denomination: 'To omit this condition would be to abandon principle, and to neglect the fondest wish of the deceased.'[11] The wishes of the children's mother, Margaret Reynolds, appear not to have been a consideration.

In October 1839, the *Achill Herald* announced the birth of a baby son to Margaret Reynolds in Westport, a posthumous son for Francis and the eighth child of Margaret and her husband. He was named Francis after his late father. Just a few months earlier, Eliza Nangle had also given birth to a baby boy, William, the couple's first surviving son.

Just over a year after his father's death, one of Francis Reynolds' sons was admitted to the London Orphan Institution. A year later, it was reported that two of the Reynolds' sons embarked on board a ship for Quebec on their way to Upper Canada where a brother of their late father lived.[12] Six of the Reynolds' eight children would eventually emigrate to Canada. Margaret Reynolds ended her days back in Donegal at the place from where Francis had whisked her away with youthful passion. The Reynolds' family ended up ruptured, split apart and scattered across the world as a result of an Achill sectarian conflagration.

It was barely three months after Francis Reynolds' death and Edward Nangle was apoplectic at the outcome of the murder trial in Castlebar. Following testimony by two witnesses, Bridget Mangan and Michael Lavelle, the judge concluded that there was insufficient evidence to convict the prisoners and that Francis

Reynolds' death was a case of justifiable homicide. The jury brought in a verdict of acquittal against the accused, Pat Lavelle and his wife.

'The trial, we say, was a mock one', Edward accused, and the fault for this lay entirely with those employed on behalf of the Crown and their total mismanagement of the proceedings. It was preposterous that the two main witnesses who the Crown called upon in making the case for the prosecution, were, in fact, the very persons whom the prisoners could have called upon in their own defence, given their connection with those charged with Francis Reynolds' murder. Worse still, he railed, the two witnesses had been under the care of the notorious Father Hughes of Newport from shortly after the date of the murder, and had been well-schooled in their evidence.[13]

The Achill Mission leader was a man aggrieved, but the *Freeman's Journal* had little sympathy with his complaints. The paper concluded that the verdict justified their view all along that Captain Reynolds lost his life in a drunken brawl after forcing entry into the house of the accused at a late hour.[14]

Achill, it appeared, was descending into chaos and George Dyer, inspecting commander of the coastguard, was worried: 'Achill contains 47,000 acres with between 5 and 6,000 inhabitants and those generally of the most lawless characters'. The security situation was volatile and unpredictable, he advised; more constabulary were urgently needed along with a petty sessions court on the island. Otherwise, law and order would continue to deteriorate and he feared that the situation in Achill would escalate out of the control of the authorities.[15] Action was needed.

CHAPTER EIGHT

Public Scrutiny

What was the truth about Edward Nangle and the Achill Mission? Perhaps a pair of skilful writer-journalists could provide an impartial answer and a balanced commentary.

The writers, Samuel and Anna Maria Hall, were aware of two contradictory views of the Achill project. On the one hand, Edward Nangle was denounced as a zealot, an intolerant firebrand and an embarrassment to his church with the extremity of his rhetoric and an absence of generosity towards the sincerely held beliefs of Catholics. For others, the Achill Mission was a sanctuary of protection against the evils of popery and the power of its priests: an impressive attempt to rescue an abject people from barbarism and idolatry and lead them towards civilised living. The Halls were on a tour of Ireland and their objective in visiting Achill was to view the colony first-hand and give readers their assessment.

The question as to whether the Halls had formed their views about the Achill Mission before they even reached the island would, afterwards, become a matter of debate. They may well have absorbed the growing establishment consensus that the colony was somewhat of an embarrassment, with its extreme methods and propaganda. For now, they sharpened their journalistic tools with a forensic examination of the evidence, reviewing material from the *Achill Herald* as well as the mission's annual reports. They conducted interviews and spoke to some mission orphans with devastating effect. They compared the Achill Mission schools unfavourably to those run by the Protestant Rector at nearby

Newport. Most significantly, they followed the money trail, tracing the flow of funds into the mission coffers for various projects and raising questions about the benefits and value for money derived from Edward Nangle's hugely successful fundraising campaigns.

Wexford-born Anna Maria Fielding Hall and her husband, Samuel, socialised in London literary circles and were prolific writers and editors, producing hundreds of titles between them. In the summer of 1842, they embarked on an extensive Irish tour with the aim of producing a guide book of Ireland for visitors; the journey resulted in the publication of *Ireland: Its Scenery and Character*, which included a harsh assessment of the Achill colony. To outward appearances the Halls had much in common with Edward Nangle. Like him, they were avid evangelical colonists, detesting what they saw as the demeaning effects of Catholicism on the lives of the Irish peasants. They were not opposed to the work of conversion since they considered that every conscientious accession to Protestantism contributed to the improved well-being and prosperity of Ireland. They represented a widely held view that Protestants in Ireland had the character and enterprise essential for economic progress, while Catholics had an innate tendency towards laziness and sloth. The Halls even claimed that they could identify if a particular inn they stayed in was kept by a Roman Catholic or a Protestant by its external appearance: 'Every traveller in Ireland is fully aware of the fact that a greater attention to appearance, and neater, cleaner and more orderly habits, distinguish the Protestant from the Catholic of every grade, below the very highest.'

Where the Halls diverged from Edward Nangle was in their view that his methods lacked 'that gentle, peace-loving, and persuasive zeal' that should characterise true Christian charity.[1] In this they were aligning themselves with the assessment of other established church figures. In questioning the use of funds subscribed by the mission's friends and benefactors, they would also ensure that the Achill Mission would find it difficult to shake off suspicions around its financial affairs. The very public criticism by the Halls brought unwelcome notoriety to Edward Nangle and his mission over a protracted period.

The Halls came to Achill just as its infant tourism industry was beginning to take hold with the establishment of a hotel by Robert Savage in Achill Sound the previous year. The first known advertisement for the promotion of tourism to Achill had appeared in the *Achill Herald* where Robert Savage thanked his patrons and informed them of tours, fishing, trips to caves and the Druid's Altar – a megalithic tomb at Slievemore. The advertisement referred to remarkable island places which included the 'interesting and fast-rising Protestant colony'.[2] Within a few years the colony would have its own hotel at Dugort and the Achill tourism industry would be well underway.

On reaching Achill, the Halls were overwhelmed by the astounding beauty of its 'naked nature', a landscape of surpassing grandeur and sublimity and a place rich in materials for the painter's pencil and brush. They arrived at Dugort and took in the amazing sight on the slopes of Slievemore, like a glossy property brochure with its terrace of alternating single and two-story slated buildings comprising a school, infirmary, corn mill, dispensary, small hotel, printing office and residences. Behind the terrace of houses ran a row of cottages for the colony workers – an impressive sight in sharp contrast to the surrounding squalor. The timing of the Halls visit was unfortunate, for a contagious disease had caused the mission schools to be closed. The visitors were also taken aback by the lack of neatness and cleanliness they observed, having expected that this would have been one of the colony's distinguishing features.[3]

From the material they had reviewed, the Halls were able to extract data for the period since Edward Nangle took over the Achill Mission stewardship. By 1842, the colony accommodated fifty-six families comprising 365 individuals. Eleven of the families, one-fifth of the total, were originally Protestant, and forty-five originally Catholic. Of the latter, only nineteen families were natives of Achill. The Halls concluded that, out of an Achill population of 6,000, only ninety-two islanders had been converted by the Mission in nine years. This was hardly a convincing track record given the temptation that had to exist for Roman Catholics to exchange their destitution and misery for employment and the material benefits on offer by the colony.

There then followed the most devastating aspect of the Halls' critique, couched almost in the form of a report by a contemporary forensic journalist. If these numbers represented the head count of converts from Catholicism to Protestantism by the Achill Mission over a nine-year period, was it not reasonable to ask what the conversion of these Catholics had cost? They turned to the mission's published annual reports in carrying out their cost-benefit assessment. They found the most recent Achill Mission annual report for 1841 to be 'a very confused document', with several separate accounting categories for Achill Mission funds between general mission expenses, the orphan asylum, the dispensary and the Achill Bible and church missionary society. The overall income for the year was approximately £3,000 and most of the money appeared to be have been spent on the Achill Mission's own infrastructure: salaries for missionaries and teachers, building construction and maintenance, the printing office and dispensary and farm costs. The Halls concluded that the substantial funds raised by the Achill Mission from generous English donors could not be considered value for money if judged in terms of either conversion numbers or any improvement in the general well-being of the Achill people.[4]

The financial affairs of the Achill Mission had come under unwelcome public scrutiny. Since January 1840, the Achill Mission had operated under a new organisation whereby the Dublin guardians had devolved considerable powers to a court of local management of which Edward Nangle was chairman.[5] The other members were the second missionary, Dr Adams, Captain Dyer of the coastguard and the mission steward. The second missionary and Dr Adams were assigned the duties of treasurer, charged with receiving all Achill Mission monies and making all payments on the instruction of Edward Nangle. It was a system that would cause concern to a modern-day auditor. The Achill Mission dealt with substantial cash receipts, most of which were collected directly by Edward on speaking and fundraising itineraries, while Eliza acted as the mission bookkeeper. Under the revised mission organisation Edward authorised all payments, which included his own salary, travel and other expenses. An unusual aspect of the accounts was the manner in which they were split between different mission activities, making it difficult to get a clear view of the financial position. It was as if the breakdown of the mission's work into different segments was aimed at 'branding' different activities to appeal to different audiences for fundraising purposes. This was particularly the case for the orphan refuge which, in the 1839 annual report, was given a central position alongside the Achill Mission itself on the report's front page. The orphan refuge became a critical target for the Halls' criticism, and their dramatic first-hand encounters with some of the orphans caused a sensation.

***

Edward Nangle laid great stress on the work of the colony's orphan asylum, which proved to be a powerful tool in his proselytising weaponry. The institution allowed orphan children of Catholic parents to be taken and educated in the principles of Protestantism and moulded in the habits of useful industry. Edward had devised an ingenious financial model for the orphanage: he estimated that £5 per annum was required for the maintenance of each child and, should there be a surplus of funds at year end, the money was lodged in a savings bank. When an individual orphan was married, bound to a trade or otherwise settled, his or her dividend from the fund would be either given to the orphan or spent in a manner that the orphanage governors thought fit. An important benefit of such a scheme, Edward told his benefactors, was that it would act as a check on the 'intermarriage of the orphans with papists' as no payment would be made where such a marriage took place. He believed that once the orphan children were settled in life, this

Eliza Nangle with her daughters Francis and Henrietta. This watercolour was likely painted by Edward Nangle in the early 1830s. (Courtesy the Nangle Family)

The Achill Mission Colony, Dugort. By the mid-1830s an impressive settlement of slated houses and reclaimed fields had grown up on the slopes of Slievemore as a result of the Achill Mission developments. (National Library of Ireland)

Keel Village, Achill. In the closing months of 1847, in the midst of the famine crisis, James Hack Tuke, a leading Quaker philanthropist, arrived in Keel and was shocked by the conditions he witnessed. (National Library of Ireland)

Slievemore Hotel, Dugort. By the 1840s the Achill Mission Colony was attracting visitors to the Slievemore Hotel and Achill's tourist industry was underway. (National Library of Ireland)

Bunnacurry Monastery, Achill. In 1851 John McHale, Archbishop of Tuam, acquired land at Bunnacurry as a base for a Franciscan monastery and school. This started a concerted effort by him to counteract the influence of the Achill Mission on the island. (National Library of Ireland)

The Achill Mission Colony with St Thomas' Church in the foreground. When the Achill Mission became an extensive landlord in Achill in 1851, it acquired the land at Finsheen across from the main Colony development which became the site for the new St Thomas' Church which opened in 1855. (National Library of Ireland)

The Fishery, Dooagh, Achill. Having acquired extensive land in Achill, the Achill Mission attracted newcomers to the island to sub-lease its assets. A Scottish man, Alexander Hector, established an extensive fishing and processing enterprise on the island in the 1850s. (National Library of Ireland)

Main Street, Dugort, Achill Island

Main Street, Achill Mission Colony, Dugort showing a feature of the development in its alternating single and two story buildings. (Mayo County Library)

Main Street, Dugort, Achill Island

Postcard photograph showing the west end of the Colony's Main Street with Temperance Bar. The settlement comprised housing, school, orphanage, post office, hotel, dispensary, corn mill and functioning farm. (Mayo County Library)

St Thomas' Church, Dugort, Achill. The church continues to be used by the local Church of Ireland community to this day. In September 2011 the local Catholic and Church of Ireland communities organised a memorial and healing service at the site and placed crosses at the unmarked graves in the adjacent cemetery. (Brian Thompson)

would counter any efforts by the priests to have them removed from the colony.

The orphanage offered a further benefit: it could be placed at the heart of the Achill Mission's appeal to its donors with powerful effect. For how could Edward's subscribers not rejoice at the spectacle of children 'rescued from the degradation of Popery' being offered education and training for a better future life? The configuration of the orphanage comprised four individual cottages, each accommodating twenty-five orphans and a supervisor. The girls were trained in sewing, washing and domestic skills, and the boys in planting and harvesting crops, cutting turf and other field labour.[6]

The mission's work with orphans was something that the Halls would have instinctively supported for they believed that 'the education of even a small part of the rising generation in good habits and right principles is a work upon which the moneys of the wealthy might be most advantageously expended'. They learned that the colony orphan children arrived from distant parts and were mainly children of Roman Catholics who had been left destitute. However, their instinctive sympathy for this work changed decisively after a chance encounter.

On their way to Dugort the visitors met a wretched-looking boy of about thirteen years of age, clothed in rags, who told them he had been dismissed from the colony. Mr Nangle had taken away his decent clothes, he told the visitors, and given him three shillings to convey him a distance of about sixty miles to County Sligo where his grandfather lived, his parents both being dead. The Halls reasoned with the boy, advised him to return to the colony and themselves brought him before Edward Nangle only to be met with an intransigent response. Edward was adamant that he would not tolerate misconduct and refused to readmit the boy into the colony. The visitors then took the boy in their car out of Achill and gave him money to support himself on the road back to his home place. The affair, however, did not end here for, driving through Newport, the Halls heard of five other boys who had also been dismissed from the colony orphanage: 'six poor little helpless and deserted children were cast upon the world, nearly naked and penniless, without parents, without homes, and without friends'. It was sensitive and controversial material.

The Halls made no apology to their readers for presenting their case, arguing that the many subscribers and patrons who sustained the Achill Mission work knew nothing of it except its name. Their verdict on the Achill Mission was unambiguous: it had, they concluded, been 'a complete failure', had not been conducted in accordance with the principles of charity and Mr Nangle did not conduct his establishment with any sense of gentle, peace-loving Christian zeal. Those who subscribed to the mission's work were spending their money on a worse than useless cause: 'No good has arisen or can possibly arise from the Colony conducted as it is.' Their censure was public, hard-hitting and damaging.[7]

***

By the close of 1842 the highly charged public squabble with the Halls was taking its toll on Edward and, not for the first time, his health disintegrated under mounting pressures. On Christmas Day, he was in Leamington, West Midlands, England on a day when a man might have been with his family. But Eliza Nangle, her three daughters and two infant sons celebrated Christmas at Dugort without their father, who continued his English tour while constantly complaining of poor health: 'I had been ill with my head for the last three or four weeks; felt as if my mind was gone; was much cast down … Could not sleep at night, and was in a miserable state.'[8]

Despite his ailments, Edward persisted with his preaching and fundraising. He preached at Trinity church in Cheltenham, collecting £47, twice as much as he expected, with money coming in afterwards which raised that collection to almost £60. While he was able to raise his energy and spirits to preach with power and passion, he afterwards relapsed, burdened with anxiety and depression, and expressing himself 'overwhelmed with cares about Achill'.

Throughout this period, in a series of letters published in the *Achill Herald*, he fulminated against Samuel and Anna Maria Hall and their criticism of his mission following their visit the previous June. He resented their denunciation of his work, seeing it as a personal reproach: 'The personal taunts and insinuations whereby you are pleased to assail my character shall go without any notice, but your misrepresentations of the principles and workings of the Achill Mission shall be subjected to searching and unsparing scrutiny.'

Edward challenged the Halls on the detail of their visit to Achill: 'Will you please to inform the public how much time you spent in the *examination* of the Settlement, and in the acquisition of that *experience* which is gravely put forth to give weight to your statements?' He proceeded to answer his own question: the Halls' stay at the colony did *not exceed two hours*, for they arrived at Dugort at half past five on Wednesday, 22 June, and left two hours later! 'Truly, sir, the rapidity with which you can acquire *experience* throws into shade the wonders of the steam press!'

Edward disputed the Halls' contention that the Achill Mission was founded 'for protestantising the Island of Achill'. While the conversion of the island had indeed been a clear objective of his mission, Edward now claimed that the most the mission ever expected was to draw some of the island's inhabitants 'out of the apostate church of Rome to Christ' and to afford shelter to persecuted converts from other parts of the country. He believed that these objectives had been more than realised. As to the Halls' sordid references to the cost of the colony's activities, he rejected these criticisms, 'as if the salvation of immortal souls for which Christ died, was not a worthy object for the expenditure of a smaller sum of the world's wealth than is often squandered without a rebuke, on the follies and vanities of this perishing world.'

Edward was clearly rattled and forced on the defensive, spelling out what had been achieved by the investment in the Achill Mission: an impressive physical infrastructure comprising a terrace of buildings with two dwellings for religious ministers, steward's house, hotel, printing press, dispensary, tuck mill, corn store and kiln. 'All of these buildings are constructed of good stone and mortar and covered with the best Welsh slate.'

As for the denigration of the orphan asylum, he robustly defended this work, asserting that the colony had lodged, clothed, educated and fed 100 orphans over the previous four years. Sensitive to the Halls' reporting of boys having been dismissed from the orphanage, he appeared to have reassessed his actions, telling his readers that the boys' expulsion had been temporary and all five had now returned to the colony. 'The six boys are now doing well, but had we weakly permitted ourselves to be swayed into an untimely relaxation of discipline by the gratuitous interference of a casual visitor ... the consequences would have been most injurious if not ruinous to these youths and their companions.'

Significantly, Nangle denied the Halls' allegation that a profession of Protestantism was extorted as a condition of receiving the Colony bounty: 'I deny with all the vehemence of honest indignation, that food, lodging, clothing, or any similar inducement was ever used by me to influence any one in his religious profession ...' This was a charge that would return to haunt the Achill Mission in the years of horror that lay ahead. Edward concluded his letter to Samuel Hall: 'I am truly sorry that anyone calling himself a protestant should appear before the public in the position in which you have rashly placed yourself ... As to your personal taunts and insinuations concerning my position and character, they give me no concern, they can only lower you in the estimation of those who know me, and whose opinion I value.'[9]

The public disagreement between Edward Nangle and Samuel Hall increased in ferocity with each exchange and Samuel Hall did not back down, repeating his accusation that the 'experiment in Achill had been a complete failure' and that the subscribers to the Achill Mission had bestowed their money for a worse than useless purpose. Samuel Hall was equal to Edward Nangle in his verbal powers, twisting the knife to devastating effect: 'Be assured, sir, that religion is strong enough to overcome your miserable attempts to degrade it – that Christianity cannot be permanently tainted by coarseness, ignorance and bigotry of which you are representative. I have done my duty. To God be the glory of the triumph I have achieved over you. May God give you a new heart, and renew a right spirit within you.'[10]

The acrimony was indicative of a prominent feature of the Achill Mission's history in the gulf that emerged between Edward Nangle, on the one hand, and leading figures of the Protestant establishment on the other. While in a later report on the colony towards the end of the Great Famine the Halls offered a more benign assessment of the Achill Mission, their earlier criticism damaged the public perception of Edward Nangle and his enterprise, drew unwelcome attention to the volume of funds raised from the mission's benefactors and raised legitimate questions about the benefits derived from the Achill Mission expenditure.[11]

CHAPTER NINE

Tenth Year

A decade into his Achill project, Edward Nangle was increasingly confident while beginning to focus on issues of land ownership and the further expansion of the Achill Mission's terrain. He was also emboldened to introduce to the colony the practice of recantations, whereby Catholics publicly denounced the tenets of their denomination in favour of those of Protestantism – an odious and humiliating ritual which he had experience of from his Cavan days. Provocatively, he also infiltrated the ranks of the Catholic clergy, securing a number of high profile priest recruits to his cause. His mission appeared to be at the zenith of its powers.

'This day I finished my tenth year,' Edward Nangle told the members of the Devon Commission on 31 July 1844. The commission was established by Sir Robert Peel to look at relations between Irish landlords and tenants and to investigate the rancorous issue of land leases. The officials would hear the testimony of over 1,000 witnesses and Edward Nangle was witness number 474. It was a confident performance from a clergyman who was now revealing his surprisingly strong commercial instincts alongside an aspiration to acquire further property for the next phase of his work.

Edward may well have swelled with pride as he worked through his evidence and described the transformation that had taken place in that part of Achill where agricultural reclamation had been carried out by his mission. To exemplify the progress made, he told the commission members that when he first arrived in Achill there had not been as much as one cart on the island;

now there were several, as well as special ploughs for drilling turnips. He listed the other improvements that the colony had been instrumental in bringing about: an island dispensary, a post office, a mail car running three days a week to Newport, two inns to accommodate visitors and a court of petty sessions to uphold the law. 'All these advances in civilisation have been made in the last ten years, and have manifestly sprung out of the Achill Missionary establishment which includes in its more important objectives – the agricultural improvement of its locality.' These were the words of an assured man, confident in his achievements.

Edward and Eliza were, by then, parents to six children. Having lost three sons during the family's early years in Achill, the family now comprised three small boys as well as three daughters approaching adulthood. Their youngest son, the delicate George, was just three months old, and Edward's evidence to the commission reveals a man alert to his responsibilities in providing for his family.

Edward had done his homework and he had a proposal for the commissioners. He told them there was considerable opportunity to reclaim land and make a return on the investment, but only if long term leases were available from the landlords. He had himself undertaken a detailed exercise in estimating the cost of reclaiming four acres of bog land and the likely crop returns. It was clear to him that nobody would wisely sink capital into the reclamation of such land unless longer leases could be secured. He was asked whether he would take on such a reclamation if he had the capital and good tenure by way of a lease: 'To-morrow, if I had a lease of it in perpetuity, for the benefit of my children, I would get a steward and say, "Here is so much money, do the best you can with it."' Edward told the commissioners that if he were a country gentleman owning his own property, rather than holding the obligations of a missionary, he would implement the proposals as he had outlined.[1]

The perennial issue of the rights of property owners versus the needs of the people was being hotly debated at the time of the Devon Commission and was reflected in an article on the state of Ireland in *The Times* a few months earlier. What was going on in

Ireland, the writer argued, was nothing less than 'a war for land'; it was a conflict between the tenants' right to live and the landlords' right to land possession. Those who were lecturing the Earl of Devon about not compromising property rights in carrying out his Irish task should ask themselves: is it the rich man's right to possess or the poor man's right to live? *The Times* writer offered unequivocal advice to Lord Devon: 'The rights of property thus abused are inconsistent with the paramount right of human beings to their existence', and if adjustments to Irish landlordism were not undertaken quickly the situation would become even more desperate.[2] These words were to prove prophetic.

The detail of Edward's evidence to the Devon Commission is interesting in hindsight in the manner in which it foreshadows certain of the Achill Mission's responses to the Famine in subsequent years. When Asked how the colony obtained labour and if the colony workers were drawn from the ordinary labourers on the island, Edward had replied: 'we have generally enough of persons connected with our own settlement to do the work, and we do not give employment to any others unless we have more than we can do, or in a scarce season'.

Did he mean that his operations on the island were confined to those connected with the colony?

The ordinary work, he said, was done by people connected with the colony but sometimes, when there was building work going on or at harvest time, they employed people not connected with the settlement.

Was it the principle of the Achill Mission to colonise the district with Protestants or converted Protestants?

'Principally converted Protestants.'

Was the colony land distributed therefore to those who conformed to the established faith?

'Yes.'

While admitting to the practice of allocating colony land and providing employment to converts, Edward was more defensive when questioned about other aspects of the colony's operations.

In providing relief from distress, were there any inducements held out to people to join the colony?

'Most decidedly not, we have frequently singled out the parties we have known to be most bitter opponents of our principles, and given them employment when the distress came.' In administering relief at the mission dispensary, was any distinction made between those who followed Achill Mission principles and those who did not?

'No,' came the reply. 'There are upwards of fifty or sixty of those who entertain different religious principles from our own for every one of our own people. There is never a question asked about it.'[3]

The issue of the perceived Achill Mission discrimination in its activities as between Protestant and Catholic was a live one on the eve of the Great Famine. It would become divisive and contested in the years immediately ahead.

Edward's testimony showed the evolution of his thinking and tactics from a concentration on schooling and scripture education to seeing land acquisition and ownership as key mission tools in his work of evangelisation and moral regeneration. Within the year, the Devon Commission published its voluminous report. It echoed the view of De Tocqueville over a decade earlier in its finding that poor relations between landlord and tenant were at the heart of Ireland's problems: 'The foundation of almost all the evils by which the social condition of Ireland is disturbed is to be traced to those feelings of mutual distrust which too often separate the classes of landlord and tenant and prevent all united exertion for the common benefit.' The paternalism, hereditary loyalty and feudal ties which existed in England between landlord and tenant were absent in Ireland.[4]

On the eve of the Great Famine, the Commission ominously warned that the country was in a perilous state. The Irish were dangerously reliant on the potato and it was 'the most dangerous of crops' for it could not be stored from one season to the next.[5] The Commission's report came too late to avert catastrophe.

***

Edward now came up with a shrewd, breath-taking tactic: he would go after the leaders of the people, their priests, entice them to his cause and establish a haven for those clerics who would renounce their faith and convert to Protestantism. The manoeuvre would be a humiliating blow to the faith and confidence of the people, seeing their own leaders cross over to Nangle's side. The problem for the Achill Mission was that the priest who was alienated enough to abandon his own church did not always prove to be the most stable individual in his new role. Edward was progressing plans to establish an asylum in Dugort for priests deserting their Catholic ministry, but he had a problem: the man who could lead the work of the asylum was himself embroiled in an embarrassing public controversy. William John Burke of Kinvara had got himself into a right mess.

On the very day that Edward testified before the Devon Commission officials, an inmate at the Sheriff's Prison in Galway wrote him a long letter.[6] A former Catholic priest at Kinvara, County Clare, William Burke, needed the livelihood and home on offer at the Achill Mission, but he had some explaining to do as to how he ended up as a prison inmate.

The trouble had erupted three months earlier when Burke, who had served as a Catholic priest for thirteen years, formally read a recantation at St John's Church, Kinvara, County Clare, renouncing the faith of his ministry and converting to Protestantism. Returning from the ceremony, a mob of nearly 2,000 pursued his carriage and hurled abuse at him: two other clergymen and police protection were needed. Further controversy followed when Burke was charged with having married his wife, Catherine, a year earlier while still a priest, leading to his prosecution for 'tendering an illegal oath'.[7]

While he was acquitted in court of the charges, trouble again broke out in the aftermath of the verdict. William Burke himself described what happened: 'we were scarcely beyond the portals of the courthouse when we were assaulted by yelling and hooting … as we entered the square near my lodgings, stones were thrown by the justice-loving Popish rabble of Galway'.[8] He was advised by the magistrate to take refuge in the sheriff's prison, it being the only place where his safety could be secured.

Edward acknowledged that Burke had been privately married the previous year in a Catholic ceremony while still a priest, but accepted Burke's explanation that he had wanted to get his affairs in order before publicly announcing the marriage. With an uncharacteristic indulgence, Edward admitted that Burke's behaviour had not been as straightforward as it should have been, and had allowed his enemies to make the malicious charges which led to the Galway trial. However, Catholic priests recanting their faith were like gold dust to the Achill Mission's cause and, within a few months, William John Burke and his family had taken up residence at the colony.

***

It had been a stormy, wet October morning at Dugort but, by midday, clouds and rain lifted as a group waited in a procession line at the colony for an important ceremony: to formally lay the foundation stone for a building to house the reformed priests' asylum. The service, organised by Dr Adams, was impressive. Three orphan boys led the parade, two carrying open Bibles and the third a globe. Came the settlement school children walking three deep and followed by three former Catholic priests: John O'Brien, formerly of County Kerry, George McNamara, formerly of Erris, County Mayo, and Solomon Frost of Limerick. An attendant walked next with a hammer and trowel followed by Rev. Lowe, Edward Nangle and the main congregation. It was a powerful coup to have lured the three clerics over from the side of the enemy, even if all did not turn out to be exemplary in their new duties.

On reaching the designated site, the children sang a special hymn composed for the occasion. Then each of the three Maynooth-educated former priests laid a stone as a testament of his goodwill and support for the priests' asylum project. The former priest George McNamara then addressed the crowd in Irish. Was it not extraordinary, he asked the congregation, that the foundation stones had been laid by three men who had renounced the errors of the Church of Rome in favour of the established church? He spoke of the personal circumstances that caused him to abandon his former faith, including the obligation put upon a priest if interrogated about a fact he heard in confession to deny all knowledge of it. He knew that some priests had been guilty of beastly immoralities that were unmentionable and, when he had reported these matters to the Pope, no action whatsoever had been taken;[9] here was a modern-day whistle-blower.

As the ceremony ended, the clouds burst open and rain descended from the mountain in torrents.

Reflecting on the event of that autumn afternoon some twenty years later, Edward regretted that neither John O'Brien nor Solomon Frost would give satisfactory service in their new ecclesiastical roles: 'O'Brien proved to be, as many of the priests are, a person of dissolute habits.' While Frost was a man of a higher order, he could not entirely free himself of the polluting influence of Maynooth, in Edward's view, and died some years later under suspicion of misconduct.[10]

The people told their stories about the priest 'jumpers' – those who went over to Nangle's faith:

> There were four priests that turned. He took the turned priests with him to England to raise money and to show the good work he was doing when even the priests came to his side. He took a priest to Liverpool once, but the priest took flight and took off to America. They brought the priests to the colony to show the people there was no harm in 'jumping'. They gave the priests the good life and they thought the people were so simple that they would believe there was no harm in it, but the people weren't taken in.[11]

***

The brown leather binding is peeling off the large heavy book: the nineteenth-century register of baptisms, marriages and deaths for the parish of Dugort, Achill. Inside the back cover is a compelling list: 'Converts who read their recantations' at the Achill Mission.[12] The list starts in November 1844, a full year before the Great Famine showed its first terrifying signs, at a time when the Achill harvest appeared abundant. In the final two months of that year, 143 people formally recanted at the colony and converted to Protestantism. It is interesting that the practice of recantation, which became notoriously linked to the charge of 'souperism' against the Achill Mission in the Famine years, had actually commenced before the onset of the Great Famine. The practice was carried on by the Achill Mission for less than two years with the final ceremony taking place on 3 May 1846 as famine tightened its grip, perhaps with the realisation that the practice was repellent at a time of such famine hardship.

According to Edward, it was the converted priests who urged on him the idea of public recantations, and he enthusiastically supported their proposal. It must have reminded him of the heady days in County Cavan, almost two decades earlier, when the people went in their droves to the Farnham estate to formally recant their faith and secure a better life. The first pubic recantation ceremonies took place at the colony on Sunday, 27 October 1844, the same month that saw the inauguration of the priests' asylum. Eleven people came forward in front of a crowded congregation, the numbers limited to allow each person individually answer the solemn questions put by Edward Nangle in English, and by George McNamara in Irish.

> Minister: That this congregation here present, may be fully satisfied that you are well acquainted with the doctrines which you renounce and also with those you come here to profess, I ask you, 'Do you utterly renounce the Sacrifice of the Mass as offered up in the church of Rome, and do you trust only in the Sacrifice of our Lord Jesus Christ, made on the Cross, once for all, and you own no other merits whereby man is saved but His only?'
>
> Convert: I do.

Minister: Do you renounce the doctrine of Purgatory, and the practice of praying to the Virgin Mary, or to Saints or Angels, or to Images or Relics?

Convert: I do.

Minister: Do you believe that in the Holy Communion there is no Transubstantiation of the Bread and Wine into the Body and Blood of Christ?

Convert: I do not believe that any such change is made.

Minister: Are you persuaded that the Holy Scriptures contain sufficiently all Doctrine required of necessity for eternal salvation through faith in Jesus Christ.

Convert: I am so persuaded.[13]

There is a searing quality to the inventory of those who made a public recantation at successive public ceremonies in Dugort in the mid-1840s. Some came from other parts of County Mayo and Ireland, driven by the economic need to seek a better life and recantation was part of the package on offer. Some came from within Achill, willing to be ostracised by their community for their actions if they could improve their personal lot and that of their families. When famine hardship intensified, the prizes of employment, food and relief were compelling. Each person had a story of need to tell.

Converted priests, public recantations by converts, the offer of more land for expansion and a thriving expanded Dugort colony – to all appearances, these were a powerful validation of Edward Nangle's work over a decade on the island of Achill.

CHAPTER TEN

The Finger of God

Asenath Nicholson, the American traveller and writer, was a figure of wonderment in Ireland in the mid-1840s as she criss-crossed the country: spectacled, with a determined air, often dressed in a polka-dot coat and carrying a parasol and bearskin muff. By the time she headed to Achill, she had already spent a year travelling throughout the country using every available mode of transport: coach, baker's cart, steamer, post-car, Bianconi car and ass and cart. But mostly she walked, reading the Bible to those she met and sharing their hospitality. She had come with a mission – to bring the Bible to the Irish poor, similar in ways to the objective of Edward Nangle but yet very different.

The Achill Mission was one of the places the American widow most desired to see and, at last, she stood before 'the indefatigable Mr. Nangle' at the colony in Dugort. There was a palpable tension in the parlour where they met, for Edward had likely been warned in advance of what had been termed the visitor's liberal and democratic views, while he was also still smarting from the Halls' criticisms of his venture. Mrs Nicholson wanted to hear about the Achill Mission from Edward first-hand but the tension soon turned to outright hostility when she put her questions. The mood darkened further into mistrust and paranoia when a woman with a 'silent fixed stare' entered the room and Eliza Nangle curtly asked the visitor: 'What brought you here?'[1] What subsequently transpired gives an insight into the mood of paranoia, and sensitivity to outside criticism, which appeared to then pervade the colony.

There is a delight in Asenath Nicholson's writings which reveals an exuberance of spirit, a passion for experience, a kind temperament and an eagerness to enter into the lives of the ordinary peasant people she met, alongside an eccentric and rather scatter brained personality. Immediately on her arrival from Liverpool at Kingstown, Dublin, she had misplaced, and later recovered, her purse and money, lost her rail ticket, run into the ticket office to pay for another and then mislaid her keys. Soon, she was walking the side streets of Irish cities, traversing the country across mountain and bog and suffering from blistered feet, fatigue and many ailments. Yet, all the time and everywhere she went, she marvelled at the Irish with their appealing 'jumble of Irish sadness and Irish mirth'.

Mrs Nicholson had arrived in Westport on 26 May 1845 and then climbed Croagh Patrick alone, later admitting that this was the height of folly and recklessness. She walked the six miles to Newport, called on the Bible reader Mr Gibbon and then headed for Achill Sound where she was received kindly at the well-ordered and comfortable hotel run by Susan and Robert Savage. After two days, feeling refreshed, she left the Achill Sound hotel early in the morning, crossed the quarter-mile sound at low tide onto the island and then set off in the direction of Dugort. She had intended to proceed on foot until the public car overtook her, but ended up walking the entire way to the colony.

Asenath Nicholson was different to other travellers of the period in the way she moved among the people, stayed in their cabins, joined in their meals and fully immersed herself in their way of life. Above all else, she valued the Christian virtues of kindness and hospitality and these she found in abundance among the ordinary people. She would be disappointed to find that, in her estimation, the Achill Mission exhibited a deficit in these qualities. The colony hotel was not ready for occupation; she was told there were no private lodgings available and she was directed uphill to Moll Vesey's shebeen where she passed an unpleasant night. The Achill Mission had failed her first crucial test in its cold lack of hospitality for the visitor.

Her first impressions of the physical aspects of the colony were positive and could not have been otherwise. The settlement appeared tidy and prosperous, barren soil converted into fruitful fields by industrious hands and the inhabitants, to outward appearances, seemingly well nourished. As an experienced educator, schooling and education were a passionate interest and she visited the colony schools before meeting Edward Nangle. She was offended by the lack of civility displayed by the teacher in the infant school, while having a better experience at the female and boys' schools.

When Mrs Nicholson arrived for their meeting at the appointed time, she was kept waiting. When finally summoned, Edward responded tersely to her questions and the exchanges became increasingly testy when she raised her concerns about adult literacy at the colony. She had come across a number of converts who could not read and she enquired if it was the Achill Mission's practice to hold Sabbath-school for adults.

'Not to teach them to read, but to read to them and instruct them in the scriptures', he replied.

'Are they not anxious to read the Word of God for themselves?' she asked.

He gave her to understand that this would be a difficult task whereupon she described to him a school for Irish people in New York where many adults of various ages had been taught to read. It was surprising and disappointing for her that the mission prioritised the teaching of the Bible over basic literacy, which she valued so highly. This was her greatest disappointment with the work of the Achill Mission. She learned afterwards that Edward Nangle considered this exchange officious, as if he was unable to properly manage his own affairs.

'What brought you to Achill?' a clearly hostile Eliza Nangle again asked the visitor.

'I came to see the colony, and to hear from the founders of it, its progress and true condition, that I might tell to my own country what good work was going on in this remote island of the ocean.'

'Let me tell you that you came on very improper business,' Mrs Nangle retorted, most likely still stinging from the negative fallout of the earlier visit from the writers Samuel and Maria Hall.

At this point Edward Nangle silently left the room.

After further sharp exchanges with Eliza, Mrs Nicholson later noted: 'I have never before been treated by any female with such vulgarity and so little courtesy.'

A nurse who waited outside the room where the encounter with Eliza took place volunteered the view that '[Mrs Nangle] has a stony heart, and I feared she would abuse you. Smiles are put on, good dinners got up, a fine story told of the colony when the quality come, while the poor servants are stinted and miserably paid.'

Eliza's outwardly rude behaviour towards the visitor appears at odds with the perception to that point of a stoically heroic figure. Her conduct could indicate a growing sense of paranoia at the external criticisms of the colony, particularly by the Halls, or a frustration and despair from personal trauma and illness as well as the gruelling island hardship. For her part, Asenath Nicholson's judgement of Eliza may have been excessively harsh, taking little account of the severe conditions under which she and her family had lived for a decade, her husband's regular absences and the recurring distress of pregnancies ending in infant deaths.

Like other visitors to the Achill colony, Asenath Nicholson was left with two very different assessments of the mission's activities. While she could not but acknowledge what had been achieved in converting a barren waste of land into a productive settlement with its neat development of cottages and cultivated fields, she appeared shocked at the deficit of Christian charity in terms of kindness, courtesy and hospitality to the stranger. Above all, she was appalled at the converts holding in their hands Protestant prayer books which they were unable to read.

Some weeks later, while visiting the Tract Depository in Sackville Street, Dublin, Asenath was presented with an article from the most recent edition of the *Achill Herald*. While Edward

Nangle did not name Mrs Nicholson but described her colourfully as a female travelling through the country, a person who lodges with the peasantry and says that her object is to become acquainted with the Irish character. He believed, he wrote, that she came with other motives and that 'the principal object of this woman's mission is to create a spirit of discontent among the lower orders'. While accepting that she was a talented and educated person, he believed her behaviour was at odds with the biblical ideal of a virtuous woman in terms of modesty and humility. Intriguingly, he added that while there was nothing 'to justify the supposition of insanity', there was, nevertheless, a strong suspicion that she was 'the emissary of some democratic and revolutionary society'.[2]

Mrs Nicholson was unrepentant: 'I make no apology to Mr Nangle, I make none to the public, for visiting Achill and visiting it as I did. I had a national right, a civil and religious one to do so, either with our without letters, as long as my conduct was proper.' She believed that she had been treated not only uncivilly, but degradingly and wickedly, at the colony and that she had a responsibility to report on what she witnessed – to tell the truth.

Asenath Nicholson had expected to find much at the Achill Mission which she could support: the teaching of the scriptures, education, and improvement in the living conditions of the people, in a word – Christian humanism. But her disappointment at what she perceived as the lack of Christian charity was palpable and contrasted, in her mind, with the cordiality and welcome she had experienced among the peasant people.

Asenath Nicholson left Ireland as the dark clouds of famine calamity edged closer and she was fearful that 'an explosion must soon take place'.[3] That explosion was just weeks away and she would later return to witness its devastating outcome.

***

The month of June, and into early July, blazed with sunshine and summer heat. It was an exceptional spell of dry weather, the likes of which had scarcely before been experienced even by the oldest inhabitants of Achill, and held out the promise of a productive autumn harvest. The Achill Mission's cultivated fields glowed with golden abundance. A new masthead proclaiming the extent of the colony development featured on the front page of the *Achill Herald,* in which the editor proudly described the extent of the work that had taken place on the mountain slopes.

On entering the settlement, the first house on the left was occupied by the inspecting officer of the coastguard. The second and third dwelling, not yet completed, would accommodate the assistant missionary and the converted priests. The next building was the farm office next to a large house comprising, in the lower storey, the kitchen and dining hall of the orphanage and, on the upper level, the male and female school rooms and a reading room.

The next range of buildings across the slope of the mountain included the shop keeper's residence, the printing office, a shop, the colony superintendent's dwelling, a committee room, a post office, a church, an infants' school and Dr Adams' home. Behind this row of buildings was the colony hospital and, further up the mountain, a row of cottages that housed the Achill Mission settlers. At the front of the settlement was a neat rectangle of cultivated ground, giving the overall vista the appearance of a handsome English village.[4]

It appeared to be a development oasis, a self-sufficient community and a beacon to the world of what Edward Nangle's civilising mission had accomplished in one of the most primitive spots in Ireland. The plan was to duplicate the colony model in Mweelin on the other side of the island about six miles from Dugort where, on additional land leased from Sir Richard O'Donnell, a small church together with a parsonage, a school house and nine cottages were under construction.[5] This impressive growth showed Edward Nangle at his best – driving the expansion of the colony with energy and vigour.

***

In July and August, the summer sunshine gave way to rain and unseasonal cold. Sheep shivered on Achill's mountains, sea birds screeched on the cliffs and fierce showers blasted the island. One night, towards the end of July or the beginning of August, the eminent physician and author, William Wilde, was travelling west by mail-coach when, sometime after midnight, the atmosphere became unusually cold and a dense fog about six or eight feet thick spread over the ground. The next day, while on a fishing excursion in fertile potato country, his group observed that a sickening stench rose up from the fields where the stalks had turned black: the potato was gone.[6]

When September came, there were a return to dry summery conditions and an alarming announcement in the *Gardeners' Chronicle*: 'We stop the press, with very great regret, to announce that the potato Murrain has unequivocally declared itself in Ireland. The crops about Dublin are suddenly perishing.'[7] The unimaginable had happened. The potato blight, which had appeared in Europe in June, had now reached Ireland. The culprit was a fungus, *Phytophthora infestans*, commonly known as potato blight. What did it mean for a country where three to four million people depended on the potato as their staple diet?

Stories from folklore would claim that the destruction of the potato crop was done suddenly, almost overnight: 'Every old person corroborated this – the blight or the 'failure' as they call it came suddenly, today the stalks were quite natural and healthy and tomorrow as they say they were black as your shoe and burned to the clay'.[8]

What did it mean for Achill? In early October, Edward Nangle was giving an upbeat report: 'We are thankful to say that the potato disease has not made its appearance in this island, although parts of the neighbouring district are suffering severely from its presence.'[9] All that was about to change.

The weather in October was so severe that worry about the crops intensified. It was the month when potato pits were opened and, in early November, *The Telegraph* confirmed the dreadful news from County Mayo: 'From accounts that have reached us from every division of this extensive county, we lament to find that nearly one half of the potato crop is totally destroyed, a great portion of the remainder is in a very precarious state.'[10] As pit after pit was opened, potatoes that appeared initially sound oozed sour-smelling liquid once touched with even a slight pressure of the finger. Henry Brett, Mayo county surveyor, wrote: 'I have to report that the prevalent disease has committed great ravages in most parts of this county, and it appears to be daily getting worse.'[11]

In mid-October, Sir Robert Peel, the British prime minister, while acknowledging the seriousness of the Irish situation expressed himself sceptical of some accounts: 'there is such a tendency to exaggeration and inaccuracy in Irish reports that delay in acting upon them is only desirable.'[12]

Edward Nangle's reaction in the early stages of the Famine was to become almost unhinged. He raged against popery and the wicked measures in the Maynooth Bill which, he had already warned, would draw down God's judgement on the nation. His prediction had now come to pass and God had delivered a practical rebuke by delivering the rot into the potato crop: 'this is God's judgement – sin has excited his wrath against us.'[13]

The Maynooth Grant Bill had been passed in the British House of Commons several months earlier and provided for the trebling of the annual grant to the seminary in Maynooth which trained the country's Catholic clergy, as well as a capital grant towards the renovation and extension of the college's buildings. The bill had infuriated Edward and he and the three Maynooth-educated ex-priests who had joined the Achill Mission – Frost, O'Brien and McNamara – had drawn up a petition of protest expressing their 'grief and alarm that it is the intention of her Majesty's Ministers to propose to your honourable house, a permanent endowment of the Roman Catholic College of Maynooth'. It was intolerable, he said, that the government would support Catholicism in this way, for popery was proven by the Bible to be superstitious, idolatrous and revolutionary. Catholicism was anti-national and the undisputed cause of Irish misery, and the endowment of Maynooth would only strengthen the people in their adherence to an utterly false system of belief.[14] He had warned that the passing of such a wicked measure would most certainly draw down God's judgement and his warning had proved correct with the emergence of the potato blight.

Edward now felt vindicated in his prediction, seeing divine vengeance, 'the finger of God', in the rotting potato crop.[15] In those early frantic famine days, he appeared frozen in his reactions, obsessed with seeing God's judgement in the potato disease, and fevered to the point of collapse.

In December, as was his custom, Edward Nangle left Achill to embark on a speaking and fundraising trip to the friends of the Mission in Ireland and England. Yet again, he would be absent over Christmas and for several months afterwards, leaving behind in Achill an ailing pregnant wife and six children. He was about to suffer a total mental and physical collapse. It was his most serious breakdown since that which he underwent as a young clergyman in County Cavan two decades earlier. It was a lengthy and devastating illness and, by his own admission, it would be several years before he fully recovered.

Edward Nangle's health crumpled just as the country was descending into chaos. At least a million people would die in Ireland in the famine years with another estimated million leaving the country. Achill would be left with its lingering bitterness and shame.

PART 2

In the evening time an old woman came up to the [Achill] cottage and once or twice in the morning as well. She pointed out the cliffs and hillside with its broken cottage walls. She spoke readily and easily about the Famine ... And then she said they were a great people, the people in the Famine.

–Eavan Boland, 'Famine Roads'

CHAPTER ELEVEN

Quicksilver Illness

'My ailment was a low nervous fever. My recovery was very slow.'[1] So wrote Edward Nangle two decades after the most serious breakdown since his collapse as a young clergyman in County Cavan. Surprisingly, his 1860s memoir placed this illness as occurring in the winter of 1846, a full year into the Great Famine, but we know that it occurred a year earlier as the food crisis began to unfold.[2] Was this a genuine mistake on his part, given the elapse of almost two decades? Or was it an attempt to gloss over the embarrassment of such a breakdown as famine was tightening its grip on the country. He may well have relied on past editions of the *Achill Herald* as the main source material for his memoir. The editions of early 1846 contain little reference to this illness, and the writing and editorial work may have been taken over by somebody else given the editor's infirmity.

As was frequently his custom, in the winter months of late 1845 Edward set out from Achill on a speaking and fundraising itinerary while once again anxious about his own wellbeing: 'My health had been declining for some time, and I hoped that change of scene and occupation might restore it.'[3] His first preaching assignment was in Belfast but, on reaching County Louth, he fell ill, complaining of a loss of appetite and a sensation of constant cold. He pushed on to Belfast and preached his sermon before collapsing at the church in an alarming state.

The Telegraph carried the news of the illness in January 1846:

> The Rev. Edward Nangle of Achill preached to the St George's congregation, Belfast, on Sunday morning, but having become seriously indisposed, he was unable to occupy the pulpit of Trinity Church in the evening. As his illness appeared alarming, the aid of Doctor H Purdon was called in. Under decided remedies, the febrile symptoms were removed. The reverend gentleman was, however, too weak to leave his bed, and the proposed meeting at the music hall could not be held.[4]

After several days recuperating, he surprisingly decided to push on to London but there was little improvement in his condition. His own descriptions of his symptoms reveal a man in emotional and mental turmoil. He described his suffering: 'a weight of despondency', a 'feeling of desolation', sleeplessness, his head distracted with an incessant rumbling, feverish symptoms, constant anxiety and unable to read or write.[5] His collapse was total – physical, mental and psychological.

Edward would remain in London for several months, mainly confined to bed, as Achill and Ireland were being overwhelmed by the potato failure. Things came to a head in March when his sister travelled from Ireland to inform her brother that his wife Eliza, then in an advanced state of pregnancy, was seriously ill and that he must return home. There are hints of family anger, irritation and even embarrassment at Edward's lengthy absence from Achill at a period of family and national crisis.

The Nangle family Bible is dated January 1830, coming into the family's possession just three months before the arrival of Edward and Eliza's first child.[6] The Bible: the book of truth – its words inspired Edward Nangle to launch his west-of-Ireland mission with enthusiasm and vigour. It was the book he had drawn upon in sermons, pamphlets and debates – the words of his God.

A handwritten page, with entries by both Edward and Eliza, lists family births, marriages and deaths. The large, heavy book with its frayed brown cover is one of this narrative's archival texts from which so much more can be gleaned than mere factual information. One can imagine the hands that leafed through its contents in times of sorrow and elation, the shelf or table where it rested in its Achill home through winter storms and Atlantic rains and a woman recording yet another pregnancy in its pages – a pregnancy ending in life or in death.

The Bible entry for 1846, as famine bit deep, reads: 'A daughter born in Achill on March 10th died immediately after its birth.' A famine daughter. It was the tenth recorded child born to the then 43-year-old Eliza: six children living, four dead. The weather in Achill was bitterly cold and she had not laid eyes on her husband in several months.

On hearing of Eliza's poor health, Edward returned with his sister to Dublin where they received a letter from Neason Adams to say that Eliza had given birth to a still born child and was dangerously ill. At last, Edward set out for Achill as an unseasonal snow storm swept across the island. He was relieved to find Eliza somewhat improved. However, the health of both would remain precarious throughout the famine period. 'It was several years,' he wrote, 'before my overstrained mind recovered its elasticity, and my excellent wife never thoroughly recovered; her illness was the first manifestation of the malady which closed her useful life some years after.'[7]

The famine years were typified by Edward's continual references to the shattered state of his physical and mental health. It is difficult to decipher if the deterioration was just another in a series of cyclical bouts of infirmity, or whether the latest illness resulted from the unfolding famine crisis coupled with family stress. By the end of 1846, he was using a Dublin address and it appears that this was now the main residence for the couple and their children.

Edward's periods of depression, alternating with manic energy, indicate symptoms associated with bipolar disorder or manic depression, which may have had roots in his childhood trauma. There are numerous references in his writings to seasonal change in mood in the winter months, while often absent from Achill, and of depressive symptoms striking at periods of personal stress. His swings of mood and energy are indicative of the cyclic upheavals associated with a manic depressive illness: restless, creative exuberance alternating with spells of unrelieved blackness and exhaustion. 'Mania is a strange and driving force, a destroyer, a fire in the blood': an illness that both kills and gives life, creates and destroys. For Edward, the periods of elevated energy produced episodes of intense activity: huge writing output, energetic travel and fundraising and fiery and agitated sermons followed by the bleak periods of depression, blackness, withdrawal and exhaustion. His was a volatile, unstable, mercurial personality, inflicted by a 'quicksilver illness'.[8]

The Achill Mission possessed the organisational structure and tools to respond to an Atlantic island's famine catastrophe. It had a powerful fundraising network spearheaded by its founder; a propaganda and communications vehicle in the *Achill Herald*; a welfare structure of hospital, dispensary, orphanage and schools; a colony farm with well-developed cultivation systems; and a resident humane physician. Edward now faced a test like never before – to marshal his personal skills and the resources of the Achill Mission in response to the potato blight and famine onslaught. Could he rise to the challenge at a time of personal frailty?

CHAPTER TWELVE

Death is Now Loose

While Edward Nangle was still laid low in London, panic and hopelessness were gripping County Mayo as the effects of food shortages began to bite. Hunger was widespread. 'We are upon the brink of famine,' *The Telegraph* reported, 'starvation and fever is upon us.' Where were the promised public works, asked the writer; the people would surely starve to death before the promised works commenced. And, supposing the poor were employed, what good would employment do if the people couldn't obtain food from their earnings? The potatoes were almost gone and the meal was being sold at a price they couldn't afford. To cap it all, grain was being shipped from Irish coasts to fill the granaries of England.[1]

One report illustrated the dilemma facing families who travelled from outside Achill to the colony seeking help. A young girl named Bridget Hiland came before the Castlebar Board of Guardians seeking admission to the workhouse.[2] Her father had taken her and the family from their home place at Tyrawley, County Mayo, to the Achill colony, she said. Her family had always been Roman Catholic and, when she refused to rescind her faith at the Achill Mission, her father had beaten her and she ran away. She had walked from the colony to the workhouse – a distance of about forty miles – supporting herself by 'killing little things' along the roads. Her application for admission to the workhouse was accepted and the clerk was directed to write to the colony and enquire into the veracity of the girl's statement.[3]

Another intriguing account concerned the benevolent Neason Adams who was not beyond *The Telegraph*'s criticism. The newspaper claimed the doctor was dispensing medicines to the islanders wrapped in proselytising texts, a behaviour the paper deemed unacceptable from a public official holding the post of medical officer in the community.[4] A benign interpretation of the incident might point to the pamphlet paper being the only available wrapping material.

On 23 March 1846, what may have been the first starvation death in the country was reported.[5] Some weeks later, on 2 May, a public recantation ceremony by fifteen converts took place at the colony church in Dugort. It was the last such public recantation ceremony, as even Edward Nangle would have understood the repugnant spectacle of suffering people publicly denouncing the faith of their birth in the hope of material benefits. In later years, obviously conscious of the criticisms voiced about the Achill Mission's actions during the Famine, Edward claimed that the colony had refused numerous requests for recantations:

> We said to the poor people, 'No; you may come to our church if you please and we will visit you at your houses ... we shall also be happy to instruct your children in our schools; we shall gladly give you all we can in this time of distress, whether you call yourselves Roman Catholics or Protestants, and then, when the famine is over, if God has wrought any conviction in your souls, you may come forward and make a public conversion before the congregation.'[6]

Food and relief in return for religious conversion became a continuous charge in famine Achill.

***

Despite Edward's poor health, the Achill Mission was closely involved in the official famine response in Achill through 1846 via the local relief committee, the public works programme and the food depot, as well as through the mission's own relief works. Much of this work fell on the shoulders of Neason Adams as Edward moved back and forth between Achill and Dublin.

The local relief committee for Achill, established in June 1846 with Edward Nangle as chairman, included the Achill Catholic parish priest, Father Dwyer, and the curate Father Monaghan, with Neason Adams acting as secretary. Dr Adams was soon writing to the Dublin commissioners complaining that the committee had insufficient funds to keep 275 people in employment, and requesting the assistance of the military in protecting the government food stores. He complained that the state of want on the island was severe, and that a much larger sum of money was needed from Dublin to provide employment for those islanders without food or money: 'we have had in employment this day 275 persons and from this number we have carefully excluded all who had food or money to purchase it'. The islanders, he wrote, are 'a population driven by famine to desperation'. A week later, Dr Adams wrote once more to say that the local relief works had been abandoned due to lack of funds.[7]

The Achill relief committee was later disbanded; it would be reformed and reconstituted six months later when the link with the Achill Mission would be almost severed, except for the presence of Dr Adams. Edward was unhappy with what he saw as his personal marginalisation from the committee, an early indication of an official unease with his divisive role.

Edward was doing what he knew best, using the platform of the *Achill Herald* to publicise the Mission's work and to attract donations from supporters. His specific appeal for money to offer employment on the colony lands was accompanied by a statement emphasising the philosophy that underpinned the colony's relief work. No gratuitous relief would be given except where the recipient was unfit for work due to old age or sickness. The view, which was in line with the prevailing official government thinking, was repeated in the *Achill Herald* many times: 'gratuitous relief shall be afforded only to those people who are entirely incapable of giving a day's work, and who have no able-bodied relative on whom they are dependent'.

In addition to providing employment on the colony farms, the Achill Mission now made a decisive intervention which would dominate its famine response and attract widespread controversy: 'We have undertaken to feed all the children who have been in attendance at our schools, during the scarcity'.[8] An entirely humane and generous gesture to provide daily food for destitute children was soon viewed as a pernicious device to woo desperate people away from the faith of their birth – a tool of evangelisation. It was predictable that the practice would intensify demand throughout Achill for admission to the colony. It was a clever policy that led to a continuous flow of converts to the colony through the Famine period.

What parent would not seek out food for their hungry children, no matter what the source? For those who chose the colony schools at this time, it was a pragmatic, hard-nosed response to a life-threatening situation. Dozens of Achill children attended the schools, received nourishment when starvation and death may well have been the only other alternatives and went on to convert to Protestantism through the Famine decade. Many would later return to the church of their birth.

***

The summer of 1846 brought the distressing news that the potato crop would fail for a second year. While about a third of the crop was deficient in 1845, this year up to three-quarters of the harvest would be lost as, across the country, fields of potatoes in full bloom were about to turn scorched black. It was, said the writer in *The Times* on 2 September, 'total annihilation'.[9] *The Telegraph* struggled to describe the terror throughout County Mayo: 'The alarm of the people, both rich and poor, is very great. One thing is certain, the staple food of the people is gone ... death is now loose! – the green church yards open their graves to receive the victims of persecution and starvation.'

By September, conditions in the west were calamitous and the words of *The Telegraph* editorial screamed from its pages: 'The People are Starving! Government! Landlords!' Throughout the rural districts of County Mayo emaciated people barely survived on black potato mash and water. There was neither food nor work; there was no grain in the government depots and the landlords were pursuing their tenants for rent.[10]

Father Malachy Monaghan, Catholic curate in Achill, could not believe his ears. He and the island delegation had travelled in hope to Dublin Castle in October to the case of the islanders directly with Sir Randolph Routh, head of the relief commissioners. They reported the failure of the potato crop and the lack of any grain crops due to the exposed position of the island. Their principal objective was to secure food provisions from the government stores for which people were willing to pay.

Sir Randolph was unsympathetic. No supplies of any consequence could be expected before the end of November or early December. It was his intention not to sell food at a price lower than that sought by the merchants for he was determined that the commercial interests of the merchants not be interfered with.

The priest asked why the new regard for free trade when the government had sold corn at cost the previous year?

That had been a 'bad decision', Routh retorted, a decision that had produced 'bad habits' in the Irish people. He was now determined to act in accordance with the 'enlightened principles of political economy'.

The priest was astounded. How could the government be fettered by notions of political economy at such a time of crisis? The people of Achill would die if food prices did not fall.

Routh was adamant: nothing was more essential to the welfare of a country than strict adherence to the principle of free trade. He had carefully read and studied Burke, the curate's 'illustrious countryman', and agreed with him that, in administering relief, the strict rules of political economy should be obeyed.[11]

The Achill priest and his delegation departed, helpless.

Around this time, Routh wrote a chilling letter to the Westport relief committee in response to a plea to open the government food depot in Westport. Sir Randolph explained the government position: 'we have a crisis of a peculiar nature to overcome, and a sudden transition from potato to grain food, for which the country is little prepared.' The principles of free trade had to be observed and he patiently explained what this meant: 'With regard to the high prices which, it is alleged, the dealers exact, we must bear in mind that, if an article is scarce, it must be dear; that a smaller quantity of food must be made to suffice for a longer period than usual, and that the high price is the only criterion by which consumption can be economised.'[12]

The obsession with free trade in food derived from a political philosophy imbued with evangelical Protestantism and a belief that the potato famine heralded a profound, and much needed, social and economic transformation in Ireland.[13] It was *laissez-faire* economics tinged with the evangelical belief in self-help, coupled with a suspicion that public assistance deprived the poor of the impetus to become self-reliant. It was a mindset with which Edward Nangle was entirely comfortable.

✳✳✳

One Wednesday in early December, three hookers with a cargo of thirty tons of meal sailed into Dugort Bay: a joyful sight.[14] The first boat made its way into the harbour, the boatmen cast anchor and made their way ashore. The second hooker was only partially unloaded when a fresh northerly wind forced the crew to raise sails and proceed to shelter at Bullsmouth. The boat ran aground and a good part of the forty-one bags of meal was damaged.

The third boat remained at Dugort with its cargo of ten tons of meal, waiting for the winds to subside. Throughout that night the colony inhabitants crowded the beach, watching on. Such was their perilous position that the crew were obliged to throw forty sacks of corn into the turbulent sea to lighten the boat but, at about two o'clock in the morning, the cable broke and the boat was swept ashore. Fifty-seven sacks of grain were saved from the wreck. Meanwhile, the hooker that cast anchor before the gale grew strong was grounded during the night with the strength of the hurricane. Two other boats, in which some of the grain had been placed, drifted two miles up the sound to the village of Salia where most of the corn was rescued.

The cargo of grain had been conveyed from Dublin port to Westport by the schooner the *Lydney Lass*, purchased with funds partly donated by Achill Mission benefactors and partly raised by Edward Nangle's own security. Edward was at pains to point out that the cargo, while destined for storage at the Achill Mission settlement, was intended to assist all the islanders: 'the benefit of purchasing food at a fair price will not be limited to persons connected with the missionary establishment but will be extended to the whole district'.[15]

This was Edward Nangle at his best: taking a risk, raising money, doing what needed to be done and getting food to the hungry. However, the suspicion that the Achill Mission's relief work was primarily directed at the settlement's own inhabitants, those with an affinity for the colony principles or those who were nominally Protestant, hovered over its enterprise.

Meanwhile, John MacHale was employing his considerable verbal and administrative skills on behalf of the wretched people of his archdiocese. He toured the worst affected areas of the west, wrote a series of long public letters to Lord John Russell, the new Whig prime minister, and spent an average of ten hours each weekday, from late 1846 through to the following year, acknowledging and distributing the donations which arrived in Tuam from around the world.[16] What can be made of the archbishop's relentless immersion in this work of financial administration when he could, presumably, have delegated it to one of his staff?

Perhaps it had to do with a desire to respond personally and with an even hand to the numerous requests for assistance from suffering parishioners across the archdiocese. Perhaps, it was a desire to wield absolute control over the administration and allocation of the resources flowing into the church coffers – to hold the purse strings close.

John MacHale's criticism of government policy in a series of letters to Lord John Russell was fierce: 'Self-reliance is a fine theme … But to tell a people to supply themselves with food, when both food and the means of procuring it are gone appears like the command laid on the Hebrews to make bricks without materials.'[17] He challenged the prime minister to fulfil his destiny by rescuing the Irish people from the jaws of famine.

It is intriguing to see each of these powerful figures – John MacHale and Edward Nangle – responding to famine pressure, each drawing on his skills in administration, fundraising, oratory and writing. John MacHale appeared to have the edge in terms of steady energy and stamina, while Edward's precarious health led to an uneven pattern in the vigour of his response.

One man, Neason Adams, would go down in folklore as the person within the Achill Mission who worked consistently and tirelessly to bring practical help to the people of Achill: 'Doctor Adams – he was a good man. It did not matter what religion a person had when he got a call from a poor person and he would not take any money for his services.'[18] The doctor acted as a local relief administrator, delivered medical services and, crucially, addressed the lack of clothing among the islanders.

In the absence of an active local relief committee, Dr Adams did his best to keep communications going with the Dublin authorities. He posted a notice dated 28 October 1846, seeking information on the land that was ready for seeding of rye or barley and offering seed which would be supplied by the government at cost price. He sent out an urgent appeal for support for 200 colony orphans who would soon be without food: 'I humbly beg that a supply of Indian or Irish meal be sent to the government store on this island so that our valuable institution may not be broken up.'[19] He complained, too, of the delay in paying the wages of those employed on public works, some of whom had been working for up to a week or a fortnight without any wages.

Neason Adams understood that the lack of clothing was an additional humiliation and personal distress to that of hunger, stripping the people of dignity, and it was an issue that he tackled with his 'Freize and Brogues' appeals. The lack of clothing was preventing the islanders from availing of employment; a freize frock coat or a pair of brogues would enable a poor man to take up employment and support himself and his family for the winter.[20]

The year ended for Edward Nangle as it had begun, with his health broken. Unwisely, like a crazed man, he returned with a demented attack on popery from his Dublin home: 'What, we ask, are the Romish priests doing for the poor in this time of their distress?' Their only response, he accused, had been to attempt to avert the calamity with blessed salt, holy water, clarified wafers and mass sacrifices.

It was a peeved response to John MacHale's accusation that he, Edward Nangle, had quit Achill and deserted the people in their hour of need. He defended himself, acknowledging that 'the state of his own health, and that of others of his family, rendered a temporary cessation from active and exciting employment indispensable'. But, he assured his readers, he would shortly resume his duties fully with renewed strength.[21] It was an admission that his presence in Achill at a time of acute distress had indeed been sporadic.

The following year, 1847, would be tumultuous and Edward Nangle and the Achill Mission were about to face some nasty accusations.

CHAPTER THIRTEEN

Buyer of Souls

If the people of Achill had expected that 1847 would bring good news, after the desolation of the previous year, they would be severely disappointed. Far worse was to come.

'The year 1846 … what horror, consternation and death have we not witnessed during its reign? Famine and starvation stalked through the land.' So wrote Mayo's *Telegraph* writer in its first edition of the New Year. '1847! You have found us subdued; you have found us crushed down by starvation, disease and death.'[1] Day after day, week after week, newspapers across county and country reported the results of coroner inquests: death by starvation; death from insufficiency of food; death from extreme hunger. Many of the dead were confined to the earth without the dignity of a coffin, often buried at the spot where they fell.

On the western seaboard, people resorted to desperate means to procure food. In April, the schooner *Mavis of Dumfries*, while sailing from Greenock to Galway with a cargo of wheat encountered some rowing boats off the coast at Achill Head. The schooner mate reported that some of the men managed to board the schooner, broke open the hatches with axes, piled the corn into sacks, loaded their boats and rowed off.[2]

Westport workhouse was in crisis with almost 1,000 inmates, and the paths to the workhouse, from the town to the quay, were crowded with the starving and the destitute. People lay on the roadway in temporary sheds constructed of weeds and potato tops. On just one day, the third Thursday of April, 'no less than fifteen dead bodies were put into one hold at the rear of the workhouse, in a sand-pit, without a sufficiency of earth to cover them.'[3]

Thousands were leaving, as whole villages were abandoned and the houses locked up. Every seaport in the country was reported full to overflowing, their quays crowded with people, as panic and hysteria were driving the people out in scenes of chaos. January 1847 saw a major influx of County Mayo natives in a miserable condition into the city of Liverpool; the city docks thronged with Irish, many taking onward passages to America, Canada and Australia.

At the Deserted Village, on the western slopes of Slievemore, there is nothing subtle about the famine traces.[4] Wind, rain and Atlantic saltwater have not obliterated the lazy bed potato ridges, cropped tight by roaming sheep. One can visualise the work of potato cultivation: heaping soil from the ridge trenches, laying on the seaweed fertiliser, setting the slit potatoes on top and covering them with mountain soil, followed by the wait for new growth. Rows of roofless bleached stone dwellings stretch westward towards the Atlantic: the ruins of over eighty cottages strung out along the lower slopes of Slievemore, haunting and empty but not yet obliterated. The famine years heralded the start of the evacuation of this and other Achill villages which became symbols of mid-nineteenth-century displacement. They became places of absence and erasure, dense with tombs and ghosts.

Edward Nangle started the year with an agitated outburst in the *Achill Herald* addressed to 'the Roman Catholics of Ireland in general and of Achill in particular'. The words convey a sense of an erratic man, out of control, roaring his tirade that God had sent the potato rot to chastise his people:

> Surely God is angry with the land.
> The potatoes would not have rotted unless He sent the rot into them.
> God never can be taken unawares; nothing can happen but as He orders it.
> God is good, and because He is, He never sends a scourge on His creatures unless they deserve it.

He is so good that He often punishes people in mercy.

When He sees them going in a bad way He chastises them to make them take a thought of themselves, that they may quit the sins which would bring on them the eternal pains of hell if they did not repent of them and forsake them.[5]

The words astound in their perceptible lack of appreciation of the famine carnage and in their deficit of empathy, pointing to an unstable personality at a remove from the day-to-day suffering of the Achill islanders.

***

In the month of May, when the early summer heat was bringing some warmth to the Achill mountainside, an official of the board of works made a strange decision. While staying at the new Achill Mission hotel on government business, and seemingly provoked by what he had observed in Achill, G.E. Bourke decided to vent his feelings in the pages of the hotel visitors' book, knowing full well that his words would quickly reach Edward Nangle. He articulated a growing unease at the Achill Mission's famine response:

I am astonished that English generosity could require the ignorant people to abandon the principles in which they were brought up and the creed which they understand, for food. Were the English people placed by providence where the Irish are, how would they like that any other nation should call on them to give up the faith of which they are justly proud, in order that they should be provided with food.

Was it true, he asked, that hundreds of Catholic children were being fed on condition that they daily attend Protestant schools, there to be instructed and brought up as Protestants?[6]

Bourke's charge was serious: school children were offered food in return for changing their faith.

Edward's response was unambiguous and he did not refute the allegation. Yes, the Achill Mission had indeed established schools in which the children of the poor were being fed, and where they received scriptural and Protestant instruction. Yes, it was also correct to say that no children were admitted to their schools except those who were willing to receive such instruction. It was also true that the children attending the colony schools were principally the offspring of Roman Catholics.

Apart from the spiritual benefit to the children from attending these schools, Edward retorted that he also believed it to be the most effective way to dispense temporal relief: 'the poor children receive two meals of wholesome food each day, by which hundreds have been saved from death by starvation'. There were strict rules for managing the schools' food allocation with a return filled in by the teacher each day, morning and evening, while the children were eating; breakfast was served at half past nine in the morning and dinner at four o'clock.

Edward made no apology for the Achill Mission's actions; indeed, their measures were entirely justified as evidenced by the fact that once food was provided through the colony schools, they were inundated with petitions from across Achill to establish even more schools and he had done nothing more than respond to these requests. He justified his actions by arguing that he had a compelling duty to repudiate the despicable system of popery by whatever means. Indeed, he believed that the Famine was 'one of the means appointed in God's providence for the accomplishment of the object contemplated in [the Achill Mission] institution'. It was as if famine had provided a lucky and unexpected opportunity to advance the work of evangelisation.

It was the response of a man so single-minded in his zeal to convert souls that he saw no moral ambiguity in enticing people to abandon their faith for food, as if this was a rational choice for a starving people. The notorious charge of souperism was becoming attached to Edward Nangle and his mission.

The Achill priest, Michael Gallagher, in a letter of appreciation for a donation of £25 to the people of Achill from the relief fund organised by Dr Daniel Murray, Catholic archbishop of Dublin, explained how the people were compelled to avail of the relief provided in the colony schools: 'poverty has compelled the greatest number of the population to send their children to Nangle's proselytising villainous schools; he has at the moment one thousand children of the Catholics of the parish attending ... and so he can, for they have no other refuge. They are dying of hunger, and rather than die, they have submitted.'[7] The priest understood that the people chose survival; they had no other choice.

**

Some weeks after the official wrote his comments in the colony hotel visitor book, *The Tablet* – a Catholic newspaper – carried a critical piece on the Achill Mission with the most prominent and forceful censure to date of Edward Nangle's famine actions. The unsavoury charge was repeated that he was a 'soul-buyer' and that money raised abroad for the relief of famine distress was being allocated to an obnoxious campaign.

> Achill – This memorable island, the scene of the greatest attempts at seductive and coerced perversion that have disgraced even Ireland. Achill, the memorable scene of the exploits of Nangle, the soul-buyer, has now we grieve to say it, become scarcely less remarkable for the miserable condition of its population. Money has indeed been poured into Achill. The propagators of perversion pay handsomely, and we learn from thence, of a date so late as Friday last, that 'Nothing is given of all the money that comes from England, and elsewhere, for the relief of the poor of Achill, except what is given in exchange for consciences. Nangle has doubled his donations in amount, but no one gets anything whatever that does not go to the Protestant school and conform to the Protestant formula.'

In short, it is given at the Protestant clergyman's discretion, and it is at his discretion to starve poor Catholics into Protestantism, or, failing that to let them starve.[8]

This was a prominent denunciation of Edward Nangle and his colony for an alleged unsavoury practice of providing famine relief in exchange for conscience and faith. It was a serious indictment, while also drawing unwelcome attention to the volume of donations being attracted from Achill Mission friends and benefactors.

The phenomenon of souperism[9] – the practice of using hunger to win converts by offering material benefits – became odious in the famine years and left in its wake a legacy of bitterness and shame. The Achill Mission was a particular target for charges of souperism given that children were fed in its scriptural schools, that employment schemes were used for the benefit of the colony, that the practice of public recantations operated and that mass conversions took place at the Achill Mission through the famine years.

The oral history concerning the Achill Mission could be likened to the broad strokes of a children's cartoon, where the action and characters are depicted in bold primary colours without much subtle detail – stories that became fused, one with the other in the telling and retelling, capturing the emotion and hurt of the times. There are numerous tales in the oral history which reflect the shame attached to 'taking the soup', and the desperation which lay behind these actions:

Some of the people turned with the soupers and remained with them till they died. A few of them went to Inishbiggle, Ballycroy, when driven from home by shame, fear or otherwise.

One man turned. He was passing by the priest's house one day and raised his hat. 'Ah', said the priest, 'you cannot please God and the devil'. 'Father,' he said, 'it's only until

the potatoes grow.' He turned back later. His son was also
a Protestant but only during the famine period.

The poor priest had no help to give but told the poor
people that if they took their needs wherever they found it
it would be no sin.[10]

There is no doubt but that the Achill Mission, through its food,
employment and general relief programmes, saved the lives of
many in famine Achill who otherwise would have died. However,
the linking of these programmes to the colony's evangelisation
mission, combined with Edward Nangle's highly charged rhetoric,
brought a notoriety and unsavoury reputation to the island colony.
Given his bouts of depressive illness, his lengthy absences from
Achill as the famine progressed and his successful and tireless
focus on raising funds for the mission, Edward may have been out
of touch with the reality of the people's suffering and unresponsive
to the growing antipathy to his methods.

***

Another controversy attached to the Achill Mission's methods
concerned the alleged numbers provided with famine relief by
way of employment at the colony. Edward claimed that the
mission employed 4,458 labourers in December 1846, of which
almost half were Roman Catholic.[11] Given an island population
of approximately 6,000, these figures attracted incredulous
comment leading to an attempt by Edward to correct the record
for the following month, when he reduced the colony employment
figures by more than half and provided a muddled and
unconvincing explanation about his earlier use of 'aggregate'
numbers.[12]

The employment figures cannot be verified and appear
exaggerated and confused. 'Mr Nangle delights in exaggeration,' a
critic would write some years later.[13] As editor of the *Achill Herald*,
which operated as a successful propaganda and fundraising

instrument for the colony, Edward may well have given in to a temptation to exaggerate his colony's relief work.

A powerful tool to appeal to Achill Mission donors was the graphic depiction of the suffering caused by the continuing famine. In May 1847, Edward printed a report in the *Achill Herald* of a day spent visiting the island's distressed and the details 'the writer' had noted in his journal. While the impression is given that it was Edward Nangle himself who called to the cabins, this seems unlikely given Edward's lengthy absences from Achill and his own prolonged bouts of illness. It is probable that the material came from Neason Adams or from some other colony staff member.

In the first scene, the visitor enters a hut inhabited by an old man, his wife and son. The man was 'much emaciated', while the woman lay on some grass in the corner of the hut with a few rags thrown over her. She also was 'wasted to a skeleton; but her suffering was not from disease; her emaciation was evidently the result of want of food'.

In the next cabin, an aged father was also wasted from hunger. There were no provisions of any kind in the house and his son was unable to work for several days past due to illness.

In the third dwelling, a 'wretched hovel not more than six feet square', a widow and three of her daughters lay on weeds in a corner or the room, sick with fever. On the other side lay the woman's father-in-law 'on the damp floor with a few rags thrown over him, also in fever'. Between them was a fire, before which sat a child of about four years old.

In the next hut were three women, a man and two wasted children, one of whom was an infant at the breast. A woman lay dying in the corner: 'she had no sickness, complained of nothing but want of food'. There were no provisions of any kind in the house.

In a fifth cabin, a man lay on the floor suffering from dysentery, and there were no evident provisions in the house. A sixth cabin was occupied by a widow with her son who lay in the corner of the house 'in a state of insensibility'. It appeared that his employment in the public works was finished and they had not eaten for three days.

Scenes of such harrowing suffering undoubtedly added urgency and emotion to Edward's continuous and successful appeals to Achill Mission benefactors.

Neason Adams continued to carry an intolerable burden with his wife at their colony home: 'From day light to the return of night, the cry of the sick, or starving seldom ceases at my window.' For Neason and Isabella Adams there was no escaping the constant cries of the people seeking food tickets: 'give me a ticket, give me a ticket'; 'myself and my family are starving'; 'dying of the hunger'. The food tickets he had been issuing would soon expire and he feared the consequences as conditions were deteriorating by the day. 'The sick, aged, and infirm, are not the only applicants for support, as heretofore. The cry for food is almost universal. Numbers that were considered to be able to hold out much longer, are now seeking relief.' Most worryingly, fever and dysentery were now general on the island.

The doctor continued his pleas for 'Freizes and Brogues for Naked Labourers' in the pages of the *Achill Herald*: 'A freize frock coat, costing seven or eight shillings, would enable a poor man to support himself and family for the winter.' From the donations received, he had already distributed 139 frock coats and waistcoats, nineteen jackets and 165 pairs of brogues.

By August, the doctor's appeals were becoming more desperate: 'The harvest has brought in no food; the turnip crop (except on the Mission land) is a failure.'[14] Sufficient land had not been cultivated in the spring with the result that there was little or no harvest to reap.

* * *

If Neason Adams was the benign face of the Achill Mission's famine response, Edward became increasingly isolated from both government and voluntary relief efforts. He was also becoming a slightly pitiful figure of peeved self-importance in his irritated reaction to the organisation of the new local relief committee.

In early 1847, he wrote to Sir Randolph Routh from his Baggot Street, Dublin residence: 'As I understand that the Government store in Achill is now supplied with food, I beg leave to inform you that I do not intend any longer to provide supplies for the population of the island ... I think it right to release myself from all participation in the responsibility by informing you of my intentions.'[15]

We can speculate as to his reasons for this communication. It may have been his absence from Achill due to ill health, his annoyance at the government response to his criticisms of the relief effort for the island or his advance knowledge of the impending reconstitution of the local relief committee.

In February, a new Achill committee was formed with Sir Richard O'Donnell as chairman, Robert Savage as secretary and Neason Adams named as treasurer.[16] There was no seat on the committee for Edward Nangle and the omission rankled. Sometime later, Edward revealed that he had been initially approached informally to act on the committee and that he had attended several meetings up to August when he was then informed that he was not included in the reformed committee. He could only presume that his name had been submitted to Dublin Castle but had not received approval. He complained that the act of parliament under which the relief committees were organised entitled the 'principal clergyman of each domination [sic]', and 'the three highest ratepayers' in the district to membership. On these grounds, he argued, he personally was entitled to a seat on the committee since he was the senior clergyman in the parish by more than ten years, yet a curate had been preferred ahead of him.

He believed that the priests were behind his exclusion: 'The Pope's priests and their dupes and partisans, who have attained positions of influence in the government, determined that the presence of a notorious opponent of the Pope and his cause would be inconvenient in the committee.'[17] As a result, he was excluded from a privilege which he considered his as of right.

CHAPTER FOURTEEN

Vicious and Rotten

On a luminous autumn day, at the edges of the swelling Atlantic, an elderly grey-haired man tottered towards a young English gentleman visitor. The old man carried what appeared to be a bundle of rags which he laid at the visitor's feet, pointing silently at the pile. It was the body of his near-dead wife. Then he lifted his arm and stretched it out towards a nearby roofless cabin – the couple's home – its charred timbers scattered in all directions. A crowd of wailing islanders pressed in on the stranger.

James Hack Tuke, a leading Quaker philanthropist, was touring Connaught in the closing months of 1847 and had reached the village of Keel in Achill where the overhanging Minaun cliffs must have filled him with awe. The scenes of evicted families and famine destitution undoubtedly filled him with horror. The old man told the visitor that he had been put out of his house for owing less than one year's rent. Another man with five motherless children had also been evicted and their boiling pot sold for 3s 6d. A widow and her four young children had lost their only possession, a small sheep seized and sold for 5s 6d. Tuke heard that, in Keel alone, at least 150 people had been put out of their holdings for not paying their rent.

Tuke was a serious young man from York, England, educated in the Religious Society of Friends, or Quakers, and he had concluded that the state of Irish society was 'vicious and rotten', and the relationship between landlord and tenant entirely severed: 'In no country in the world are these duties less recognised than in

Ireland.' He had concluded that the landlords of County Mayo, and other areas in Connaught, were pursuing a course which could only add to the universal wretchedness and poverty. Every direction in which he looked, the landlord agents were at work seizing crops and turning out tenants. Whole villages were being swept away by starvation and emigration, and those who remained were surviving on turnips or turnip tops boiled with a few half-decayed potatoes.

Tuke learned more about Achill when he attended a meeting of the board of guardians at Westport workhouse, forty miles away. Of the one hundred people admitted on the day of his visit, almost half were the evicted tenants of Keel. In the previous week an additional seventy-five people were admitted from Achill, the majority tenants of the same landlord, who were driven out, he heard, by the landlord's agent.

The landlord for almost the whole of Achill Island was Sir Richard O'Donnell who, Tuke acknowledged, had done much to promote the cultivation of flax close to his Newport home with up to one thousand women engaged in harvesting the crop. This contrasted with the situation in Achill where land seizure and eviction were practised daily. Sir Richard would protest to the visitor that he could not be held personally responsible for the Achill evictions for he was only the nominal owner of the land, which was under the court of chancery, and he was entirely ignorant of what had occurred. Tuke was sceptical: had the poor Achill creatures, in coming to the workhouse, not passed through Newport, the town where the landlord himself resided?[1]

James Hack Tuke had witnessed first-hand another phenomenon piled on to famine hunger – that of mass evictions, forever associated with the Great Famine. The Irish landlords, especially in the west, faced the dual problems of collecting unpaid rents and finding the means to discharge heavy poor rates, and Sir Richard was no different.[2] Sometimes, no formal evictions were necessary as tenants were induced to leave their land and seek admission to the workhouse, or were assisted with the cost of their passage out of the country.

One of the reasons evictions soared in 1847 was the introduction of the quarter-acre Gregory clause which became law in June, just weeks before James Hack Tuke arrived in the west of Ireland.[3] The law stipulated that no tenant holding more than a quarter-acre of land was eligible for public assistance or admission to a workhouse and, to qualify for such assistance, the tenant had to surrender the holding to his landlord. The provision facilitated landlords in clearing their estates of the poorest tenants who were faced with the decision of having to either surrender their holdings or starve. When tenants were formally evicted, it was frequently the practice for landlord bailiffs to burn the vacated dwellings.

Edward had no difficulty in securing more land for the Achill Mission that autumn: 'I only asked for twenty acres, and Sir Richard's reply was – you shall have as many twenties as you like in any place you choose.' The landlord would let him have as much land as he could cultivate in the vicinity of each village and he would employ the poor people in reclamation work. Edward had a clear plan for the use of this additional land.

His proposals were decidedly linked to the mission's evangelisation work. The poor would be employed in fencing and reclaiming the fields, and also in building a school house: 'This will create a means of support for the maintenance of scriptural education through the district when the present distress is over.' The labourers would be paid not in money but in food: a quarter of a stone of meal for each day's labour, 'just enough to appease the cravings of hunger'. Feeding the labourers in this way, together with the food given to the children in the schools, would suffice in Edward's plans to support an entire family.

Edward set out the principles underpinning his strategy, principles resolutely built on his guiding evangelical perspective. Firstly, 'gratuitous relief is ruinous to a people, especially to those with whom indolence and improvidence have become habitual'. Secondly, the low rate of wages on offer to the labourers would enable relief to be given at a moderate cost. Thirdly, the low wage rate would also effectively deter all but the really destitute from seeking access to the programme. Fourthly, the scheme would provide a future permanent benefit through the operation of the new school to be constructed as part of the proposals.[4] It was an innovative scheme tainted by its links to the Achill Mission's evangelising campaign.

The famine years triggered an upsurge of development not just at the Dugort colony, but also at the Achill Mission site across the island at Mweelin where, by mid-1847, a clergyman's house, a school, cottages and farm buildings had been constructed.[5] If the impressive funds collected by Edward Nangle enabled employment to be given to the poor, it had the additional benefit of improving the colony infrastructure as more ground was reclaimed, drained and fenced, and roads built. Edward was able to confidently predict that, for the 1847 season, the colony would produce thirteen acres of potatoes, eleven of turnips, thirty-seven of oats and one of parsnips and carrots: 'we shall have more than enough for the support of our own people during the coming year.'[6] The demands placed on the colony, particularly in feeding the children in the mission schools, was a stimulus to this development.

***

On a Tuesday morning in November, the thunderous noise of the previous night's storm was replaced by the calm of a molten sea. But the stillness was broken by other sounds: the wails of the crowd, mostly comprised of women and children, who pressed into Savages' hotel at Achill Sound. Asenath Nicholson stirred large pails of Indian meal gruel, then moved quietly among the famished people, feeding them from tin cups until their hunger was satisfied. She looked at the wretchedness about her, the degraded islanders in their soaking rags, and her heart went out to the islanders who had suffered yet another tragedy, heaped upon their famine misery.

The woman with the Bible was back in Achill having spent most of the year, since January, on a tour of famine-ridden Ireland.[7] Apart from a short time spent in Scotland, she had now been in Ireland continuously for almost three years. The previous day,

Monday, she had finally got a passage from the Mullet in Erris to Achill Sound, when she stepped into a dirty boat with filthy-looking men jabbering in Irish and sat down on a pile of wet straw. The boat travelled throughout the day, the rain and the sea splashing over them until they were totally drenched by the cascading waves. Close to sunset the weather improved, the sun came out and the boatmen rowed into Achill Sound on motionless water.

The island fishermen had already loosened their boats and gone out with their nets into the calm seas, not knowing what was to erupt in the darkness of the night, for they needed the fish to feed their families. Only months before, Robert Savage – proprietor of the Achill Sound hotel – had equipped fourteen men from Keel with boats and fishing nets funded by the Society of Friends.[8] It was the type of practical support in self-help that Asenath admired; the men were set up and trained to go out to sea to fish for herring and mackerel.

The storm struck almost as soon as Asenath stepped ashore and before she had time to change out of her wet clothes. She looked out from the hotel window overlooking the Sound and watched apprehensively as the black clouds tossed and rolled and 'the earth seemed moved as if at the coming of Christ'. Soon slates were hurtling from the hotel roof, window glass splintered, doors crashed open and waves smashed over the nearby pier. So black were the clouds, Asenath Nicholson afterwards wrote that 'had the graves opened, and the sea given up her dead, the living would not have known'.

The following morning, the scale of the nocturnal tragedy unfolded. Of the fishing boats that had gone to sea, just one returned safely to the island: one boat had disappeared and was seen no more; a second was wrecked on the shore, and the three men who escaped and crawled up on to the cliffs had perished on the mountain. The body of one of the fishermen was washed up on land, while another was located under the wreck of his vessel. In all, nineteen fishermen had died.

Neason Adams was quick to respond: 'I have just returned from the melancholy and afflicted village of Keel, where I made the following list of nineteen men drowned, leaving fourteen widows and thirty-eight orphans.' It was, he said, one of the most distressing scenes he had ever witnessed, having listened to the cries of the widows and the screams of the children. He had arranged to send the families a ton of Indian meal – a pound of meal a day for each adult, and a half-pound for each child up to Christmas.[9]

From her visit to Erris, just weeks earlier, Mrs Nicholson was familiar with the fierce desire among the people to 'put a board' on the dead and to bury the deceased in a proper coffin. Failing this, the families would sometimes leave the dead body at a door in the hope that someone might 'put a board' on them. In the absence of a coffin, a corpse was wound about with the remnant of a blanket or sheet, and carried to their resting place. These burials, she said, told more of the paralysing effects of famine than anything else, for the Irish in all ages were celebrated for their attention to the interment of their dead.[10]

A fortnight after the boating tragedy, while Mrs Nicholson was still at Achill Sound, the widow of the fisherman who had been washed ashore and buried without a box bought a white coffin and took it to the spot where her husband's remains were interred. With her bare hands, she dug him up from his grave, 'proved' or identified him by a leather button she had sewed on his clothing and then had him buried with the dignity of a coffin.

James Hack Tuke and Asenath Nicholson had earlier met in Rossport, from where they had travelled together to Ballina in north Mayo. Like Tuke, Asenath, while acknowledging the positive work of the landlord Sir Richard O'Donnell in offering flax production employment at his Newport estate, was appalled at the role of his agents in the eviction of tenants, like those in Achill. How could it be tolerable for those 'drivers' to cast out people and destroy cabin after cabin, and sometimes whole villages, while the landlords claimed ignorance?[11]

She was respectful of the Quakers' work: 'The Society of Friends in Ireland stand out, as they do in other places, distinct.'[12]

Not for them vain boasting about the growth of their denomination or the error of the ways of others. She witnessed this work first-hand in Achill in the efforts of her hosts, Robert Savage and his wife. It was practical assistance imbued with compassion – a virtue, she had reluctantly concluded, that was lacking at the Achill Mission colony.

December in Achill was cold and stormy and Asenath Nicholson planned to return to Edward Nangle's colony once more, eager perhaps to make her peace with him and his wife before she left the island. There is no indication that she understood the pressure the Nangle family was then experiencing, or that Eliza had, only two weeks earlier, given birth to a stillborn baby. The following was reported in the *Achill Herald*: 'In this Settlement, on the 10th inst., the Lady of the Rev. E. Nangle, [delivered] of a still-born child.'[13]

Mrs Nicholson's experience was somewhat better than that of her earlier visit to the colony: 'I passed the Christmas and New Year's Day in Achill in the colony of Mr Nangle, and to the honour of the inhabitants would say that they did not send me to Molly Vesey's to lodge, but more than one family offered to entertain me.' She listened to Edward preach, but he did not speak to her even though he had an opportunity to do so. There was evidently no rapprochement between the pair. When the superintendent of schools informed the clergyman that Mrs Nicholson had visited the colony schools and provided clothes for the most destitute children, she heard that Edward had coolly replied, 'If she can do any good I am glad of it.'

Asenath Nicholson was critical of the quality of the food in the mission schools, and of the scanty food allowances which kept the children in a state of 'lingering want'. It was no better for the colony workmen in the bogs who were paid so skimpily – three pence a day – that 'some would have died but for the charity of Mrs Savage'. The men, she learned, had to work until Saturday and then travel nine miles to the colony to procure the Indian meal for the week's work. She complained, too, that the relief shops were selling damaged and unground Indian meal which 'a good American farmer would not give his swine'; such provisions would only result in dysentery among the half-starved people, she believed.[14]

Mrs Nicholson reflected on what she referred to as 'proselytism', and what she viewed as the misguided attempts in Achill and elsewhere to bribe the people away from their own church with offers of food and other benefits. The light-hearted responses she received from some children gave her an insight into the thinking of those who accepted instruction, clothing and food on condition that they read the scriptures and attend a church not of their own faith. 'We are going back to our own chapel or our own religion when the *stirabout* times are over', they told her, when the 'bread's done' and when 'the potatoes come again'.

When asked about their instruction in the scriptures, the children's replies were cheerful and pragmatic, seemingly untouched by any sense of shame: 'We shan't say the prayers when we go back,' they said, 'we'll say our own then.' The children understood that, by attending the colony schools, they would be fed and 'they could keep the life' until better times came round. Asenath understood that the parents of these children would not have made such comments, and were more likely to present themselves as true converts while 'receiving the stirabout'.

'Rice, Indian meal, and black bread would, if they had tongues, tell sad and ludicrous tales,' was Mrs Nicholson's pithy comment. They did what they needed to do to stay alive.[15]

Asenath left her mark on the ground of Mayo before taking her leave. Near Murrisk Abbey, at the foot of Croagh Patrick and close to the ocean, she helped gather stones and lay a garden rockery at the home of her hosts, and wrote: 'Stand there, when the hand that raised you shall be among the dead; and say that Asenath Nicholson, of New York, raised these stones as a memento of the suffering country she so much pitied and loved ...'[16]

She left Ireland the following year, never to return: 'The dark night had come, my trunk was packed, and the vessel was in readiness that was to bear me away.' The unusual, eccentric and generous American widow, imbued with Christian charity, is a unique and compelling witness of famine Ireland. On 27 December, while Mrs Nicholson was still at Dugort, Edward Nangle sat down to write yet another appeal for donations to the Achill Mission friends. Conditions in Achill were appalling, he told them, and the mission's store of Indian meal needed to be replenished urgently. 'If I can only manage to keep the poor people alive until the latter end of next August, I trust that all will be well, as even now several are making preparations for sowing their land next spring.' He was anxious to purchase a supply of corn without delay: 'I solicit a prompt response to this appeal.'[17] Even when thrown down with illhealth and family troubles, Edward never lost his ability to keep famine donations flowing into the Achill Mission coffers. However, he would soon be embroiled in a new rancorous public dispute.

CHAPTER FIFTEEN

Feed the Children

Edward Nangle was not the only outsider with an agenda to feed the famine children. An exotic Polish count now turned up in the west of Ireland to match the Achill Mission tactics and his programme of school food soon provoked the Achill clergyman's ire. Edward was incensed when the colony schools were excluded from a new relief scheme on the basis that they were already well supported by charitable donations to the Achill Mission.

Count Paul de Strzelecki was the agent of the British Relief Association, the private charitable organisation which raised the largest amount of money for private famine relief in Ireland. A handsome, physically fit, renowned explorer and a resourceful man, he had travelled to the west of Ireland during extreme winter conditions, his carriage at one stage stranded in snow drifts. On reaching County Mayo, he made Westport his base and was immediately horrified by the scenes of hunger and suffering: 'No pen can describe the distress by which I am surrounded. It has actually reached such a degree of lamentable extremes that it becomes above the power of exaggeration and misapprehension. You may now believe anything which you hear and read, because what I actually see surpasses whatever I read of past and present calamities.'

Strzelecki was particularly concerned by the famine distress of the children and, in the spring of 1847, he pioneered a system of feeding school children in the Westport Union. At a daily cost of one-third of a penny for each child, pupils were given clothing and food and – in an effort to improve hygiene – were required to wash their hands and comb their hair in the schools before eating. The food relief consisted of a daily ration of rye bread averaging ten ounces, and a half-pint of warm broth. The British Association would supply the rye meal, and pay the expenses of baking the bread and buying meat for the broth. All the bread would be baked in Westport and delivered weekly to each school.[1]

Edward Nangle was peeved that while Charles Seymour, Protestant rector of Achill, had received the British Association circular about the school relief programme, he himself had not. Given that Charles Seymour had a defined parochial role as Achill rector, in contrast to Edward Nangle's positon working with a missionary agency, Edward could be said to have over reacted. He was peeved to learn that the Achill schools which would receive assistance were listed as Dooega, Keel, Kildownet and Corraun, while all the Protestant and Achill Mission schools were excluded. He vented his indignation on Lord Sligo, chairman of the Westport Board of Guardians who were administering the programme locally on behalf of the British Association. The exchanges between the pair – Lord Sligo and Edward Nangle – indicate the extent to which Edward's famine activity had become repugnant even to other members of the Protestant establishment.[2]

John George Browne, 3rd Marquis of Sligo, was a young man in his twenties with a soft round face and a heavy burden of responsibility, having succeeded to the Westport estate following his father's death just two years earlier. Together with Richard O'Donnell, based nearby in Newport, he was one of the two main County Mayo landlords. Already, he had been lauded for his support of the people in the famine, no less than in the House of Commons where it was commented that the Marquis had sacrificed 600 head of deer from his estate for the soup kitchens. He was also a man deeply in debt.

He and the other members of the Westport Board of Guardians had struggled to keep the local workhouse operational.[3] At the start of the year, he himself had agreed to support its operation for three weeks out of his own resources, but the workhouse conditions continued to deteriorate until, by April, there was no milk to feed the inmates at the workhouse hospital and eleven dead bodies were waiting to be buried.

In addition to these pressures, he had to deal with Edward Nangle's attacks when their antagonism exploded in a series of angry exchanges. Why, demanded Edward, was the British Association school relief, which the board of guardians administered, confined to Achill's national schools to the exclusion of the colony schools? The Achill Mission, he complained, was now facing a situation where the priests were using the better relief available in the national schools to tempt children away from his schools. This was an intolerable situation for the colony, especially given that the British Association funds were largely sourced from English Protestants.[4]

Lord Sligo defended the practice, countering that the colony schools already benefited from large flows of money from English benefactors: 'You have thought fit to accuse the Roman Catholic clergy of proselytism by means of increased temporal advantage. In my humble opinion such a charge comes ill from the Protestant missionary settlement, where temporal advantages have long been considered as an inducement to starving peasants to desert the faith of their fathers.'[5] This was a severe reprimand of the Achill Mission from an establishment figure.

Edward denied that he had ever seduced the people to change their religious beliefs by offering temporal benefits. Indeed, in the previous two years, he insisted that he had restrained people who wished to make a public recantation of popery.

It was a nasty confrontation.

Some months later, Lord Sligo chaired a meeting of all the local relief committees, including that from Achill, at Westport Courthouse. They passed a resolution of thanks to be conveyed to the British Association in London, and to its representative Count Strzelecki, 'whose urbanity, courteous demeanour and anxiety for the destitute is deserving of our heartfelt gratitude.'[6]

By the summer of 1848, the British Association had suspended its relief work and its schools food programme as its funds were exhausted. Count Strzelecki reported that, since the previous October, £78,666 had been spent on the schools programme. In all, 8,380 children in the Westport Union had benefited from the scheme by the time Count Strzelecki left Ireland in September, his mission in Ireland substantially over.

The following year, giving evidence before a parliamentary select committee, he would declare: 'the calamity which has befallen to Ireland is an Imperial calamity.'[7]

***

Change was afoot at the Achill Mission itself when, in a significant move, its administration offices were transferred to 14 Holles Street, Dublin. It had been a tempestuous few months for Edward and his family: a stillborn Nangle child; a tense return visit to the colony by Asenath Nicholson; and Edward's disputes with the local relief committee, Lord Sligo and the British Relief Association. Meanwhile, Edward continued to be plagued by depressive symptoms: 'The illness which obliged me to leave England still continues to oppress me; but my medical advisers assure me that nothing is needed to restore me but a total suspension of business for some months. I am therefore restrained for the present to absent myself from Achill.'

There was a new Achill Mission management committee comprising Rev. Charles Seymour, Achill rector, together with Rev. Edward Lowe and Thomas Longley from the colony. There were changes, too, in the financial management systems, perhaps triggered by external criticisms of the use of Achill Mission donations. In future, all funds received by Edward and the Achill Mission would be lodged with its bankers, and drawn down by order of the colony committee with the signature of two of its members.

Added to these changes, the colony now had to contend with internal financial pressures: 'our treasury is not only exhausted but we are in debt'. The cost of sustaining over thirty schools, of feeding over 1,000 children and paying mission staff and farm labourers was straining resources. Edward's anxiety over the colony's financial affairs was compounded by another difficulty: he was dealing with the fallout from having given an ill-advised personal guarantee to finance a shipment of Indian meal.[8]

That summer, the dreaded blight had reappeared and Edward again called on the assistance of the Achill Mission friends. 'God has again sent the fatal rot on the potato crop,' he told them, and unless they could continue to feed the children for another year, many of them would certainly die of starvation. 'I want you to help me to collect money to feed these poor children. The cost of the education and food of each child will be about one penny per day.'[9]

Edward had a proposal, but not one which he had fully thought through. He would secure a shipload of corn for Achill before the winter set in if the funds could be raised. He entered into a verbal agreement with a merchant in Dublin to import 220 tons of Indian corn on the basis of phased payments as he raised the necessary funds. However, when Edward eventually received the contract for signature he was held to be personally liable for full payment once the cargo arrived. Rather naively, he had assumed that the document would not supersede the verbal agreement and put his name to the contract.

The shipment of corn reached Ireland in November 1848, after a journey of thirty days from Philadelphia. Edward then received a letter from the merchant demanding a settlement of £400 immediately, coupled with a personal security to pay off the balances of £700 and £800 in three and four months. Edward had no option but to immediately set out with Charles Seymour on a programme of preaching and meetings across England and the Channel Islands to raise the required funds.

He later felt compelled to give a detailed explanation to the Achill Mission friends about what had happened, lest he be charged 'with indiscretion and rashness'. The cargo of Indian corn, he explained, had saved many Achill lives through the winter of 1848, supplying food to about 1,800 children daily and supporting an average of seventy labourers on the colony lands.[10]

The assistance received had another more enduring benefit, he told the donors, in the diffusion of scriptural knowledge and the consequent weakening of popery on Achill Island. When he first arrived in Achill, he had found that the majority of the children wore neck amulets, charms and scapulars sold by the priests as a preservative against misfortune. Now, it was difficult to find any child with 'these trinkets of knavery and superstition' which had been laid aside or thrown into the fire. The improvement of the children's literary proficiency was also heartening, particularly in reading English. 'Several of these poor children could not have put two sentences together in the English language three years ago.'[11]

**

The Fifteenth Report of the Achill Mission for the famine year 1848 makes for interesting reading. It shows a spectacular level of fundraising from the mission's benefactors, largely outside Ireland and mainly in Britain, alongside commercial revenue from its own activities. Total income for the various Achill Mission funds amounted to an incredible £6,000, with approximately 60 per cent of this accounted for by collections, donations and subscriptions. The report paints a picture of an impressive flow of resources into Achill via the Achill Mission with these funds being allocated across infrastructure, schools, commercial enterprise and famine relief.[12]

This is the aspect of Edward's famine labour which can be submerged in the overlay of sectarian rhetoric and sentiment. A remarkable programme of fundraising, backed up by clever communications and emotive messaging, brought considerable resources to Achill and undoubtedly saved lives and improved the conditions of the people. While many queried his motives and methods, his organisational and entrepreneurial attributes were unquestionable.

In addition to subscriptions and donations, the Achill Mission generated over £1,000 of other income in 1848 from substantial commercial activities: the colony farms, sales in its shops, cattle sold and other income. On the expenditure side, almost £2,000 was spent on colony buildings and farm infrastructure, the printing press and salaries. By then the Mission had a wide physical reach across Achill with farms at Dugort, Mweelin and Inishbiggle, as well as an office premises in Dublin.

There is separate information in the accounts for the Achill Temporal Relief Fund. Over half the income, approximately £1,000, was allocated towards clothing and food relief programmes in the colony schools. The report acknowledges that 'a share of the funds entrusted to us for the temporal relief of the poor was expended in giving employment on the farms belonging to the mission' and building up the colony infrastructure, indicating a dubious overlap between the mission's philanthropic famine relief work and its quasi-commercial mission activities.

Edward described how the famine had produced some painful effects, including the moral degradation of the people. 'We know how the cravings of unsatisfied hunger have forced even parents to devour their offspring, and although our population has not been driven to such extremity of wickedness, there has been a general deterioration of character.' Thieving had become so widespread that it was difficult to uphold and defend the crucial rights of private property.

Another failure of the potato in 1848 sent a wave of alarm and panic across the country. The coming months into 1849 would result in as much suffering as at any time since the start of the famine. Count Strzelecki would afterwards state that 1849 was the worst year of all: that the effects of the famine were cumulative as the people endured the fourth year of distress and they were now 'skinned to the bone', worn down by workhouse and relief tests and by the Gregory clause and evictions. The people had declared, 'the land is cursed'.[13]

CHAPTER SIXTEEN

Workhouse War

At 4am on Friday, 21 September 1849, a Bianconi horse-drawn car set out from Westport in the thick darkness. On board were two sisters, Mary and Bridget McNamara, aged nineteen and eighteen, with eight other girls. They were accompanied by Mrs Bell, matron of Westport workhouse where all had resided.[1] Each girl had a lockable trunk, with her name painted on the outside, and a checklist of clothing items inside the lid, including a suite of new clothes provided by the Westport Guardians: six shifts, two flannel petticoats, six pairs of stockings, two pair of shoes, two gowns, chemises, bonnets, gloves, combs, brushes and knitting needles. The cost to Westport Union of providing clothing, transport to Dublin, and subsequent passage to Australia was estimated at £5 for each girl.[2]

The story of the girls' journey started the previous month when the emigration agent, Lieutenant Henry, visited several workhouses in Mayo seeking girls for the Earl Grey female orphan scheme to the Australian colonies. The agent had expressed some disappointment with the general level of education: 'we regret that from the large number of persons brought forward for inspection, but one young girl could read and she was educated at Achill colony. The gallant officer expressed surprise that education shall be hidden from such intelligent persons as the Westport paupers seemed to be.'[3]

Between 1848 and 1850, over 4,000 Irish orphan girls were brought from Irish workhouses to Australia through the scheme, 136 of these from four Mayo workhouses: eighty-six from Ballina, twenty-five from Ballinrobe, fifteen from Castlebar and ten from Westport.[4] For the Australian authorities, who paid the girls' passage fares, the programme provided an opportunity to redress the gender imbalance in the country. For the Irish local guardians, it enabled them to reduce the workhouse numbers who would be a long-term burden on their resources. Largely illiterate, the orphan girls were leaving a destitute and impoverished country on a three-month sea voyage with high expectations of a better future.

Mary and Bridget McNamara were Achill orphans – their parents, Thomas and Honora, were dead and it's likely that both spent time at the Achill Mission orphanage.[5] Despite Lieutenant Henry's assessment, each of the McNamara sisters was noted as being able to read but not write, on the shipping list. Mary gave her religion as Church of England while Bridget is recorded as being Roman Catholic. Five years earlier before famine took hold, in one of the controversial Achill Mission recantation ceremonies, two of those listed as formally recanting their faith were Bridget and Mary McNamara. There is a reasonable possibility that these were the McNamara sisters later selected for the Earl Grey scheme. If so, the sisters would have been aged fourteen and thirteen at the time of the recantations. The fact that Bridget identified herself as Roman Catholic suggests that she reverted to the denomination of her birth afterwards, possibly in the workhouse where the battle for souls appears to have been as fierce as on the island of Achill itself.

On reaching Mullingar, the girls boarded the train to Dublin, then crossed by steamer to Plymouth where, over two weeks later, they boarded the *Panama* which departed port on 6 October 1849. There were 157 orphan girls from Ireland on board – over half of these from County Mayo. Before their arrival in Sydney three months later, on 12 January 1850, the girls took their trunks from the ship's hold and spent time getting themselves clean and respectable before putting into port. On arrival, they walked the quarter of a mile from the harbour up to Hyde Park Barracks where they were housed until hired out as domestic servants.[6]

Bridget gained employment in the household of J. Nathan at Hunter St, Sydney, at a wage rate of £8 p.a., while Mary was employed at the McLean residence on King St, on similar terms. In these, their first paid employments, the sisters were within a ten-minute walk of each other.[7]

The stories of Mary and Bridget McNamara encapsulate the complexity of the Achill Mission's activity. Two young orphan girls had moved, through necessity, from their own community into an unfamiliar one, had publicly rescinded their faith and, in turn, had received the benefits of education and literacy in English – factors which undoubtedly acted to their benefit when they were selected for the Earl Grey emigration scheme. One sister, perhaps pressurised within the workhouse community, returned to the faith of her birth. Both left Ireland with bright hopes for a better future.

***

A month earlier, an unusual meeting took place in the first-floor board room of the same workhouse which had been home to the McNamara sisters. It was a summer's morning in August when the glow of Atlantic-infused light seeped into the tall stone structure. Viewed from a distance, the complex of rectangular slated workhouse buildings rose above the town against the dramatic backdrop of Croagh Patrick. Built to accommodate up to 1,000 inmates, it was one of the largest workhouses in the country and, since opening its doors four years earlier, had witnessed some ghastly famine scenes. Now, a battle for souls was raging within its walls as the sectarian contest moved from Achill to inside the forbidding walls of Westport workhouse.

Seated around the board room table were Captain Farren, poor law inspector; two vice guardians of the union; Edward Nangle; and the Catholic and Protestant workhouse chaplains, Rev. Jackson (assistant Protestant chaplain at the workhouse) and Father Gibbons (the Catholic chaplain). The purpose of the meeting was to enquire into the treatment of Protestant inmates from Achill at the workhouse following a formal complaint by Edward Nangle. After the priest objected to Edward Nangle taking notes, Captain Farren asked that no notes be taken as he did not wish any of the proceedings to be published by the press. Edward responded that he had no confidence in the government or in its agents where Protestantism was concerned, and he believed that the only security persecuted Protestants had was in the power of public opinion influenced by a free press. He would not surrender his right to use the free press for the protection of the friendless converts who looked to him as their advocate, and he refused to provide a pledge not to publish any of the evidence produced at the enquiry.

One of the first witnesses called was Neal Grealis, an Achill convert to Protestantism. Edward Nangle's accusation was that, when the islander refused to attend mass the Sunday after he entered the workhouse, he was severely ill-treated by other inmates. A group had run at him, taunting: 'There is the jumper – the turncoat – the devil of a Protestant.' Such was the abuse the man had suffered, claimed Edward, that he himself had no choice but to remove the man from the workhouse and support him directly with Achill Mission funds.

Michael Malley of Dugort was another witness. He described how he had entered the workhouse as a Protestant sometime before Christmas, but left soon afterwards because other inmates beat him up, kicked him, pulled his hair and called him 'sammey' and 'jumper'. He used to stay at Savages' hotel in Achill Sound before he moved to the workhouse, but had lost his place there when Mr Savage moved away to another part of the country. When he was obliged to leave the workhouse, he went to the colony because that was where he was best treated.

Edward Nangle told the enquiry that there were many such witnesses with similar stories. 'Until some alteration is made in the administration of the poor law I cannot send any Protestant pauper to the workhouse. I do not believe that, unless they denied Christ, their lives would be secure in such a den of iniquity and violence.'

It was three months before Edward received details of the outcome of the investigation:

> The commissioners have arrived at the conclusion that although the statements which accompanied Mr Nangle's complaints were exaggerated as a general description of the ill usage and entire absence of protection for persons of the class referred to [as Protestant inmates of Westport Workhouse], quite enough appears on credible testimony to show that certain of the Protestant inmates, converts from Roman Catholicism, were exposed to annoyance, and on some occasions beaten by the Roman Catholic inmates of the workhouse.

Edward was unhappy at the commissioners' assertion that some claims about the workhouse events were exaggerated. As for a recommendation that the vice guardians be more diligent in the future in protecting workhouse inmates from ill treatment, this was insipid and weak in the extreme, in his view. He was particularly infuriated at the feebleness of the commissioners' reprimand of the Catholic chaplain who had 'struck one of the nurses who was a Protestant because one of the paupers in her ward died without being anointed'.[8]

At the height of famine suffering, the sectarian conflict in Achill reached beyond the island and inside the walls of the institution that was the last refuge for destitute people, Catholic, Protestant and convert alike.

***

Two days before Bridget and Mary McNamara left Westport on the first leg of their long journey, there was wild excitement in their native Achill. At noon, on a day of clear blue skies, a large congregation pressed into the colony church at Dugort for what was to be one of the largest confirmation ceremonies carried out by Thomas Plunket, Bishop of Tuam, anywhere in his extensive diocese.

Those who couldn't be accommodated inside the building waited outside. There were 400 candidates for confirmation, twenty-eight of whom were the children of Protestants and 'the remaining 372 were converts from the Church of Rome'. Children who had flocked to the colony schools for nourishment in the famine years were now confirming their adherence to their new faith.

Surely, observed Edward Nangle, the fact that so many Achill children were permitted by their parents to come forward to commit themselves to Protestantism illustrated 'how Popery [had] lost its hold on the adult population'. An alternative opinion might point to the irresistible draw of the soup schools for those on the edges of starvation. The decision for many was to seek life or famine death.

The confirmation celebrations continued into the evening with an explosion of colour and celebration. In front of the Nangle house, a huge pile of turf was kindled into a monster bonfire; guns were fired, rockets were set off by a cutter out on the bay and the verses of 'God save the Queen' rang out as Bishop Plunket walked among his congregation. Edward was beside himself with elation and eloquence: 'The lofty mountain Slievemore,' he afterwards wrote, 'was thrown into the most graceful relief on the cloudless sky and itself lit off by dark contrast the illuminated colony of its base.'[9]

Bishop Plunket had another important task to perform the next day in laying the foundation stone of a new church at Achill Sound, to be known as the Holy Trinity Church, in the presence, it was claimed, of one of the largest crowds ever seen in Achill. From early that morning the colony was abuzz with excitement, and soon the road from Dugort to Achill Sound was thronged with people on horseback, in carts and on foot, with every available vehicle, horse and pony brought into use. Others, including the orphanage children, travelled by boat along the Sound. The site chosen for the church was picturesque and elevated, with extensive views from Achill Sound back to Slievemore and across to the mainland. A coastguard galley, with a Union Jack at the stern, awaited the bishop's arrival.

Edward was emotional as he surveyed the scene: 'It was delightful. As we stood upon the eminence where the church is to be erected, to see the crowds of old and young pressing to the place of meeting, by the roads and over the strands ... about two o'clock, between twelve and thirteen hundred people were assembled.' Prayers were read and William Stoney, rector of Castlebar, delivered an address. Hymns were sung, and Bishop Plunket proceeded to lay the foundation stone and to give the customary benediction.[10]

It was a triumphal moment, a public signal of what had been achieved on Achill Island over almost two decades by Edward Nangle and his ministry. An important guest, Rev. William McIlwaine of St George's church, Belfast, articulated the sense of what a glorious time it was for the Protestantism on the island. Seventeen years previously, he said, there was not a solitary instance of a member of our Protestant established church among the thousands of native inhabitants of Achill, while the popish chapels were crowded with those who were among the most abject and superstitious slaves of the Roman Catholic Church. There was then little tillage on the island, no enterprise whatsoever and not a slated house to be seen. What a transformation the Achill Mission had wrought!

The Belfast clergyman was overjoyed to see the process of evangelisation that continued throughout the whole island: five places of Protestant worship had been established; 1,500 children were attending the scriptural schools, all learning the English language and expressing their loyalty to the British Crown. The clergyman was lavish in praising the work of his colleague Edward Nangle and his colony: 'Wherever the Mission farm is seen, there is an oasis in the desert. The Colony is a lovely and comparatively prosperous, comfortable, and rising village, with its Church, Schools, Hospital, Orphan Refuge, Dispensary, Post-office, and Printing-office.'[11]

The tone of the ceremony exuded a sense that a wild and uncivilised island had finally taken on the enlightened mantle of British culture and Protestant civilisation. Edward Nangle, it appeared, had achieved his vision, assisted greatly by the flow of famine converts to his colony in their hour of need.

CHAPTER SEVENTEEN

Three Women

Each column of the *Achill Herald* edition for June 1850 is framed by a thick black boundary line. It is sombre and carries a brief statement announcing Eliza Nangle's death:

DIED

On the 19th inst., at Peafield Terrace, Blackrock,
near Dublin, after a long and painful illness, in the sure
and painful hope of a resurrection to everlasting life
through Jesus Christ, Eliza, the beloved wife of the Rev.
Edward Nangle.

She had not yet reached her fiftieth year, and was the mother of three adult daughters and three small sons. Five of her infant children lay in Slievemore graves where she, too, would shortly rest.

For six years, since the birth of her last living child, George, her health had been in decline. Indeed, it appeared as if her mental and physical health had been fragile ever since the family's arrival in Achill. From 1848 onwards, she had resided permanently in Dublin.

In an obituary, Edward described his wife's debilitating final illness. In the summer of 1849, she developed severe swelling from dropsy, accompanied by breathing difficulties. By the spring of 1850, her symptoms had become alarming, with no hope of recovery. The news was difficult to bear, and she was distraught at the prospect of leaving her small sons motherless. The final months of her life were wretched, filled with sleepless nights and days of suffering, 'her naturally placid countenance wrenched with anguish'.

A few days before her death, Eliza took leave of her three sons, William, Henry and George, telling them 'she had much more to say to them but was unable', overwhelmed as she was 'with the load of bodily suffering and mental anguish'. At the end, she asked the nurse attending her to wet her lips and spoke her last words to her sister, Grace Warner, before falling into a slumber. She breathed her last at nine o'clock on the evening of 19 June.

Edward's obituary referred to his wife's virtues of faith, kindness and perseverance, also acknowledging 'her singular skill in account keeping' which, for many years, 'saved the mission the expense of book-keeping'. He added the interesting comment that she was 'in every respect a woman of masculine understanding' and that her most astute piece of advice to him at the beginning of the famine was to administer relief by feeding the children in the colony schools. The impression created is of a practical woman struggling to keep the family's life intact in the face of immense difficulties. The reference to Eliza suggesting that the children in the mission schools be fed during the famine could either be taken as an expression of Eliza's practical and caring nature, or an attempt by Edward to share responsibility for a practice which later became tarnished.

Eliza's life and well-being were not helped by Edward's own volatility of temperament, frequent bouts of depression and ill health, and long absences from the family home. He himself acknowledged the latter. 'Another trial to which the faith and fortitude of this excellent woman was exposed originated in the necessity which obliged the writer frequently to leave Achill for the purpose of collecting funds to carry on the Mission. In these tours, she could not accompany him, domestic duties requiring her presence at home; still, she never complained.' In the end, it all proved a burden too difficult to bear.

Eliza Nangle's remains were taken across the entire width of Ireland for interment next to her infant children. 'The funeral,' wrote her husband, touched by the condolences of the islanders, was 'attended by a large concourse of people of all classes; few indeed have been followed to the grave by a larger company of sincere mourners.'[1]

***

The first page of the Nangle scrapbook carries a dedication: 'Matilda Nangle, from her affectionate Mamma in remembrance of kind attention in hours of illness. April 19th 1850.' A gift to her third daughter, seventeen year old Matilda ('Tilly'), from her mother just two months before Eliza's death.

There is a series of watercolour pieces pasted into the book, pictures that capture a family's life in Achill: children playing and riding horses on Dugort strand, several views of the mountainside Achill Mission colony, Achill Sound and Bullsmouth viewed from the vantage point of Inishbiggle, boats being rowed on Atlantic waves and a woman and child standing at Keel beach in the shadows of Minaun cliffs.

The most striking illustration is entitled 'Missionary Settlement in the Island of Achill'. It shows a grey-purple mountain with a necklace of clouds at its summit and cultivated fields descending its slopes. The settlement itself is neat and enclosed, with its two rows of slated houses looking out on the straight lines of symmetric gardens, like a pleasant plantation village. A man with a hat – perhaps Edward Nangle himself – rides his horse in a westward direction along the road in front of the colony. In the foreground of the picture, a woman with a basket walks over a small bridge against the backdrop of the mountain, rows of cultivated ridges stretching away on either side.[2]

It could be a picture of Tilly herself, in the place that was her home for almost her entire life. She arrived at Slievemore in the summer of 1834 with her parents and two sisters before she had yet reached her first birthday. She grew up on the slopes of this mountain, played on the silver strand at its base and – all the time – watched on as her father's vision materialised before her eyes. It was said that she had an artistic gift and a fine singing voice and that, from an early age, she assisted in the colony infant school and orphanage. She undoubtedly also witnessed appalling famine distress.

The picture captures in space and time the good moments, freezing them in the imagination, but indicates nothing of life beyond the confines of the picture's borders – nothing of the dark days endured by the Nangle family itself, nothing of the vicious sectarian strife and nothing of famine horrors. It is a representation of an idyllic oasis where all pain, strife and controversy are hidden from view.

**

The columns of the *Achill Herald* for June 1852 were once again edged with mourning black for a tragic notice: 'On the evening of Saturday, 5th inst., a sudden gloom was cast over every countenance in this Settlement, by the arrival of a special messenger with the melancholy announcement of the death of Rev. Mr. Nangle's youngest daughter, who had gone to Dublin in charge of a sick brother on the Tuesday week previous, apparently in good health.' Tilly Nangle had travelled to care for her sick brother, George.

On Tuesday, a week later, she was out and about but complained of a slight cold; on Wednesday she received medical attention but nothing serious was suspected. On Thursday, when she complained of a violent headache, the physician returned to provide medical attention and left her that evening with the intention of seeing her early on Friday. By then, Tilly Nangle had passed away. The following Sunday, her remains arrived at Dugort for burial next to her mother.

The Nangle scrapbook has an unfinished pencil drawing of a landscaped driveway. Somebody – possibly Frances or Henrietta Nangle – had written beneath the drawing: 'MN June 24 1852 aged 19 years.' Tilly died just two years after her mother, leaving the scrapbook drawing unfinished.

On the slopes of the mountain is a cemetery, the *Sean Reilig*, containing the Nangle grave, almost hidden from view by the encroaching growth. It is the month of May but the place feels cold, as if all warmth has been sucked into the mountain mass. The setting is quiet except for the birdsong, and the sounds of water plunging through the drainage network of stone dykes created by the Achill Mission in the early years. It is the final resting place of Eliza Nangle, her daughter Tilly and five infant children – a lonely mountainside place of repose.

***

Grace Warner was there to support the motherless Nangle children, in particular the delicate George, youngest child of Eliza and Edward, born on the eve of the Famine. He would suffer continuous poor health and mental illness as a youth and young man, spending periods in mental institutions in Sligo, Dublin, and later in Wales. In medical assessments and hospital admission papers, his ailment was described as 'melancholia', his countenance as 'vacant though placid with persistent taciturnity', a young man staring vacantly ahead when addressed.[3] Almost two decades after her sister's death, Grace would sign admission papers for his entry as a private patient to the County Asylum at Denbigh, in north Wales, where she was then resident. The mental frailty experienced by each of his parents, combined with the loss of his primary carers – first his mother, then his sister – were likely factors in his unstable condition.

Grace Warner appears to have made the care of her delicate, sensitive nephew the main focus of her later life. Three decades after Eliza's death, while still listed as resident in Bangor, Wales, she signed an agreement to make weekly payments of seventeen shillings and six pence to cover the costs of her nephew's continued asylum upkeep and care.

In her final years, Grace would return to Achill where she died on 1 December 1890. Her death certificate lists her profession as 'private lady' and the cause of death as 'old age'.[4] The witness to her death was John P. Sheridan, then proprietor of the colony's Slievemore Hotel which appears to have been Grace's final place of residence. We can speculate as to why she returned to Achill in her closing years. Did she have a desire to be close to her sister Eliza and her deceased children? Was it an opportunity to avail of favourable accommodation terms given her association with the Achill Mission? Or, perhaps, she had an enduring attachment to the wild place where she came as a young woman with youthful idealism in support of Edward and Eliza's daunting enterprise.

George Edward Nangle died at the County Asylum, Wales, in 1895 five years after Grace's death. He is buried in an unmarked grave in north Wales.

It would make for a neat symmetry for this story if Grace Warner were interred on the slopes of Slievemore next to her sister Eliza, her niece Tilly and the Nangle infants. But her final resting place is unknown. What we do know is that, in her compassion, she consistently picked up the pieces of shattered Nangle lives. Eliza, Tilly and Grace were three women caught up in a mighty clash of belief systems in nineteenth-century Ireland. It was as if their lives were squeezed out and smothered in the rage of an historic clash on an Atlantic-drenched island.

CHAPTER EIGHTEEN

Battle of Stones

It was a Friday, in the month of September 1851, when an excited crowd accompanied the archbishop and a half-dozen of his priests around a property at Bunnacurry, Achill. Those who gathered were animated as they walked the elevated site with its fine vista northward to Slievemore and eastward to Blacksod Bay. John MacHale and his archdiocese had recently become the owner of 1,200 acres of island land with excellent development potential and, importantly, its own access to sea manure to fertilise its soil when they built a road connecting the site with the sea. The archbishop was enthusiastic, buoyed up with plans. There would be a monastery to accommodate Franciscan friars, a school for the local children, a glebe house for two priests and a model farm to provide education in modern systems of agriculture. He promised to enter into arrangements with the twenty tenants on the site with regard to rent and tenure.[1]

John MacHale's fightback against the Achill Mission was underway and he was determined to beat Edward Nangle at his own game. He planned to counteract 'the mischievous speculators, who, more than twenty years ago, bought a farm in Achill and planted themselves there to drive a lucrative trade on English credulity', particularly in the famine years.[2] This time the fight would centre on land: the two militant clergymen were about to become ecclesiastical landlords.

The Encumbered Estates Act of 1849 had provided the archbishop with his opportunity. The Act established a new tribunal with drastic powers to dispose of the estates of indebted landlords which could be compulsorily sold on the petition of a creditor.³ Once lands in Achill were advertised for sale, John MacHale was quick off the mark in bidding for and acquiring the Bunnacurry property, making him a neighbouring landlord to the Achill Mission. John MacHale's bold purchase prodded Edward Nangle into action.

Ireland was entering a new era of assertive Catholic nationalism articulated at the national synod of the Catholic Church in Thurles a year earlier under the direction of Paul Cullen, the new archbishop of Armagh. The synod took strong positions on church discipline, on education and on the need for measures to counteract Protestant missionary efforts that had gained momentum during the famine. John MacHale was under pressure to counter the spread of Protestant proselytisation in his extensive western archdiocese.⁴

For now, as he walked his elevated site in Achill, he may have felt a growing confidence that he could finally halt and reverse the inroads made by Edward Nangle and his mission. He believed that just as 'hunger and weakness were the only arguments by which they assailed the faith of the people', now the courage and resistance of the people were again returning.⁵ John MacHale believed that they now had the tools to defeat the enemy. He had the land.

The building of Bunnacurry monastery was marked by a fierce battle, which 'like the night of the Big Wind is a landmark in the memories of the people'.⁶ It was the *Battle of the Stones*, which took on a powerful resonance and figurative value in post-famine Achill. Stones from the island land, smoothed by weather and time and symbolising strength and resilience, were fought over with passion by colliding Achill interests. The crash of pelted stones rang out for days on end in a factional skirmish that brought to mind the biblical words: There shall not be left one stone upon another that shall not be thrown down (Matthew 24:2).

The trouble started soon after John MacHale's visit when Bunnacurry workers attempted to carry off stones from dilapidated houses at nearby Cashel, from land owned by the Achill Mission.

A letter was quickly issued from the colony to the priest warning against the 'illegal invasion of our property' with no effect. Representatives of the Achill Mission then sought a legal warrant and, on Wednesday, 7 October, went with the police to Bunnacurry, pointed out the alleged stolen property and a man found in charge of the heap of stones was arrested. Some of the Achill Mission party, without the police, then proceeded to Cashel where a number of men were again found to be carrying away stones and loading them onto carts. Following an order to throw down the stones, two men who violently resisted were arrested by the police.

The next day, when two Achill Mission workmen returned to Cashel, they encountered more resistance and one of their men received a wound to the head. 'They committed this outrage,' reported the *Achill Herald*, 'in the full knowledge of the fact that our men were removing the stolen property under the authority of a magistrate's warrant'. Word of the Mission was dispatched to the superintendent who arrived with more men and, after some persuasion, the colony was allowed to continue its work.

That evening, word reached the colony that a number of men from the mainland were to join the resistance the following day. During the night, a messenger was sent by the Achill Mission to Sir Richard O'Donnell, the nearest magistrate, requesting his presence with the police the following day so that the warrant preventing the removal of the stones could be executed. On Friday, when Sir Richard O'Donnell arrived accompanied by eight policemen, the colony workers were allowed to continue with their work without interference.

On Saturday morning, when there seemed little likelihood of further resistance, Sir Richard and his party started back for Newport but soon encountered a belligerent crowd of men who were associated with the Catholic landlord, William McCormack, approaching Achill from the direction of Corraun on the mainland and intent on supporting the resistance to the colony workers. The presence of the police contingent prevented further hostilities and all was peaceful on Sunday and in the following days as the work of removing the stones back to Cashel continued without further resistance until the work was completed.

Edward Nangle gave his verdict on the strange hostilities: 'We believe that many see the gross inconsistency of building a *holy house* for *holy monks* with stolen goods. Laying the foundations of such an institution in robbery, must indeed appear incongruous to the unsophisticated mind of an honest layman.' As for the priests, he claimed that not one of them had made an appearance during the confrontation, preferring to put forward their blind and unsuspecting faithful to do their dirty work while they themselves skulked behind.[7]

Not for the first time, Edward would be furious at the outcome of the petty sessions court at Achill Sound the following April. He was appalled at Daniel Cruise's decision to dismiss the court case on the basis that 'both parties were equally to blame'.[8]

The latest battle between John MacHale and Edward Nangle had ended all square. In a strange way, this phase of hostilities was appropriately accompanied by a sound track of crashing rock and stones as the contestants took on new weapons of land, building and churches.

***

John MacHale and Edward Nangle again attacked one another publicly and traded insults in sharp exchanges reminiscent of those between the two protagonists almost a quarter of a century earlier. On the Feast of the Epiphany, in January 1852, MacHale wrote a pugnacious letter to the *Freeman's Journal* castigating Edward Nangle and the Achill Mission for its behaviour during the Famine.

'Notwithstanding,' he wrote, 'their long residence in the island, and the volumes of lies and calumnies they have circulated, and the heaps, amounting to thousands of England's mammon which they have received, and the six years of excruciating famine with which the country has been affected, they have made no inroad on the Catholicity of the natives.' Provocatively, he continued, the colony missionaries are 'the off-scourings of society'; their scholars 'imported vagrant-orphans or the orphaned children of negligent parents, whom, like gypsies, they contrive to gather from other quarters'. The Achill Mission, he concluded, 'is a detached and isolated thing of long legal standing amidst a Catholic population without hold on the hearts of the people or sympathy with their affections'. The Achill Mission, he asserted, had pathetically failed to make inroads with the Catholic population of Achill.

Edward was goaded by John MacHale's criticisms of his missionaries and 'their lack of gentle birth and rank'. What about the archbishop's own priests, he retorted. Was his own curate on the island not 'taken from the peasant class, and that not of the highest grade', while the parish priest was the son of a lowly native? As for the archbishop himself, was he not 'the son of a poor peasant who lived in a cabin in the bogs of Nephin where he kept a *shebeen* house'? Furthermore, if conclusive evidence was needed of the continued good health of the Achill Mission, surely Dr McHale's own decision 'to build an ecclesiastical barrack for the accommodation of a troop of Monks' was proof of this.[9]

John MacHale had a few more tricks up his sleeve. He was determined that those who converted to Protestantism during the famine should return to the Catholic fold and express their regret publicly for their association with the 'soul-destroyers'. He took his opportunity on a bright summer's day at Dookinella in the new church that stood between the mountain bulks of Minaun and Slievemore. Attired in his episcopal robes, as he had done on several occasions in the past, he ascended the altar and addressed the congregation in Irish. After concluding a confirmation ceremony, forty-nine people came forward to make a public declaration on bended knee, each expressing profound regret at having been driven by dire distress to attend the proselytising schools. Each acknowledged guilt, asked for pardon and implored the archbishop's benediction.[10]

Archbishop MacHale's most significant move in this new phase of resistance to the Achill Mission was the appointment of a young priest, James Henry, to a curate position on the island.

'Father Henry took up the work with the zeal of a saint and the soul of a hero,' as if he combined the energies and traits of both John MacHale and Edward Nangle.[11] He set to his task with energy and determination and was about to become a formidable figure on the Achill stage. He visited the parents of children attending the 'stirabout and soup schools' and extracted a promise that the children would be withdrawn.[12] He boasted that, over a period of ten days, four colony schools had closed their doors, and not only had the children returned to the faith of their birth, but their teachers also had asked to be readmitted to the Catholic Church.

James Henry adopted Edward Nangle's own tactics by pulling at the heart strings of English benefactors in soliciting funds: 'It is really impossible to picture the naked state of these poor children, who have left those proselytising schools – their members shivering from the piercing blast of winter, and their souls just rescued from a state, a relapse into which might prove fatal, are more powerful appeals to the hearts of the good and the charitable than my humble advocacy.' He let his benefactors know that the children, once clad, would have the opportunity to attend the school of the Franciscan friars who were already employing the poor and providing the children with a religious education.[13]

Today, the buildings at the former Bunnacurry monastery are roofless ruins, apple windfalls strewn across the ground of what was once a picturesque walled garden. The small monastery cemetery, still intact, runs parallel to what was once the chapel, its windows now boarded up. The cemetery area is cared for, the ground freshly gravelled and the walls recently whitewashed. There are nine Franciscan friars buried here, including Bonaventure McDermott, 'founder of this monastery in 1852'.

It is intriguing that John MacHale wanted the Franciscan friars to take on the Achill Mission with its own methods – education of the young, agricultural improvement and employment. Like the Dugort colony, it was an oasis of development and plenty in its day.

The road where the friars walked, downhill to the sea, is quiet and deserted today, except for the cattle who raise their heads and look on with curiosity as grey clouds gather above. Men who came from outside the island to join the battle for Achill souls rest peacefully, undisturbed.

✶✶✶

Edward Nangle took fright at John MacHale's purchase of the Bunnacurry land. The colony was threatened and he feared that his bitter enemy, the archbishop, was setting his sights on the purchase of Sir Richard O'Donnell's Achill lands which included the colony. He penned an urgent and anxious plea to the Achill Mission friends who had supported him so generously in the past. The best years of his life had been devoted to the Achill project, he told them. Much had been achieved, but now the whole of his work was in serious jeopardy. Achill Island was about to be sold in the Encumbered Estates Court and, should the land fall into hostile hands, there was a real danger that the Achill Mission could be ejected and their buildings 'desecrated by Roman idolatry'. The danger could only be averted by the Achill Mission itself purchasing the advertised land, but the situation was urgent and the required funds would have to be raised within a fortnight.

Acquiring the land would offer considerable benefits, he told his supporters, by providing the colony with a rent-free property which would secure the mission's future. In addition, the land offered significant potential for improvement and would put the mission in a position of being self-reliant and able to support itself from its own resources. If acquired, the property would be vested in trustees for the perpetual benefit of the Achill Mission.

'I saw Sir Richard O'Donnell, the proprietor of Achill, last week and he informed me that he expected the arrangements for the sale would be perfect in about a month.'[14] There was no time to be lost, and the very survival of the mission depended on the goodwill of the Protestants of Great Britain. He was calling on their generosity once more if calamity was to be averted for his mission. The impending threat had roused Edward into a frenzy of action in a new phase of his vision: to secure his enterprise into the future by owning and controlling not just the colony lands, but much of the island of Achill.

1 April 1851 was a landmark day as Edward Nangle confirmed that the Achill Mission was to become the major landowner in Achill: 'The Trustees of the Achill Purchase Fund beg leave to inform those kind friends who contributed to it, that the private contract into which they had entered with Sir Richard O'Donnell for the purchase of the Achill estate received formal sanction of the Encumbered Estates Commissioners on the first of this month.'[15] The agreed purchase price was £17, 500, and this amount had been lodged with the Commissioners.

It was a daring move, the scale of which caused Edward sleepless nights. The Achill Mission had acquired the whole of the island with the exception of the lands at Bunnacurry now owned by John MacHale, and two townlands in the east owned by the Marquis of Sligo. Edward had raised approximately £11,000 towards the purchase price and the shortfall was contributed by three gentlemen, William Pike, Thomas Brassy and Samuel Holme, to whom two-fifths of the property was then transferred, while three-fifths of the land became the property of the Achill Mission. William Pike later bought out the other two and became the second largest landowner on the island after the Achill Mission.

By the end of 1852, all the purchase legalities were complete. The change in land ownership took effect quickly and was dramatically illustrated when the Achill Mission then advertised to sublet portions of its new extensive estate, including a substantial area at Keem:

TO BE LET, THE MOUNTAINS AND
VALLEY OF KEEM[15]

This is the most picturesque spot in Achill, and affords a
most desirous situation for a Summer Residence, or
Bathing Lodge. The Mountains of Keem are celebrated for
the excellence of the mutton fed upon them. There is also

in the Bay a SALMON FISHERY, which if worked by a
skilful fisherman, would yield from nine to ten ton of
salmon in the season. There are also other unoccupied
lands; the particulars of which may be had on application
to Mr. Issac Johnston, Dugort, Achill, Newport, Co Mayo.

The purchase of the Achill land, even if prompted by the perceived
threat of John MacHale's plans, was bold and audacious and
another indication of Edward Nangle's fearless drive, his ability to
take risks and his monumental energy when not laid low with
illness. But it also signalled a new, very different phase for the
colony when estate management came to the fore and took
precedence over missionary work. Throughout the second half of
the nineteenth century, there were three major landowners in
Achill: William Pike, the Achill Mission and the Archbishop of
Tuam. The Achill Mission would lease large tracts of land to
approved outsiders to boost returns on its investment, thus
opening up a new era of land control in Achill alongside new
conflicts.

CHAPTER NINETEEN

Root and Branch Change

The Achill Mission was about to undergo profound organisational change with the overall focus shifting to its landlord and estate management functions while its missionary work was outsourced, and the role of its charismatic founder declined. This transformation could be compared to a modern corporation moving beyond its founding mission in favour of a property development function. The change brought a new type of conflict to Achill.

The Catholic backlash against the Achill Mission and its famine conversions intensified through the archbishop's episcopal visits, ecclesiastical construction and confirmation services. Achill would witness the incongruous sight of two bishops – John MacHale and Thomas Plunket – simultaneously visiting the island on a weekend in early August 1852, as the competition for souls in post-famine Achill deepened.

Bishop Plunket was in Achill Sound on the Sunday to consecrate the new parish church in the presence of a large congregation, and afterwards confirmed 167 people at the colony church in Dugort.

Not to be outdone, John MacHale arrived in Achill from Belmullet the same day and presided at a Catholic confirmation ceremony at Dookinella church on the Monday. A biased writer in the *Achill Herald*, who passed the church during the ceremony, remarked how few young people were present: 'we did not see six people under the age of eighteen, a fact which confirmed us in the opinion which we have held for some time that the convictions and affections of the rising generation are on the side of Protestantism.'[1] The Archbishop, however, was fired up, stung by charges that he had allowed proselytising Protestantism to spread without resistance across his archdiocese.

Present at the Achill Sound new church consecration by Bishop Plunket was a bearded English clergyman in his fifties: Alexander Dallas, an even more aggressive and unpalatable evangelical than Edward, who had established an evangelising mission in Connemara at the outset of the Famine, with mission stations manned by clergymen and preachers entrusted with funds to advance the work of education and evangelisation.[2] One of his claims to fame was the use of the postal service in January 1846 to deliver 90,000 copies of a religious tract, A Voice from Heaven to Ireland, throughout the country.[3] So successful was his campaign that a new organisation, the Society for Irish Church Missions, was established in 1849 and it was to this group that the Achill Mission now turned as it came to terms with its new tasks. Absorbed by its new landlord and estate management efforts, it decided, in a radical departure, that it would now delegate the missionary work which had fired the energy of its founder.

The bones of an agreement had been put in place three months earlier when Bishop Plunket and Alexander Dallas held a meeting in Achill. They had spent three days at Mweelin, the outlying Achill Mission colony in the west of the island, where they witnessed a buzzing, impressive development: a new church, rectory and steward's house; a row of cottages housing eighteen families; a school with forty pupils (children of converts from the surrounding villages); and a training school with fifty boys being trained as school masters and scripture readers. It was here that Alexander Dallas, on behalf of the Society for Irish Church Missions, undertook to take responsibility for the missionary work in Achill, including the clergymen, scripture readers, teachers and the Mweelin training school.[4]

Anne Dallas afterwards spoke of the considerable stress the new Achill responsibilities placed on her husband's shoulders, causing him much 'mental anxiety' and involving many long journeys to the island, often in the depths of winter. She pointedly referred to one aspect of the arrangement which would eventually lead to its demise: 'It was important that the principles of the Society should be faithfully adhered to; and as in this [Achill] Mission there had been a considerable mixture of temporal relief with the spiritual agency, it was exceedingly difficult to work through the complications of the combined departments.'[5] In the end, the issue of the allocation of money from the Achill Mission's overall income for the Society's Achill work would become fraught and problematic.

The arrangements with Alexander Dallas were part of a root and branch reorganisation of the Achill Mission structures in the wake of its substantial land purchase. A Dublin-based committee would oversee the management of the estate and rental income, which would be used for the benefit of the tenants and the enhancement of the value of the property. It had the potential for a new beginning whereby the Achill Mission could manage its estate in a productive and exemplary way and, in the process, improve the lot of its Achill tenants after the experience of famine wretchedness. This potential, however, did not materialise.

There was a clear intention in purchasing the Achill estate to keep the property out of Roman Catholic hands and to 'let out to respectable Protestant tenants'.[6] This would result in many mission tenants claiming that they were forced to send their children to the mission schools or face effective eviction. The tight control that the Achill Mission exerted on its lands was reflected in its lease agreements, specifying that no Catholic buildings would be permitted on their lands and any activities antagonistic to the mission would be prohibited.

All was about to change, too, for Edward Nangle. In May 1852, as the Achill Mission's purchase of Sir Richard O'Donnell's encumbered estate was being finalised, Bishop Plunket assigned Edward to a new post as rector of Skreen, County Sligo, a position

The interior of the St Thomas' Church contains many memorial plaques to members of the Achill Mission community, including Edward and Eliza Nangle. (Brian Thompson)

The gravestone at the small cemetery on the slopes of Slievemore at the rear of the Colony development marks the resting place of Eliza Nangle, her daughter Tilly, and five of the Nangle infant children. (Brian Thompson)

Edward Nangle died in September 1883 and was buried in Deansgrange Cemetery, Monkstown, Dublin where his second wife, Sarah, was also later buried. (Brian Thompson)

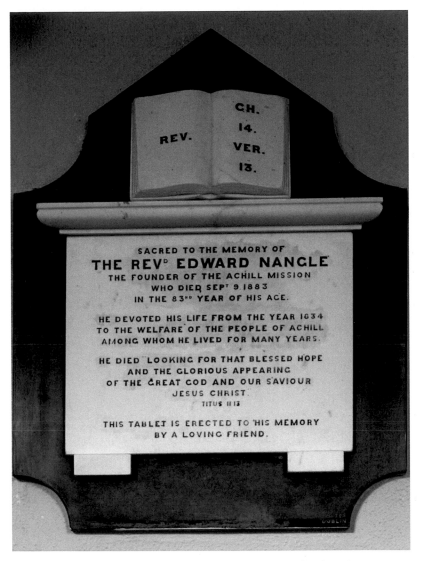

Edward Nangle memorial plaque at St Thomas' Church, Dugort.
(Brian Thompson)

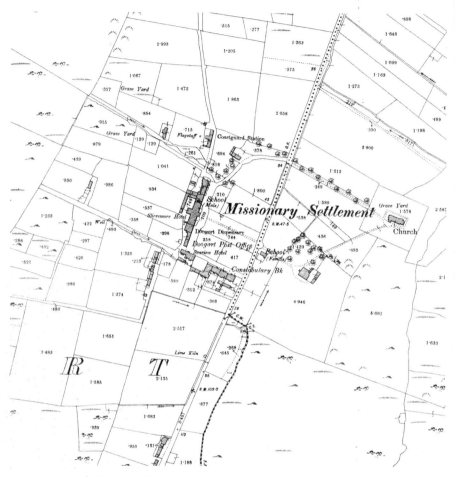

Layout of the Achill Mission Settlement from Ordnance Survey 25th series, 1897–1913. © Ordnance Survey Ireland/Government of Ireland. Copyright Permit No. MP 000218

The mountain, Slievemore, dominates the Achill landscape and became the location for Edward Nangle's evangelical colony. On the western slopes of the mountain can be seen the Deserted Village with the remains of dwellings abandoned during or immediately after the Great Famine. (National Library of Ireland)

Main Street of former Achill Mission Colony as it is today with Slievemore in the background. (P. Byrne)

Picture of Edward Nangle from memorial plaque in St Thomas's Church, Dugort. (P. Byrne)

SACRED TO THE MEMORY OF
ELIZA
THE BELOVED WIFE OF THE
REVᴰ EDWARD NANGLE
AND HIS FELLOW HELPER IN THE ESTABLISHMENT
OF THE ACHILL MISSION.
SHE FELL ASLEEP IN JESUS
IN THE FULL ASSURANCE OF FAITH
JUNE 19ᵀᴴ 1850.
HER BODY LIES IN THE ADJOINING BURIAL GROUND
AWAITING THE RESURRECTION AT THE ADVENT
OF JESUS CHRIST.
THE CONGREGATION ASSEMBLING IN THIS CHURCH
HAVE ERECTED THIS TABLET AS A RECORD.
OF THEIR AFFECTIONATE REMEMBRANCE
OF THE DECEASED.

Plaque to the memory of Eliza Nangle who died in Dublin in 1850 and whose remains are buried in the cemetery behind the former colony buildings on the slopes of Slievemore. (P Byrne) he would take up before the end of that year. It was a significant moment of personal change and Edward is said to have remarked: 'I will never lose my interest in Achill, and it is my intention to visit it every year.'[7] The reasons for his transfer are unclear: perhaps the burden of poor health, or the changed Achill Mission role with its expanded estate management functions, or the fallout from criticism of his actions in the famine years or, indeed, the need for his evangelising zeal in a new location.

Years later, reflecting on his departure from Achill, Edward gave his personal response to the move: 'I have felt for many years that I had not the strength for so weighty a burden', and so he had decided that he should 'seek out a field of less labour and responsibility and resign the superintendence of the Achill Mission'.[8]

Before the year was out, he also had a new wife. On 20 October 1852, Edward – then in his fifties – married Sarah Fetherstonhaugh in the Protestant church in the parish of Ardnurcher, County Westmeath. He gave his address as Skreen, County Sligo – which would be the couple's home for the next two decades and where they would raise their new family, as four more Nangle offspring – three daughters and a son – joined the five Nangle children still living.

***

There was change afoot also at the *Achill Herald* which had a 'new dress', represented by its new masthead. Edward reassured his readers that the journal would continue to be published at the Achill printing press after his departure for Skreen, with no change to his role as editor and principal contributor. There would be no abandonment of the 'old principles', which were those of the Reformation. Neither would he shirk from again asserting that the Catholic Emancipation Act of 1829 had been a fatal error, the point of the wedge which had slivered Protestant institutions and 'Protestant sovereignty' into atoms. He promised that the *Achill Herald* would continue to expose the errors and delusions of popery, and to further the cause of the Protestant movement. The change in location and role had not lessened Edward Nangle's zeal for the Protestant evangelical cause and his war against Roman Catholicism.

The new vignette in the *Achill Herald* masthead captured the Achill places into which he had poured his energies during the prime years of his life. It was a picture of magnificent natural scenery: mountain, ocean, sandy beach and swirling clouds. Slievemore dominated the vignette with the Atlantic Ocean below, Minaun in the distance and Finsheen Hill to the left. At the centre can be seen the outlines of the Achill Mission colony on the mountain slopes – the place built through his direct efforts.

In the foreground of the vignette stands a man with a hat, arm outstretched towards the panorama in front of him.[9] It could be Edward himself surveying his work. He may well have swelled with pride at his achievements, with a sense of having realised the vision in his head when he landed on Dugort beach two decades earlier. He may have experienced a profound sense of satisfaction at his endeavours, as well as a confidence that the structures he had put in place for the Achill Mission estate and missionary work would sustain his enterprise into the future.

Possibly there were other, darker, emotions: sorrow at his family's personal tragedies; sadness that he was leaving behind a wife, a daughter and five infant children in their mountain graves; an awareness of his own demons through the Achill years when words and pen were his only protection against the agitation and depressive illnesses that wracked his being; and regret, perhaps, for the long winter absences away from his vulnerable family.

Edward may have dwelt on the island's recent famine trauma with which he would forever be associated. In front of him was a landscape that held the emaciated corpses of the famine dead, the deserted and roofless cottages of those who were driven out or fled to the paupers' workhouse, and the expanse of ocean crossed by others desperate to get away. He may have believed that he could have done no more when working night and day to solicit funds to bring sustenance to the Achill people, to feed the children in his mission schools and to employ the people in the colony fields. He may have felt justifiably confident beyond doubt that he and his mission had saved the lives of islanders who otherwise would have faced starvation and certain death.

There may, or may not, have been an intuition on his part that he might have done some things differently: that his approach could have been less belligerent and less offensive to the beliefs that the islanders held dear; that, when famine struck, he could have quietened his vitriolic rants and offered food and relief with no strings attached, not linking them to membership of his church; and that he might have imbued his good works with other virtues – those of empathy and compassion.

Edward Nangle departed Achill with its trauma of famine horrors, its deserted places and its people lost to starvation and emigrant ships. While his influence over the Achill Mission would now be at a remove, he would always be the figurehead associated with its history.

PART 3

Ailt was an old village of Kildownet. There is four Ailt, one of them called Ailt an Sagart. There was a mass path through the hills from Dooega, there was a mass rock in Ailt an Sagart where they would say mass. On the top of the hill there was a stone chair called Cathaoir an tSolas, if you sit in it you will get peace. There are twelve heaps of stone where the people from Dooega rested the coffins of the dead on their way to Kildownet graveyard. There is a round pound where Pike would put the donkey and the cow from Ailt in it and they would have to pay money to get them out.

–Folklore Achill, 1989

Nangle raised the rent on the Slievemore tenants, and they had to leave. They went to Dooagh, and Pollagh, and made bothans for themselves. Some of them did that. Some of them went all over the world. They reclaimed the bog at Dooagh, all that is reclaimed of it. That was the beginning of the village of Dooagh.

–National Folklore Collection, MS 1348

CHAPTER TWENTY

Clearances

All was changed in Achill. Evictions, emigration and famine deaths had taken their toll and whole villages were disappearing. The land clearances which started in the famine years, as the quarter-acre Gregory clause and starvation loosened the smallholders' grip on their plots, continued under the new regime of landowners.[1] The two main landlords, William Pike and the Achill Mission, needed to make a return on their investment and the Encumbered Estates Act gave them new powers to evict tenants, pursue arrears of rent, and refuse to renew leases which ran out. Purchasers had the power to look for cleared properties.[2]

But the Achill landowners had to contend with the fiery militant priest, James Henry, who strode the island stage with a ferocious energy, a figure who represented the resurgent and militant Catholic counter-attack against the Achill Mission. In the early 1850s, religious acrimony in Achill would evolve into land agitation, both becoming intertwined, as the swerves and loops of the Achill Mission story followed the broad sweep of Irish history.

The first public controversy involving William Pike concerned not land but a burial ground and it would, surprisingly, bring the two main Achill landlords into direct confrontation. It was a dispute, also, with a residue of shame, guilt and family division from the practice of religious conversion in famine times. William Pike was drawn reluctantly into the conflict in his capacity as the only resident magistrate on the island.[3]

On a chilly Thursday in late January, he found himself standing in the cemetery at Kildownet in the south of the island, close to the water's edge, within sight of Gráinne O'Malley's castle. The grief and dignity of a burial had given way to an unsavoury dispute between the island's two religious groups who contested the burial place of a recently deceased man. It was an episode that exposed not only family divisions, but deep psychological wounds from the recent famine. Michael Heanue had converted to Protestantism and, when he died at Mweelin, the Achill Mission agent sent a horse and cart to convey his remains to the colony where, it was claimed, the deceased had requested to be buried. The man's family objected, and let it be known that they wanted him buried in Kildownet with his own family. Fearing trouble, the Protestant rector, James Baker, requested the intervention of the magistrate and the police. William Pike, a newcomer to Achill, was faced with a difficult situation and he would later plead in his own defence that his only interest was to 'restrain fanaticism on both sides'.[4]

On arriving at the cemetery with four policemen, William Pike sent for the sister and brother of the dead man and asked what they knew of their dead brother's wishes. He wished to be buried with his own people in Kildownet, came the reply. James Baker reluctantly accepted this on condition that he was allowed to read a Protestant burial service. However, commotion erupted when he attempted to speak, the clergyman was pushed and jostled and some attempted to pull the prayer book from his hands. William Pike tried to intervene, waving his hat in the air to get the crowd's attention and then pleading with the people for calm. When it appeared that the situation could get out of control, he approached the rector: 'I said I cannot keep the peace. There may be unpleasant consequences if you continue to read the prayers.' Rev. James Baker acquiesced and William Pike asked the crowd to leave quietly.

Edward Nangle added his voice to the dispute with an attack on William Pike and his role in the conflict. Why had Mr Pike not upheld the law rather than give in to a lawless mob? Instead of supporting Rev. Baker in the performance of his religious duties, he had sided with those intent on violence and addressed the mob 'in language more suitable to a popularity hunting demagogue than a gentleman holding Her Majesty's commission of the peace'. If he had carried out his duties as magistrate properly, he ought to have warned the people that they were committing a serious violation of the law, which he would not tolerate, and if they did not conduct themselves peacefully he would order the police to clear the burial ground. Instead, he had capitulated to the mob. 'No district can prosper where legitimate authority is not upheld, and lawless violence repressed and punished.'[5]

The *Mayo Constitution* reflected the fury which Edward Nangle had unleashed against William Pike from his new base in County Sligo in deploring the new Achill landlord's lack of firmness in dealing with the burial controversy and in succumbing to mob violence and clamour. The only excuse William Pike had offered for his actions was his fear of bloodshed, when he had the option of summoning the rioters to the petty session's court. Edward Nangle believed that Achill needed a magistrate with a better knowledge of his duty than William Pike, and more firmness and courage in executing it.[6]

William Pike would soon encounter a more serious conflict in Achill, this time when he himself would be a central protagonist rather than a mediator. The burial ground incident brought the new landlord face-to-face with Achill religious tensions and animosities in a dramatic way. It also illustrated, once again, how Edward Nangle could pick fights not just with adversaries, but also with those who might be expected allies.

Within months, the religious battle in Achill had moved from burial ground to hospital in the continuing island struggle for souls. It was an incident which revealed emerging fault lines within the Achill Mission itself in its transition to a fully fledged landlord, in a growing disenchantment on the part of the ageing Neason Adams and in a continued Catholic challenge to the Achill Mission, personified by the priest James Henry.

On a blustery Friday morning in November 1853, the Achill Mission colony was thrown into a state of fevered activity when a boat carrying sixty people in a distressed condition landed at the nearby Dugort strand. They were survivors from the *California* emigrant ship that had been travelling from Sligo when wrecked about 150 miles from land. Fifteen people died, some at sea and others after arrival in Achill. The survivors, many in a pitiful condition, were cared for at the colony hotel and hospital, and in private houses.[7] But this tragic event would also become the source of another sectarian outburst.

James Henry arrived at the colony, following the request of some of the shipwreck survivors to see a Catholic clergyman, and called on Dr Adams, a man whom he greatly admired for his medical services to the sick on the island. The priest availed of the doctor's offer to accompany him through the infirmary to see the patients but was soon astonished to find his entry barred by Dr Montgomery, who had recently taken over the position of medical officer, along with a threatening crowd. 'I asked him on what authority he presumed to interfere in this manner as a paid officer of the district,' James Henry later reported, and the doctor replied that he had a letter of instruction from Edward Nangle in Skreen not to admit the priest. James Henry had to retreat and had no choice but to return home.[8]

The disagreement revealed internal stresses within the Achill Mission. 'Dr Adams said that no one had control over that hospital but himself, and that the Infirmary was built for all classes without reference to creed or sect', while Rev. James Baker, who was now head of the Achill Mission, claimed that the hospital was built with colony funds and was not a public institution. It was an interesting divergence of views, bringing into prominence issues that continue to be debated to this day about the overlap of public and private institutions – between the publicly funded role of a medical officer and the private control of a hospital institution. ·

In a subsequent court case, Rev. Baker's testimony provided an insight into what happened, and into emerging friction within the Achill Mission itself. He claimed that, while Dr Adams was a member of the newly formed Temporal Affairs Committee, the doctor had declined to have any involvement in its work, and that Dr Montgomery had taken over the role of hospital superintendent. Yes, he agreed, there had been a disagreement between Neason Adams and Dr Montgomery about admitting James Henry to see the *California* survivors: 'I heard that Dr Adams, on that occasion, abused Dr Montgomery at the hospital; I heard that Dr Adams wanted to get Mr Henry in there to go to the sick people.'[9]

It appears that Dr Adams was an unhappy and aging man, having to deal with the departure of Edward Nangle from direct Achill Mission supervision, and an erosion in his own personal autonomy. Possibly exhausted by two decades of medical work in Achill and by the trauma of the famine years, the life of his beloved wife Isabella was also ebbing. His influence at the Achill Mission appeared to be at an end.

James Henry was challenging the establishment at every opportunity, shrewdly writing a defiant letter to the poor law commissioners to confront them about their responsibilities in administering the law, and in the provision of dispensary services in Achill. If Dr Montgomery was to continue to carry out his duties as a paid officer in a bigoted and partisan way then, the priest argued, a sub-dispensary had to be established on the island so that his parishioners did not have to resort to the colony dispensary for medical aid. He knew of several islanders suffering from fever and other diseases who would go without medical aid rather than attend the colony dispensary. 'The working of the Medical Charities Act in this district is,' wrote the priest, 'most unsatisfactory, and shall continue so as long as Dr Montgomery remains their Medical Officer.'[10] It was a shrewd and effective line of attack.

The *California* incident brought into the open developing strains within the Achill Mission following Edward Nangle's departure. Administration of the religious aspects of the mission's work was now with the Society for Irish Church Missions, but mistrust was also emerging in that relationship with complaints that the funds flowing to the Achill Mission 'have not found their way into the treasury of the Society for Irish Church Missions', leading to difficulty in funding missionary work on the island.[11]

∗∗∗

The removal of tenants from the estate of William Pike would become notorious in Achill folklore in a narrative that James Henry had a prominent hand in shaping. Trouble had been brewing for some time on the estate and came to a head in the autumn of 1854 when the priest alerted *The Telegraph* to the plans of Pike, 'a specimen of an English landlord'. It was a notice to tenants from Pike's agent, Owen Lavelle:

> Notice is hereby given that if the tenants on said land give up peaceable possession, and go elsewhere, on or before the 30th October next, their crop will be given to them, and no rent will be charged from 25th March last. All who remain will be ejected after that date by the Sheriff.
>
> Dated this 19th day of September 1854.
>
> Owen Lavelle for William Pike, Esq.[12]

Pike asserted his right to vacant possession of his property under the terms of the purchase from the Encumbered Estates Court two years earlier. He protested that he held an injunction whereby he could have turned out eighty families, yet he had turned out neither Catholic nor Protestant but held the right to 'eject some of the worst characters' who were troublemakers and contaminated the neighbourhood.[13]

News of evictions on Pike's estate surfaced over the bitterly cold Christmas period and James Henry was quick to communicate to the newspapers his version of what had happened. He wrote that he had, in recent days, witnessed 'those cruelties which my poor parishioners in Upper Achill have been made to suffer by wholesale eviction'. These were pathetic events, he said, after what the people had endured through the famine from a previous regime of landlords and middlemen. The sheriff, he charged, and a posse of police were brought 'to eject an entire district of Achill ... when frost and snow covered our hills'. Yes, he acknowledged, it was true that some were allowed to stay in their houses at the landlord's pleasure, but the crowbar did its work in levelling to the ground the cabins of many, with some of the evicted families being forced to take refuge in Kildownet chapel and school.[14]

William Pike reacted with a fierce condemnation of Henry who had, he alleged, done everything possible to turn his tenants against him, and were it not for the priest's urgings he would not have needed to eject a single tenant. In his own defence, Pike claimed that all except two of his tenants, when removed, were allowed back into their holdings. The landlord expressed his appreciation for the support he had received from the *Mayo Constitution* newspaper: 'I shall ever feel grateful for the manner in which you upheld me when right, as one of a class of recent purchasers in this country whom it had been sought to intimidate and annoy by every species of threats and calumny.'[15]

The story of the Achill evictions was passed down through the generations in words of powerful emotion, even if the narratives were inconsistent:

In Kildownet, on the hillside above Kildownet cemetery, lies the remains of an old village which was known as Baile na hAilte. This was a fairly big village because we know that in the year 1854 there were more than fifty families living there. William Pike was the landlord in the area and according to the old people he was a cruel and greedy man. The people of Baile na hAilte had to pay rents for poor land.

Mr Pike and his friends from Glendarry House often hunted fox and shot game birds on the mountainside near Ailt. The dogs from the village always attacked Mister Pike's beagles and this annoyed him very much and he decided to evict the people in order to get rid of the dogs. The eviction took place on Christmas Eve 1854. All the houses except one were knocked and burned by the sheriff and his men.

Part of the oral history refers to a classic ploy of protest – that of removing one's cloth:

> The only house left standing belonged to two widows. These women took off all their clothes and in that way, according to the law, they couldn't be evicted without being dressed. To this day there is a place in the village called Ailt na mBraintreach – the glen of the widows. The evicted people settled in Dookinella, Cashel and Currane. Others emigrated.[16]

Evictions at Ailt were certainly carried out, while assertions as to the numbers involved differ. The people told stories of how stones from the levelled houses were used to construct a perimeter fence around the site and that, while all of the tenants may not technically have been evicted, the results were apparent – the people from those parts were dispossessed and scattered.

What was happening to Achill tenants was part of a pattern across the country as new land owners sought to consolidate their estates into larger holdings. Between 1849 and 1854, close to 50,000 families and almost a quarter of a million people were permanently dispossessed in Ireland. County Mayo accounted for approximately 10 per cent of all evictions in the country in that period, with its higher-than-average share of insolvent proprietors resulting in widespread clearances in the early 1850s as entire villages were erased from the map.[17]

If the story of land clearances in Achill in the early 1850s was dramatically illustrated in the case of William Pike and Ailt, the Achill Mission attracted similar charges of 'driving out the people' from their land, with the added sectarian religious dimension to its actions. James Henry complained that the Achill Mission, through its agent John Carr, was doing all in its power to prevent the children of their Catholic tenants from receiving a Catholic education, and had served notice on tenants to prevent them from giving the priest a school house, or a site for a school. The Achill Mission, he accused, had become an 'evangelical landlord.'[18]

When the Achill Mission began to sublease, or renew leases, on its newly acquired estate, it stipulated strict requirements on the lessors in relation to the use of those lands. No portion of the property could be sublet without the Achill Mission's approval. No land or premises could be used for any 'Popish Mass House, Monastery, Nunnery or Seminary', or for the celebration of any Catholic rites. No school was permitted on the property unless the Authorised Version of the Bible was taught to all scholars. This indenture referred to the sublease of over 4,000 acres of Achill Mission lands at Keem in 1853 by Murray Blacker who had been farming in Norfolk. Within two years he, in turn, would sublease half his Achill acreage to one Charles Cunningham Boycott.[19]

The acquisition of Slievemore lands by the Achill Mission coincided with the movement of people from the eastern end of the settlement to the west, and the reallocation of the eastern lands of *Faiche*, the field of giants, to a small number of individuals. Soon, the western end of the settlement, now known as the Deserted Village, was abandoned as people moved to Dooagh but continued to use the properties at Slievemore for seasonal pasture in the practice of transhumance known as *booelying*.[20]

A visitor in 1855 reported that the village of Slievemore was almost totally depopulated 'by the cholera, and famine, and fever'.[21] Another visitor was unimpressed by the village, suggesting that it was a most unpleasant sight and that the ruined cottages should be removed from the landscape.

Some of those leaving their land in Achill and elsewhere in the late 1840s and early 1850s may have comprised voluntary surrenders rather than official evictions, as people died from starvation, headed for the workhouse or the emigrant ship, or simply resorted to begging on the streets. The pressures of heavy poor rates and lost rents on landlords, combined with the Gregory clause and the destitution of tenants meant that, in many cases, no formal evictions were necessary as tenants were induced to leave for small sums.

The legacy of bitterness pertaining to the Achill Mission landlord resulted from the perceived practice of giving preferential tenant treatment to those who conformed to the missionary principles of the colony. Land and religious agitation became infused, one with the other.

The question of whether Edward Nangle and the Achill Mission evicted people from Achill lands became a fraught and contested issue. In the folklore of the people, where legends rolled off tongues through the generations, there were many tales of *the Mission wanting the land* and taking it from the people, and of those dispossessed having to move to Dooagh and build up soil for survival with peat, sand and seaweed.

The Achill Mission's acquisition of land spanned over two decades and comprised several locations: the main colony site at Slievemore, lands at Inishbiggle and Mweelin, the Finsheen site where St Thomas' Church now stands, and areas on the western slopes of Slievemore in the vicinity of the Deserted Village. The time span over which the Achill Mission acquired these lands ranges from the 1830s through the Famine years and into the post-Famine era of the encumbered estates.

In the cases of the main colony site at Slievemore, as well as the Mweelin and Inishbiggle lands, these were acquired by way of lease from the landlord Sir Richard O'Donnell, who was well disposed toward the Achill Mission and was in a position, through whatever means, to make these sites available to the colony.[22]

In the instance of the Finsheen St Thomas' Church site, opposite the main colony settlement, Edward Nangle revealed that he and the colony had spent several years attempting 'to procure a perpetuity of a couple of acres of land' on which to build a church.[23] The status of Sir Richard O'Donnell's encumbered estate at the time did not allow the landlord to give a tenure beyond thirty-one years, which would not have justified the expenditure involved in constructing the church. This difficulty was resolved when the Achill Mission acquired the land from the Encumbered Estates Courts and so had full control over the site.[24]

In the case of the area on the western flanks of Slievemore, once the Achill Mission acquired its extended estate it had control over all leases as these came up for renewal. From the evidence of the Keem sublease, these lettings were skewed against Catholic tenants in favour of those who were either nominally Protestant or supported the Achill Mission principles.[25]

A combination of factors led to tenants being dispossessed of land which ended up in the ownership of the Achill Mission: the lease of lands directly to the colony by Sir Richard O'Donnell; the dislocation of tenants arising from the famine; the Encumbered Estates Act and the resulting reorganisation of land ownership; and the Achill Mission's own landlord activities in sub-leasing or renewing/not renewing leases.

For those who eked out an existence on poor plots in post-famine Achill, it was understandable that tales of eviction, or constructive eviction, would enter the oral history as the people came to terms with the dispossession suffered by their forebears, and the wrongs which they believed had been visited upon them.

These were contested sites. In the years immediately following the famine, in the place across from the main colony settlement, a new dark-stoned church was rising up, its spire beckoning to the mountain.

CHAPTER TWENTY-ONE

Achill Transformed

St Thomas' Church, Dugort welcomes 'friend and stranger', its doors open to visitors all through the year. Its rust-charcoal stone reflects the exposed rock on the mountain which appears to cover the building with a protective cloak. The gravelled avenue, shaded by overhanging foliage, leads to a heavy wooden unlocked door. There is a donation box for support towards the upkeep of the church, and rows of the Book of Common Prayer on a shelf. The interior is cold, the light filtering through three stained-glass windows that glow with crimson-clad biblical figures.[1] Through the side windows can be seen black-faced sheep grazing against a backdrop of white-walled holiday homes dotted around the bay. On either side of one of these windows are two white marble plaques – one each to the memory of Edward and Eliza Nangle. Further up, next to the church pulpit, is a bronze plaque with a picture of Edward. He has the look of a benign patriarch – silver hair and beard, one hand resting lightly on a Bible, his gaze whimsical and nostalgic.

It was a fine sunny morning on Sunday, 18 March 1855, and the bells of the new St Thomas' Church rang out across the fields and bog land of north Achill for the church's first divine service. The crowds had made their way from across the island and further afield until every available seat was occupied and temporary seating was set up in the aisles, and on the steps of the chancel, to accommodate a congregation of almost five hundred. The choir exuberantly sang the words of *Venite*, *Te Deum* and *Jubilate*.

Edward Nangle had travelled from Skreen for the event and preached the sermon, reminiscing on the years he had spent in Achill. He recalled that the site of the new church in which they worshipped that day was once a village, 'inhabited exclusively by devoted adherents of the Roman Antichrist'. There was no mention of the former villagers or of their fate. Contrasting the state of the island at that time with what it had been on his arrival, Edward exclaimed to the congregation, 'What has God wrought!'[2]

St Thomas' church was erected using donations from a generous benefactor: a widow in Cheltenham, England, had donated a sum of £2,400 to the Achill Mission to be expended on the construction of two churches in Achill on condition that the endowment required to pay running costs, the clergyman's stipend, church repairs and other expenses would be separately raised.[3] Edward had expected that these costs would be financed out of the Achill Mission's rental income until some legal issues were raised around this approach.

Several months later, in August, Bishop Plunket consecrated the new church while Edward Nangle was on his annual summer sojourn in Achill with his wife Sarah and baby daughter Catherine. Afterwards, the bishop conducted a confirmation ceremony for 106 people; '104 were converts and two were original Protestants'. The Bishop proceeded to Mweelin where the young men being trained as scripture readers and teachers were examined in grammar, logic, astronomy, geography, science and the scriptures. But Edward was worried about the future of the Mweelin project since the Society for Irish Church Missions, for financial reasons, was planning to amalgamate it with a similar institution in Dublin. He fretted about the implications of 'placing a number of unsophisticated youths, just rising into manhood, in the midst of the temptations of a licentious city'. He feared that Mweelin would be sorely missed as a valuable resource for providing teachers and scripture readers for the island's missionary work.[4]

As was by then customary, John MacHale arrived in Achill during Bishop Plunket's visitation. If the Achill Mission could have a new church, then so could his Catholic congregation. In the presence of a large crowd, the archbishop laid the foundation stone for a new chapel at Bunnacurry, where the Franciscan monastery was already under construction. Edward Nangle reverted to type in an open letter provocatively accusing MacHale of having deserted the Achill people in their hour of need and of not showing his face on the island during the six years of famine. In that time, he accused, no monks or Redemptorist missionaries had come to minister to the people, and the priests could scarcely take the trouble to anoint the dying. 'Your zeal and that of your priests, your monks, and your missionaries has revived with the return of plenty.'[5]

Five years after famine had devastated Ireland and Achill, an impressive suite of ecclesiastical constructions rose high above any other buildings on the island: a new church and parsonage at Achill Sound; St Thomas' Church at Dugort alongside the Achill Mission settlement; and an emerging complex of monastery, chapel and school at Bunnacurry. The opposing religious sides in Achill faced up to one another with new tools, symbolised by the edifices and steeples that reached to the island skies.

***

In an uncanny coincidence, Isabella Adams died at her home in the colony, Dugort, on 18 December 1855, twenty years to the day since she arrived on the island with her husband to support the Nangle family and the Achill Mission.

Edward's obituary captured the qualities which Isabella exuded in tough conditions: 'kindness of heart', 'sweetness', 'maternal affection', 'gladness' and 'cheerfulness'.[6] The children of the poor in Achill were the beneficiaries of a love which she might, in other circumstances, have bestowed on her own children. She had worked for a number of years as superintendent of the colony's infant school, where she was much loved. Some years before her death, she suffered what appears to have been a stroke which left her speechless and paralysed. Although she rallied after the attack, she did not return to her full self and had to give up her school duties. She seldom left her home except to take a drive in her pony phaeton, or a short walk in the garden of her colony home, supported by Dr Adams.

On the morning and evening of Sunday, 16 December, Isabella attended divine service at St Thomas' church. The following morning she suffered another stroke, was attended to by the colony clergyman and, shortly afterwards, lost consciousness and died the following day. Her funeral was attended by a large crowd including the island's parish priest and a large number of Catholics from across the island, an indication of the esteem in which both Isabella and her husband were held. She was buried in the graveyard on the slopes of Slievemore, with her remains afterwards transferred to the family burial plot at Knockbride, County Cavan.[7] A mound of memorial stones to Isabella Adams today stands on Slievemore, almost hidden from view, not far from the resting place of Eliza Nangle and her children.

Neason Adams would soon depart Achill, and the Achill Mission accounts for 1856 show a settlement payment of £200 for his Dugort residence. He died on 21 August 1859 in Dublin, aged eighty-four. Edward Nangle acknowledged the support of the couple through bouts of illness and other difficulties: 'How often, when the writer lay prostrate by sickness, was the gloom of the sick chamber dissipated by the cheerful visits of the beloved physician and how when in seasons of spiritual depression was he refreshed and strengthened by the confiding faith of his excellent partner.'[8] Today, inside Knockbride church, a wall plaque commemorates the lives of Neason and Isabella Adams and their work on Achill Island.

The departure of Neason and Isabella Adams, following the relocation of Edward Nangle to Skreen, removed an essential glue in the fabric of the Achill Mission. The couple had managed, through the years of crises for the Nangle family and through the onslaught of the Famine until Eliza Nangle's death, to present a humane face and an example of Christian charity in their medical, educational and relief work. It was another step in the decline of the Achill Mission which faced problems on several fronts. Overall income was falling, with the total income for 1855 amounting to less than a third of what it had been five years earlier, as the optimistic projections of income from the newly acquired estate failed to materialise.

Another pressing problem was that of emigration, with Edward worrying that 'within the last few years upwards of one hundred persons were obliged to leave the Settlement at Dugort'.[9] The *Galway Vindicator* carried a story of thirty-two 'Protestants from Achill' passing through Tuam en route to Galway port and hence to America.[10] Edward had his own views as to the reasons for the emigration: 'We incline to think that the desire of the converts to emigrate originates in a wish to better their condition rather than a dread of persecution.'[11] However, it is likely that some Achill Mission converts faced pressure from a more forceful approach by the Catholic authorities and, perhaps, some hostility from within the community. The population of the colony would decline by almost 300 during the 1850s.

In July 1856, Alexander Dallas informed Edward Nangle that the Society for Irish Church Missions would withdraw from Achill after managing the missionary and education facilities of the Achill Mission for just four years, citing financial difficulties and the need to consolidate its activities. Edward quickly responded by expressing his reservations about the Society's work on the island, particularly the closure of the training school at Mweelin and the practice of removing ministers from Achill at short notice. He was also concerned that there was no resident clergyman for the new St Thomas' church.

For its part, the Society was uneasy about the fundraising activities of the Achill Mission for various activities, giving the impression of separateness between the Achill Mission and the Society. Alexander Dallas had expressed his unease about 'the mixture of temporal relief with the spiritual agency' of the Mission and the difficulty of working through the complications caused by the mingling of the two.[12] The withdrawal would have serious repercussions since the missionary activity of the Colony would now have to be maintained largely out of the estate income which, complained Edward Nangle, 'after paying head rent, income tax, poor rates, county costs, agent's fees, law costs and other charges, will barely suffice to keep the buildings in repair.'[13]

The summer of 1856 inspired nostalgic reminiscence for Edward Nangle – not surprising given that it was twenty-five years since he first laid foot on Achill soil. Despite the intensity of problems facing the mission, his dominant emotions during his annual summer trip were a mix of wistful melancholia alongside pride at what he perceived as his accomplishments over a quarter of a century.

'There is something indescribably sad in revisiting a place with which the earlier part of our life we were intimately acquainted, and where every object can trigger a memory of times past.'[14] The best years of his life had been spent in Achill, years of care, anxiety and labour mingled with joy and enjoyment. It is the voice of a man no longer immersed in the day-to-day activities of the colony, standing back to take a broader view in a tone that appears calmer and less pressurised.

Achill was transformed beyond recognition and Edward believed that men of enterprise were bringing improvements which would not have happened were it not for his personal resourcefulness in founding the Achill Mission and purchasing the island property. The evidence was all around him. Immediately on crossing over from the mainland into Achill Sound was Glendarary, the fine residence of William Pike. Across the island, high above the Atlantic at Keem, was Corrymore House, occupied by Charles Cunningham Boycott who had sublet 2,000 acres from Achill Mission's tenant Murray McGregor Blacker – a man whose name would become a byword for cruel landlordism in Ireland. The Pike and Boycott residences were of a building scale scarcely seen before on Achill Island.

Especially pleasing to Edward was the work underway by the Scottish man, Alexander Hector, who had 'rented the shore of Achill' from the Achill Mission, and was now harvesting the salmon that 'had been left in undisturbed possession of the deep' in the Achill seas.[15] The Scotsman's investment was impressive, covering the full spectrum of a vertically integrated enterprise, from the purchase of boats for the fishermen, the introduction of a new fishing device known as the bag-net, the construction of onshore processing stations and the development of overseas markets. At the height of the operation Alexander Hector was leasing the former hotel premises at Achill Sound where he invested in a fully operational cannery for processing not just fish, but game and vegetables. It was akin to bringing an inward investment project employing several hundred people to Achill Island today.

Unlike Captain Boycott, Alexander Hector was a popular figure in Achill and skilled in public relations. An example of his community involvement was his organisation of a summer party for up to 150 children from the colony school at Dugort where the tables were covered 'with a plentiful supply of salmon, bread, and potatoes', and the children feasted and enjoyed themselves until darkness fell.[16] Even the priest, James Henry, praised Hector's work in providing food for the people, including the Achill Mission tenants, in their time of want.

The fishery proved to be unsustainable in the long run with the enacting of a new Fishery Bill in 1860 designed to protect river fisheries being damaged by bag-net fishing, which was intercepting salmon en route to their spawning grounds. One visitor to Achill would give a scathing view of Alexander Hector's work, claiming that the businessman had taken control of the island's important fishery resource for a paltry sum, that these fish were being sucked from the island seas and despatched all over the world while the islanders were left without 'a winter stock of dried and salted fish' to ease the food scarcity.[17]

There was yet another pleasant change in Achill that Edward noted – that of an evident growth in civilised living and refinement. As he travelled around the island and attended Protestant services at Dugort, Achill Sound, Cashel and Inishbiggle, he noted with pleasure several persons of a class far superior to the Achill peasantry. He believed this to be the type of social advancement and refinement which invariably followed the introduction of scriptural Christianity to a community, and he was gratified that Achill had lost the character of barbarism which it possessed before he commenced his mission. The island improvements he entirely attributed to 'the impetus originating in Protestant energy and intelligence'.[18] Edward clearly saw this vein of refinement as a confirmation of his Achill work since he had always sought that his missionary programme would not simply evangelise, but would also be a civilising influence.

Unlike Christopher Anderson or Asenath Nicholson, and despite being a man of culture, Edward had shown little enthusiasm for, or delight in, the way of life of the Achill people. His use of the Irish language for the purpose of evangelisation did not mean that he absorbed or appreciated to any extent the indigenous mores of those among whom he ministered. Civilisation and refinement, in his world view, sprang from British and Protestant cultures, and Achill was benefiting from such refinement both as a result of the Achill Mission's endeavours as well as the recent influx of new landlords and enterprising people.

One commentator has maintained that the Achill colony – and its counterpart in Dingle – were, in essence, an attempt to change the nature of Irish peasant culture, and to submerge it in an English way of life: that it was, at heart, a colonising project which represented 'cultural as well as religious imperialism', and which had less to do with improving the social and spiritual wellbeing of the people than upholding and extending the existing social and cultural hierarchy.[19]

It could have been a golden era in Achill, with the Achill Mission as the largest landowner, enlightenment and education for the people through improved access to education, capital flowing into the island, new projects of enterprise and innovation as never before and the island's natural resources being developed. But these changes barely impacted the lives of the majority of the islanders, those who had survived famine starvation and were not forced onto the emigrant ship, and whose economic wellbeing was stunted. It was also ironic that, while Achill was bursting with development, enterprise and entrepreneurship, the Achill Mission organisation was straining under the pressure of internal tensions, while the conditions of its tenants was attracting unwelcome external attention.

CHAPTER TWENTY-TWO

Implosion

The Achill Mission implosion, when it came, was a classic stakeholder struggle that raised pertinent questions about the colony's role. For whose benefit did the colony exist: its founder and his church, its tenants, its lands and estate or those targeted for its missionary activities? It was also telling that, while more than a decade had elapsed since Edward Nangle left Achill for new duties, he was still the public face of the Achill Mission and continued to attract direct and personal criticism for the perceived shortcomings of the colony.

Not surprisingly, the conflict among those responsible for the Achill Mission's governance boiled down to a power struggle about money and a conflict about the allocation of the estate's resources. At its core was a dispute about the extent to which the mission's income should be used to improve the conditions of the estate's tenants, as against being expended on its own internal activities and its evangelisation work. The spotlight was firmly on the Achill Mission's role as landlord and the perceived poor state of its tenants. Allied to this were several prominent public denunciations of Edward Nangle's activities in continuing to seek donations for the Achill Mission while its own tenants received little or no benefit from these funds.

On 20 January 1857, three of the Achill Mission trustees – Somerset Maxwell, George Alexander and Edward Nangle – met in Dublin to consider the accounts for 1856, while a fourth trustee, Joseph Napier, was absent. The meeting was tense and simmering disagreements soon developed into serious rancour. As a result of a settlement with Neason Adams for his Dugort home, the need to provide some resources for the colony agricultural school and the payment of other estate expenses, it appeared that there was little surplus available for missionary activity. Some trustees raised concerns about the form and presentation of the Achill Mission accounts, where income and expenditure related to the estate and missionary activities appeared mixed up and confused. It was clear, too, that the trustees – other than Edward Nangle – were becoming embarrassed at what they viewed as the unacceptable conditions of the colony tenants.[1]

Edward insisted that the trustees were acting beyond their proper writ when they attempted to allocate expenditure for estate improvement, this being the function of the management committee.[2] He believed that if the trustees were to take control of, and manage, funding in this manner, it would prove detrimental to the colony's missionary work. The power struggle had come to a head and it was decided to seek the views of legal counsel as to the interpretation of the deed of trust on the respective duties of the trustees and the management committee. Sir Hugh Cairns was consulted.

The trustees, other than Edward, appeared sensitive to the public perception around their positions, and embarrassed by negative commentary on the conditions of the Achill peasantry: 'The names of the trustees are well known to the public, and some odium has already attached to them, from sufficient exertions not having been made to raise and improve the conditions of the tenantry'. They believed that the religious improvement of the Achill Mission tenants could not happen while the people barely survived, and they considered it their duty to be satisfied that the money subscribed for the purchase of the Achill estate should lead to proper living conditions for the colony tenants.[3] To add to the controversy, there were worrying accusations for Edward Nangle personally.

The *Belfast Daily Mercury* newspaper led the onslaught with a personalised attack on Edward and a claim that his own son-in-law, John Wilson, had been forced to cease all connection with the Achill Mission. The allegations were serious: that Edward had purchased the Achill property with funds raised from English benefactors and, having acquired the estate, the colony was now turning out tenants who would not attend the mission schools. It was also alleged that Edward Nangle was continuing to raise funds for a non-existent agricultural school on the island, and that, several years after securing the funds to purchase the Achill estate, he was still wandering around England with a begging bowl.

Provocatively, the paper taunted Edward with a series of open questions:

Where were the practical results of the clergyman's labour in Achill over twenty years?

How many bona fide converts had been made by the Achill Mission and could Edward Nangle provide a list of these converts?

In whom was the Achill property vested – the mission trustees or Edward Nangle himself?

Would Edward Nangle provide a full statement of Achill Mission accounts over the previous twenty years with unambiguous details of receipts and expenditure?

Why had the Society for Irish Church Missions withdrawn from Achill in such an abrupt manner?[4]

The newspaper called on Edward Nangle to publicly respond to these questions. A respected Protestant philanthropist, following a ten-day visit to Achill, joined in the fray with an accusation that the Achill Mission would give no lease to any Catholic, and that the leases to Protestants forbade the holding of Catholic rites and the provision of Catholic education on their land. 'I call that bigotry,' the visitor asserted, 'and I believe it is unlawful.'[5]

As was his style, Edward accepted and dealt with the criticisms head on. Yes, he acknowledged, it was true that the Achill Mission would not give leases to Roman Catholics; it was also true that any leases they did enter into included a clause forbidding the erection of any Catholic chapel, monastery or schoolhouse on the colony's property. He made no apology for this approach, as he believed it essential that the Achill Mission retained the power to remove from its estate 'any turbulent person who, at the bidding of the priests, invaded the religious liberty of his neighbour'.[6]

It was in mainland Britain – in the pages of the *Liverpool Mercury* – that the most sustained attack on the Achill Mission as a landlord took place in a series of contributions penned by an anonymous Protestant Englishman who claimed to have lived in Achill for a year. Not the slightest effort was being made by the Achill Mission, he asserted, to improve the condition of its tenants. Had those English benefactors, he asked, who financed the purchase of the Achill Mission estate ever imagined that it would become such a notorious and disgraceful landlord?

Once more, the criticisms were personalised around the figure of Edward Nangle who was accused of being a bitter, malignant polemicist. What had he been doing for almost thirty years if the tenants of his colony were in such a desperate state? How could a landlord with an estate of 15,000 acres, populated chiefly by Roman Catholics, deny these tenants such basic rights as education? A narrow, exclusive bigotry continued to be attached to the Achill Mission and Edward Nangle ought to be shamed into changing his ways: 'No man has business with an estate that he can turn to no better purpose that the rearing of broods of paupers.'[7]

There was some good news for Edward and his management committee when Hugh Cairns found against the trustees in their claims about their functions. In the counsel's legal opinion, the Achill Mission management committee had the right to levy and collect estate rents, and also to determine how the colony resources were allocated between various demands such as estate maintenance and missionary work. The trustees were acting outside their legal rights by refusing to hand over the rental income to the management committee providing the income was being applied for proper purposes. The legal counsel added the comment that it was somewhat unsatisfactory to have so much power vested in a management committee with such a loose structure.[8]

It was a significant legal victory for Edward Nangle but the internal conflict was far from resolved. Two of the trustees, Joseph Napier and George Hamilton, decided to further consult Hugh Cairns in relation to the executive functions of the management committee and the adequacy of its structure. The counsel maintained his view that the Achill Mission legal structure was loose and ambiguous, and that it was advisable that the management of the colony funds be secured by 'an executive body whose title to deal with them shall be unquestionable'.[9] The matter would eventually be settled in the Court of Chancery at considerable financial and reputational cost to the Achill Mission.

The crafty Achill priest saw an opportunity to exploit the cracks within the colony governance structure to highlight charges of sectarian practices in Achill. On a winter's day in December 1859, James Henry, having made the long journey from Achill, waited outside an elegant house at 4 Merrion Square, Dublin, determined to communicate with its occupant, Joseph Napier. He had travelled with a purpose. There was a house in Dooagh, on the Achill Mission estate, that accommodated a national school under Catholic patronage, and he feared that the Achill Mission would serve a notice to quit. He appealed to Joseph Napier, in his role as a colony trustee, for support in preventing such action. Joseph Napier assured the priest that he wished to keep the management of the Achill property clear of all controversial squabbling and that he would not support any action that was unjust or unfair to the Achill tenants.

Edward Nangle was enraged when news reached him of this encounter. Wasn't Joseph Napier fully aware that the priest was an untiring and unscrupulous enemy of the Mission? He had no business discussing the internal affairs of the Achill Mission with the priest, or indicating a conflict among the colony trustees, which appeared to have happened. 'Mr Napier stands convicted before the public of having held a confidential conference with a known enemy of the institution, the interests of which he was bound by every tie and honour and duty to have upheld.'[10] The Mission's internal relationships appeared fractured beyond repair.

It was several years before the conflict between the Achill Mission trustees and management committee was finally resolved. One lengthy legal affidavit was met with a counteraffidavit until, when the case came up for hearing, the brief prepared for counsel amounted to one hundred pages. After the long and expensive litigation, the decree of the court confirmed that the Achill Mission management committee had the powers to appoint trustees, and also to disburse mission funds in accordance with the original deed. Joseph Napier retired from his role as trustee and Edward wrote that the mission was happily rid of him. All parties were entitled to their costs from the Achill Mission estate.

The protracted dispute undoubtedly drained the Achill Mission of energy and financial resources, and drew unwelcome attention to issues around the allocation of mission resources at a time of growing agitation nationally about tenant rights and land ownership. Two years after the chancery decision, Edward Nangle estimated the litigation costs to have totalled £300–400, of which more than two-thirds was still unpaid.[11]

For almost a decade, the Achill Mission was consumed by internal conflicts which went to the heart of its competing roles as between a property owner requiring a return on investment, a landlord with responsibilities to its tenants and a missionary agency needing to fund its religious activities. In the end, these conflicting roles were irreconcilable and the Achill Mission went into terminal decline, negatively impacted by internal strains, income decline, emigration of converts and sectarian tensions.

∗∗∗

'The English Government has sown the wind, and they must reap the whirlwind.'[12]

Edward Nangle was referring to the Irish Church Act introduced by William Gladstone's administration which came into force on 1 January 1870 and ended the legal links between the Church of Ireland and the state. The disestablishment of the church, and the ending of laws requiring church tithes to be paid, is seen by historians as an event of huge significance in the history of nineteenth-century Ireland.[13] The anomalous position of the Church of Ireland as the established church in a predominantly Catholic country came to an end and state support for the Church of Ireland as well as parliamentary authority over its affairs ceased. Henceforth, all religious denominations in the country were equal before the law. The Church of Ireland would be responsible for its own governance and the church's corporate property was transferred to commissioners who would compensate the clergy, school masters and others.

Predictably, it was a policy which Edward bitterly opposed, going against what he saw as a continuum comprising the Protestantism, the state, Britain and, indeed, civilisation, and he greeted the new law with howls of protest. In the hope of 'creating contentment in the Roman Catholic mind', he complained, the government had only succeeded in nourishing 'the bitter root whence all their discontent springs'. The source of that discontent, in his view, was Maynooth, 'where priests [were] trained to maintain the towering pretensions of the Papacy'. He was in no doubt that the Irish Church Act would prove to be a grievous mistake.[14]

The Achill Mission continued to finance its missionary activities from its own internal resources. According to its 1870 report, these costs included the salaries of three ordained ministers, four scripture readers and five teachers. However, Edward was soon complaining that the Commission of Irish Church Temporalities, established after the passing of the Irish Church Act, had refused the mission's application for assistance towards the costs of a curate's salary which the Achill Mission could not afford to pay. Even more irritating for him was the fact that the bishop 'has expressed a hope that the trustees of the Mission might be able to supply the curate's stipend out of the Mission fund'. Edward Nangle responded that the mission was unable to pay the curate's stipend until it had cleared a litigation debt from the earlier trustee dispute.[15] The Achill Mission was caught in a hard place of declining income and a hangover of litigation costs, while unable to access any funds from the new commission and, apparently, an unsympathetic bishop.

Edward's active four decades as a clergyman in mid-nineteenth-century Ireland were bookended by Catholic Emancipation and the Irish Church Act. It was a period during which he sought to hold back, almost single-handed, the tide of history that eventually swept away colonial domination.

The changes brought about by the Irish Church Act, and subsequent land acts, would sound the death knell for the Achill Mission. An enterprise which spanned the mid-nineteenth-century period, and followed the tempestuous contours of Irish history, was now in terminal decline.

CHAPTER TWENTY-THREE

Weapons of His
Own Forging

Blasts of winter wind howled day and night in Achill. So severe was the weather that the smaller birds were dying from lack of sustenance, while swans and ducks searched in vain for food on frozen waters. The winter of 1879/1880 was one of crisis after a third year of poor harvests and Edward Nangle, back in Dugort as an old, frail man, found himself in the thankless position of pleading for support on two fronts: for funds to keep the Achill missionary activity going, and support to relieve the suffering poor. It was his final burst of activity on behalf of his beloved colony, as the start and finish of his association with Achill were marked by famine and distress.

He had spent much of the previous two years in Achill with his wife Sarah, responding to a situation where there was then no clergyman in either Dugort or Achill Sound due to the Achill Mission's inability to pay proper stipends. In contrast to his previous roles as founder, trustee, advocate and main fundraiser for the colony, and not renowned for his hands-on day-to-day work, he was now struggling stoically to provide a minimum level of religious services while offering support to the local vestry. He did his best to carry on the work of ministry but, much to his disappointment, many Saturdays and Sundays passed without any Protestant service on the entire island. He asked himself how much longer, exhausted by a life of toil and anxiety, he could struggle to keep the mission's work going.

The signal that Edward's Achill work had finally ended came the following summer with an advertisement in the *Irish Church Advocate*:

Bathing Lodge in the Island of Achill:

To be let, the house formerly occupied by the Rev E
Nangle. It contains two sitting rooms with four
bedrooms, with kitchen, store-room, and servant's
apartment. The house is plainly furnished, it is situated in
the Missionary Settlement, commanding a view of
Dugort Bay, and the coast of Ballycroy and Erris.

Applications to be made to Rev E Nangle, 23
Morehampton Road, Dublin.[1]

By the end of the year, Edward admitted that his health was deteriorating: 'As I have now completed my 80th year, and am very infirm, I am unable to work for our dear people in Achill as I did for upwards of forty years of my life.'[2]

As he retreated finally from public life at his Dublin home, William Gladstone introduced one of the most significant pieces of legislation in the history of modern Ireland. The 1881 Land Act conceded the long-sought-after 'three Fs' for Irish tenants: fair rent, free sale and fixity of tenure.[3] While greatly curtailing the powers of Irish landlords, the new act crucially granted tenants a form of ownership of their holdings. The law had an immediate negative impact on the finances of the Achill Mission and became its final death knell.

Soon, the Achill Mission trustees were expressing their profound alarm at the impact of the Land Act on its work: 'The revolutionary doctrines so widely disseminated in Ireland within the last few years … have not been without disastrous effect upon this property.'[4] Arrears of rent had been cancelled, and the reductions in the Achill estate income was estimated at 30–40 per cent, making it necessary for the trustees to fundamentally review every aspect of its work including the employment of clergy, scripture readers and teachers.

As the old order was disintegrating, William Pike – the main Achill landlord, along with the Achill Mission – died. A memorial stone at St Thomas' Church would describe him as 'a man of refined taste, well informed mind, generous heart and truly hospitable and friend of the poor and distressed'. It was an assessment that grated with the folk memory of the islanders.

***

That autumn, the health of John MacHale was also deteriorating. Gladstone's legislation may well have been a great source of satisfaction to him, embodying as it did many of the things he had campaigned energetically for through his life. By late October 1881, the archbishop's condition weakened and he died on the evening of 7 November, having reached his ninetieth year. Soon afterwards, the cathedral bells rang out loudly through the town of Tuam.

The *Freeman's Journal* was, perhaps, excessively exuberant in its praise: 'A pillar has fallen in the temple. A tower has tottered to the ground in Israel ... In his learned leisure, or in the fierce arena of polemics or politics, John of Tuam was an Agamemnon, king of men, and stood towering head and shoulders over the crowd.'[5]

The Irish Times, not given much to praising the prelate in his lifetime, was not ungenerous: 'A leading Irishman of a long past generation, who had retained his marvellous intellectual and physical vigour to the age of ninety passed yesterday out of life.' He was, the writer said, the most energetic representative of militant ecclesiastics'; his pen and letters were his vehicle of expression, 'the short paragraph terse and epigrammatic or witheringly fierce'.[6]

John McHale was remembered as the 'patriot bishop' – an enthusiastic nationalist and the personification of the clergy in politics. Gifted and formidable, he was driven by the quest for justice for tenants and the poor even as he railed against the

Protestant evangelisers and set his face against government policies for interdenominational education. In his later years, he had become increasingly difficult and quarrelsome, reduced to 'a sullen, sulky obstructionism' and an isolated figure in his western diocese.[7]

We are not aware of Edward Nangle's thoughts on hearing of his old adversary's passing. A couple of years earlier, he had penned a final open letter to his opponent in a meandering missive in which he launched a tirade against the recently introduced Catholic doctrine of papal infallibility. He concluded his letter with a milder tone than might have been expected when addressing John MacHale, acknowledging that they were both now old men reaching the end of their lives: 'You, sir, and the writer are far advanced in life – our earthly pilgrimage must soon close, and our day of probation end for ever.' He signed off with 'sincere good will', a realisation, perhaps, that the time had come to lay aside angry words.[8]

Around the time of Edward's final stay in Achill, a strange item had appeared in the pages of the *Irish Church Advocate*. Referring to the uninterrupted fine weather on the island over the summer, and the influx of tourists to the colony hotel from various parts of England and Ireland, the correspondent noted that one important visitor to the colony hotel had been none other than Archbishop John MacHale, 'who came and departed almost unobserved'. The writer contrasted the low-key visit with the crowds who once welcomed the prelate to Achill with banners and exuberance.[9]

Was it possible that John MacHale had taken a break at the colony hotel? If, indeed, it did happen, it would be intriguing to visualise a possible encounter between him and Edward Nangle on the latter's own ground in the shadows of the Achill mountain. Perhaps they passed one another by with a curt nod, unable to engage except through polemical jousts of oratory and pen. Perhaps they shook hands with courtesy and moved on, each carrying a grudging admiration for the other's life work. Maybe their greeting was more intimate, like two boxers who have slugged it out in the arena only to embrace, exhausted, when the contest is done. For decades, they had participated in a fierce battle for the minds and souls of the Achill people. Now, two old men were at that stage in life when they had time for reflection on past deeds. Each clergyman may have glowed with pride at the edifices to his work across the island, like a modern-day developer surveying high-rise buildings and construction cranes on the skyline and seeing there a justification for his toil, little matter that the essence of the Christian message may have become blurred in the course of their lifelong antagonism.

∗∗∗

The weather in Dublin was unsettled – showery and blustery – as Edward Nangle lay unconscious for two days in his home at 23 Morehampton Road, his breathing laboured and heavy. On Sunday morning, 9 September 1883, he took his last breath. 'Mr Nangle ought to have been buried in Achill', wrote his biographer Henry Seddall afterwards, but the Nangle family decided against this, possibly for financial reasons, and his remains were interred in the Fetherstonhaugh family plot at Deansgrange Cemetery, Monkstown, County Dublin.[10]

As he had done in his life time, Edward elicited opposing views in death, even from within the Protestant community. The *Church Advocate*, with its roots in the evangelical *Achill Herald*, lauded Edward's intellectual power, his clear exposition of scripture and his powerful writings: 'few clergymen of the Church of Ireland were better known or more highly valued in his day'. He was praised for his 'bold and uncompromising exposure' of the errors of Rome and Catholicism and his ardent evangelicalism.[11]

The mainstream Church of Ireland paper, the *Irish Ecclesiastical Gazette*, took a different view in its critical obituary. 'The Rev. Edward Nangle was an Evangelical of the old school. His magazine was chiefly engaged in the discussion of abstract questions of little practical use or value, and it was strangely deficient in church teaching.'[12] Sharp criticism.

The *Gazette* returned with an even more strident critique the following year in a review of the recently published Nangle biography by Henry Seddall. 'Everyone has their own idea of heroism, and practices hero-worship after their own fashion. We are free to confess that the late Rev Edward Nangle was not a hero to our mind ...' Yes, the writer acknowledged, there were positive aspects to the clergyman's Achill work, particularly in the famine years, but his stewardship was harsh and lacking in compassion. He was 'a perfect type of the rugged, uncompromising polemic ... [who] fought the battle against Rome with weapons of his own forging', when a gentler and more tender campaign might well have achieved better and more permanent results.

It was a hard-hitting assessment from within the Protestant establishment, not just of Edward Nangle's career but also of the general evangelical proselytising movement. 'Extravagant views of history, and unfulfilled prophecy, strong Puritanical opinions, want of sympathy with what may be called the richer and fuller side of Catholic doctrine, and a stern imperialism which frowned upon the faintest aspiration towards a national life have characterised that section of our church which has devoted itself most entirely to the evangelization of Ireland.'[13]

In the end, the main shortcoming identified in Edward Nangle and his mission was a dearth of compassion – of the type exemplified, for instance, by the evangelical Asenath Nicholson. His was a crusade that failed to touch the sinews of empathy, as a powerful vision dissolved in sectarianism and a praiseworthy idealism was seduced by the commercial dictates of landlordism and property management.

The month after Edward Nangle's death, a memorial committee gathered in 17 Upper Sackville Street, Dublin, to raise funds for a suitable permanent memorial, a campaign which led to the erection of a commemorative stone at St Thomas' Church, Dugort, across from the colony which Edward spearheaded in the shadows of Slievemore.[14]

Visitors to St Thomas' Church, Dugort, today can look up at the white marble tablet:

> Sacred to the memory of
> The Rev Edward Nangle
> The founder of the Achill Mission
> who died Sept 9, 1883
> in the 83rd year of his age
> He devoted his life from the year 1834
> to the welfare of the people of Achill
> among whom he lived for many years.
> He died looking for that blessed hope
> and the glorious appearing
> of the great God and Saviour
> Jesus Christ
> Titus 11.13.

***

Edward Nangle's headstone has toppled from its perch and rests, slightly raised, on a concrete ledge in Row J, South Section, of Deansgrange Cemetery, County Dublin. It is difficult to locate the grave, dappled by the light of the afternoon sun, amidst the overgrown foliage a dozen or so steps from the small mortuary chapel. There are no sounds of Atlantic waves here, nor howling winds, nor shrieking seagulls; no clamour of rage or frenzy – an almost silent spot except for the distant hum of traffic on the nearby Stillorgan Road, a fallen tombstone in an undisturbed place, a restless spirit stilled.

Epilogue

Now the estate is sold and the powerful story of the Achill Mission has at least had a pleasant ending. Let us hope that this union of Protestants and Catholics of Achill is an augury of brighter days awaiting long-crushed Ireland.

–Anita McMahon, 'Sale of the Achill Mission Estate',
Catholic Bulletin, December 1915

I tap my toes to the music of jig and reel in St Thomas' church, Dugort. Violin, uileann pipe, concertina and harp notes soar through the air in the fading evening light. Visitors and islanders alike drum their feet with enjoyment as the talented musicians from the island summer school exhibit their musical skills.

I sit beside an elderly man and we talk at the interval. I tell him I have been writing the story of the Achill Mission.

He looks at me, then says, 'I hope you have told the truth.'

'That's easier said than done,' I reply.

'I hope you have listened,' he says, 'I hope you have listened to the stories of the people.'

I have indeed heard the folklore stories and the narrative retelling, evoking how those past times felt and the trauma of those years. The stories carry an island's pain:

> They were afraid hunger would tempt them to take the soup so they decided to go up to the top of the hill and die there before they would put themselves in the way of temptation. And they went up and they died.[1]

To the old people, the land of Slievemore was a like a
blessed place. They had their houses and living, and their
graveyard and everything else there and everything was
taken off them.[2]

Earlier that day I had climbed Slievemore for the first time, making
my way along the mountain ridge in an east-west direction. It was
a clear summer's day with no hint of cloud at the summit, yet the
ground was often soft underfoot. I felt cupped in the hands of the
mountain in the company of a robin who threaded the heather
nearby. It seemed that I had the slopes to myself until I came upon
two men and a dog herding black-faced sheep downhill. 'You're
almost at the top,' one shouted encouragingly, as they continued
on their way.

The expanse of Achill Island was visible from the summit. I
imagined the imprint of history on the mountain, the memory of
those who lived and died on its slopes and within its range: the
ghosts of those who inhabited these places, whose flesh fell away
from their bones and whose blood ran along the veins of this earth
– a mountain that holds its skeletons close.

Scattered around the cemetery at St Thomas' Church are plain
wooden crosses. They mark the graves, without headstones or
names, of those buried here towards the end of the Great Famine
and afterwards. I walked in the presence of the nameless dead. The
crosses were erected as part of a commemorative and healing
service organised by the local Catholic and Protestant
congregations. The church's registry lists the name of many of
those buried, but in the case of the unmarked graves it is not
known whose remains rest where.

The words in the service booklet have been put together with
care, worked upon and reworded over and over, I suspect. They
are an attempt to steer a path through the historical hurt and pain,
to move beyond the competing narratives, beyond anger and hate.

Some Achill people buried here had become Church of
Ireland members, inspired by Reverend Edward Nangle

and his community. It is probable that others lying here, who likewise changed denomination or were linked closely with the Mission, would have lived and died in the Roman Catholic community had the times not been so desperate materially and polarised spiritually. There were high feelings of anxiety, hurt and anger about both groups for many years, and a mix of anger and admiration about the Mission's work and methods.[3]

Trauma rippled through the generations. It was time to be unbound from the past.

Concert over, I make my way down the aisle of the church. There is a large, rusted metal container in the corner close to the exit door. 'That's a soup urn,' a woman tells me, 'from the famine time. They found it at the colony and brought it here. Those were bad times.'

The traces and marks of the story I have followed are all around: in this church and its cemetery, on the mountain with its deserted villages, in what remains of the colony settlement that appears as if it might merge back into Slievemore – the mountain a depository of the bones of history.

The great Irish nineteenth-century conflicts around education, religion, imperialism and land were fought out on this island. Responses to the Great Famine seared and divided a community. The Achill Mission story is at the heart of these events: a microcosm of a bitter history.

Outside, the car headlights tunnel a light through the darkness along the church avenue. I look up at the black towering form of Slievemore as I pass through the gates. I have a sense that, having immersed myself in the traumatic charge of this island's history, I have become reconciled with my own past. In retracing this narrative, it is as if I have walked through my own history.

I drive away from the island mountain.

ENDNOTES

Chapter 1

1 *Freeman's Journal*, 2 February 1827.

2 This text will generally use the term 'Catholic' to indicate the Christian persuasion of 'Roman Catholic', and 'Protestant' to denote a Christian belonging to the Church of Ireland which was the official established church in Ireland until disestablished by the Irish Church Act 1869.

3 N.J. Halpin (ed.), *Authentic Report of the Speeches and Proceedings of the Meeting held at Cavan on the 26th January, 1827* (Dublin: Richard Moore Tims, 1827).

4 For a comprehensive account of the 'second reformation' in Ireland see Irene Whelan, 'The Second Reformation 1822-7' in Irene Whelan, *The Bible War in Ireland* (Dublin: The Lilliput Press, 2005), Chapter Five.

5 For Lord Farnham's communication with his tenants, see E. McCourt, 'The Management of the Farnham Estates during the nineteenth century', *Breifne* (Journal of the Breifne Historical Society), 16 (1973–5).

6 Ibid. p. 547.

7 Halpin, 'Authentic Report'.

8 Details of William Krause's early years in Cavan from C.S. Stanford (ed.), *Memoir of the Late Rev. W.H. Krause* (1854).

9 Ibid. p. 168.

10 Arva detail from F.J. McCaughey, *Arva: Sources for a Local History* (1998).

11 Nangle family details from P. Comerford, 'Edward Nangle: The Achill Mission in a New Light (1)', in *Cathair na Mart*, 18 (1998).

12 H. Seddall, *Edward Nangle, The Apostle of Achill: A Memoir and A History* (Dublin: Hodges, Figgis & Co., 1884), pp. 40–3.

13 C. Anderson, *Historical Sketches of the Ancient Native Irish and their Descendants* (Edinburgh: Oliver & Boyd, 1828), p. xvi.

14 *The Achill Missionary Herald and Western Witness*, March 1852. (Hereafter, this publication will be abbreviated in endnotes to *Herald*).

Chapter 2

1   John MacHale letter to Earl Grey in B. O'Reilly, *John MacHale, Archbishop of Tuam: His Life, Times, and Correspondence*, I (New York & Cincinnati: 1890), p. 221.

2   See O. McDonagh, 'The Economy and Society, 1830–44' in W.E. Vaughan (ed.), *A New History of Ireland V* (New York: Oxford University Press, 1989), pp. 218–22.

3   *Mayo Constitution*, 24 March 1831.

4   See *Herald*, July 1864 for an account of *Nottingham* trip.

5   *Herald*, July 1850 (Edward's obituary following his wife's death).

6   See Anderson, *Sketches*, p. xiii.

7   Detail of Frenchman's visit to Ireland in E. Larkin (ed.), *Alexis de Tocqueville's Journey in Ireland July–August 1835* (Dublin: Wolfhound, 1990).

8   O. O'Hanlon, 'An Irishman's Diary on Alexis de Tocqueville and Ireland in 1835', *Irish Times*, 29 December 2015.

9   *Herald*, August 1864.

10   W.H. Maxwell, *Wild Sports of the West* (Dublin: The Talbot Press, 1832), p. 54.

11   *Herald*, October 1864.

12   Ibid.

13   *Evidence taken before Her Majesty's Commissioner of Inquiry into the state of the law and practice in respect to the Occupation of Land in Ireland* (1845), p. 432.

14   See interview with Sean MacConmhara, 87-year-old Irish-speaking Achill resident, in *The Connaught Tribune*, 13 October 1834.

15   H. Anderson, *The Life and Letters of Christopher Anderson* (Edinburgh: William P. Kennedy, 1854), p. 140.

16   Seddall, *Edward Nangle*, p. 57.

Chapter 3

1   *Herald*, October 1864, carries an account of the journey to Dugort and Edward Nangle's early days at the colony.

2   *Herald*, October 1864.

3   N. Costello, *John MacHale, Archbishop of Tuam* (Dublin: Talbot Press, 1939), p. 39.

4   B. O'Reilly, *John MacHale, Archbishop of Tuam,* I (New York & Cincinnati: F. Pustet and Co., 1890), p. 250.

5   John MacHale letter and Edward Nangle's series of seven letters of reply included in E. Nangle, *Dr. MacHale's Letter to the Bishop of Exeter Dissected and the Established Church vindicated in Seven Letters* (Dublin: T.J. White, 1834).

6　*Herald*, November 1864.

7　S. O'Sullivan, *It's All in your Head* (London: Penguin Random House, 2015), p. 177.

8　*Herald*, November 1864.

9　*Connaught Telegraph*, 8 April 1835.

10　Details of Tuam celebrations for Archbishop MacHale from *Freeman's Journal*, 20 & 27, October 1834.

Chapter 4

1　For an overview of Jane Franklin's life, including her travels on the Nile, see A. Alexander, *The Ambitions of Jane Franklin, Victorian Lady Adventurer* (Sydney: Allen & Unwin, 2013).

2　Details of Jane Franklin's visit to Achill from J. Barrow, *Tour Round Ireland, throughout the Sea-Coast Counties in the Autumn of 1835* (London: John Murray, 1836), and also from an Appendix to that book, 'Letter from a Lady who visited the Island of Achill in September 1835'.

3　*Telegraph*, 16 September 1835.

4　For an overview of the Stanley scheme, see G. Fitzgerald, *Irish Primary Education in the Early Nineteenth Century* (Dublin: Royal Irish Academy, 2013).

5　*Herald*, November 1864.

6　'Letter from a Lady who visited the Island of Achill in September 1835' from appendix to Barrow, *Tour Round Ireland*.

7　For an account of the dispute between Edward Nangle and the school master, James O'Donnell, see P.F. O'Donovan, *Stanley's Letter: The National School System and Inspectors in Ireland 1831–1922* (Galway: Galway Education Centre, 2017), pp. 53–6.

8　Excerpts of Edward Nangle's evidence before the Select Committee taken from E. Nangle, *The Origin, Progress, and Difficulties of the Achill Mission: As detailed in the minutes of evidence taken before the select committee of the House of Lords, appointed to enquire into the progress and operation of the new plan of education in Ireland, and to report thereupon to the House* (Achill: Achill Mission Press, 1838).

9　Detail of Achill school numbers from M. Ní Ghiobúin, 'Social conditions in Achill in 19th century', unpublished PhD thesis, National University of Ireland, Maynooth, 2005, Part 2, pp. 179–87.

10　See P. Byrne, 'Women and the Achill Mission Colony', *The Irish Story* (30 August 2015). http://www.theirishstory.com/2015/08/30/women-and-the-achill-mission-colony/#.WhlqCEpl_IU, accessed 14 Dec. 2017.

11.　'Letter from a Lady' in Barrow, *Tour Round Ireland*.

Chapter 5

1   See Seddall, *Edward Nangle*, p. 86.
2   See *Herald*, May 1865, for Edward Nangle's account of Bridget Lavelle episode and of Bridget's deposition before a magistrate.
3   *Herald*, April 1865.
4   *The Achill Missionary Herald and Western Witness* is hereafter referred to in the text as the *Achill Herald*.
5   Details of Isabella Neason letter from *Herald*, October 1864.
6   Edward Nangle recounted the circumstances under which Neason Adams and his wife travelled to Achill in *Herald*, March 1865.
7   MacConmhara, *Connaught Tribune*, 1834.
8   B.W. Noel, *Notes of a Short Tour through the Midland Counties of Ireland in the summer of 1836* (London: Nisbet, 1837), pp. 159–216.
9   C. Otway, *A tour in Connaught comprising sketches of Clonmacnoise, Joyce County and Achill* (Dublin: Curry, 1839), pp. 346–427.

Chapter 6

1   Details of debate from D. McElwee & J. Baylee (eds), *Authentic Report of Important Discussion held in Castlebar between the Rev. W.B. Stoney and Fr James Hughes* (Dublin: William Curry, 1837).
2   *Mayo Constitution*, 20 December 1836.
3   *Protestant Penny Magazine*, Vol. I, No X, April 1835.
4   Ibid.
5   Debate detail from McElwee & Baylee (eds.), *Authentic Report*.
6   Anecdote recounted in *Herald*, June 1865.
7   K. Toolis, 'The Prophet in the Wilderness', RTE *Sunday Miscellany* (10 May 2015).
8   *Herald*, July 1837.
9   *Herald*, September 1837.
10 Letter reproduced in *Herald*, March 1865.
11 Ibid.

Chapter 7

1   Details from P. Mullowney, 'Life in the Coastguard in County Mayo in the 19th century', www.townlandhistory.netfirms.com/coastguard/francisrey nolds.htm, accessed 29 October 2012.
2   E. Nangle, *Origin of Achill Mission*.
3   Family legend details from Mullowney, 'Life in the Coastguard'.

4   The Archbishop's visit was described in *Herald*, November 1865.

5   Detail of statements to the jury from 'Outrage Reports', County Mayo, 1839, National Archives of Ireland, 21/1–21/54.

6   *The Telegraph*, 9 January 1839.

7   National Folklore Collection, MS 1348.

8   E. Nangle, *The Achill Mission and the present state of Protestantism in Ireland: The Statement delivered by the Rev. Edward Nangle at a meeting of the Protestant Association in Exeter Hall, 28 December, 1838* (London: The Protestant Association, 1839).

9   The incident was recalled by one of Edward Nangle's followers after the clergyman's death and was reported in the *Church Advocate*, November 1883.

10   Nangle, *Protestant Association*.

11   *Herald*, February 1839.

12   *Herald*, June 1841.

13   *Herald*, April 1839.

14   *Freeman's Journal*, 1 January 1839.

15   *Herald*, April 1839.

Chapter 8

1   Details of Halls' account taken from Mr & Mrs Samuel C. Carter Hall, *Ireland: Its Scenery and Character* (London: How & Parsons, 1843).

2   *Herald*, July 1841.

3   Hall, *Ireland*.

4   Ibid.

5   There is a description of the changed management structure in an Appendix to *6th Annual Report of the Achill Mission, for the year ended 31 March 1839* (Achill: Mission Press, 1840).

6   The Achill Mission 1839 report included a description of the orphan asylum and the goals of the institution.

7   Hall, *Ireland*.

8   *Herald*, April 1866.

9   *Herald*, December 1842.

10   *Herald*, February 1843.

11   For an appraisal of the Halls' critique of the Achill Mission, see D. Bowen, *Souperism: Myth or Reality?* (Cork: Mercier Press, 1970), pp. 93–5.

Chapter 9

1   Edward Nangle's testimony is documented in *Evidence taken before Her Majesty's Commissioners of inquiry into the state of the Law and Practice in respect to the Occupation of Land in Ireland*, II (Dublin, 1845), pp. 430–3.

2   *The Times*, 6 February 1844.

3   *Evidence - Occupation of Land in Ireland*.

4   Ibid.

5   C. Woodham-Smith, *The Great Hunger: Ireland 1845–1849* (London: Penguin Books, 1991), p. 35.

6   William Burke's letter appeared in *Herald*, August 1844.

7   Details of the incident from *The Warder* account taken from I. Ní Dheirg, *Emily M. Weddall, Bunaitheoir Scoil Acla* (Dublin: Coiscéim, 1995), p. 4.

8   *Herald*, August 1844.

9   *Herald*, October 1844.

10 *Herald*, June 1866.

11 Paraphrased from MacConmhara, *Connaught Tribune* interview.

12 Register of Baptisms, Marriages and Deaths for the Parish of Dugort, Achill; Representative Church Body Library, Dublin.

13 Format of recantation ceremony from *Herald*, May 1846.

Chapter 10

1   This chapter draws on the accounts of Asenath Nicholson's visit to the Achill Mission and her dealings with Edward Nangle from M. Murphy (ed.), *Ireland's Welcome to the Stranger – Asenath Nicholson* (Dublin: The Lilliput Press, 2002), and M. O'Rourke Murphy, *Compassionate Stranger: Asenath Nicholson and the Great Irish Famine* (New York: Syracuse University Press, 2015).

2   *Herald*, July 1845.

3   Murphy (ed.), *Ireland Welcome* pp. 337–40 contains Mrs Nicholson's remarks about Edward Nangle and Ireland.

4   The new masthead first featured in the *Achill Herald* in February 1846.

5   In a letter to Sir Richard O'Donnell on 27 April 1845, Edward Nangle requested a lease on the Mweelin lands for the colony development.

6   *Dublin University Magazine*, 43, 1854, p. 134.

7   The quote from the *Gardeners' Chronicle* edition of 13 September 1845 is taken from E. Delaney, *The Great Irish Famine – A History of Four Lives* (Dublin: Gill & Macmillan, 2002), p. 77.

8   National Folklore Collection, MS 1072.

9   *Herald*, October 1845.

10 *The Telegraph*, 12 November 1845.

11 National Archives of Ireland, 23 November 1845 RLFC 3/1/101.
12 Woodham-Smith, *Great Hunger*, p. 40.
13 *Herald*, November 1845.
14 *Herald*, April 1845.
15 *Herald*, November 1845.

Chapter 11

1 *Herald*, August 1866.
2 Edward Nangle's 1866 account of this illness suggests that his breakdown occurred in early 1847. However, *The Telegraph* report of January 1846 and the fact that Edward wrote of returning to Achill in March when Eliza gave birth to a stillborn child both point to his breakdown happening in early 1846.
3 *Herald*, August 1866.
4 *The Telegraph*, 21 January 1846.
5 *Herald*, August 1866.
6 The family Bible was viewed in February 2017, courtesy of the Nangle family.
7 *Herald*, August 1866.
8 K. Redfield Jamison, *An Unquiet Mind: A Memoir of Moods and Madness* (London: Picador, 1997), p. 123.

Chapter 12

1 *The Telegraph*, 21 January 1846.
2 Ibid.
3 The parish register for Dugort lists Mary and Michael Niland, possibly Bridget's parents, as having publicly rescinded their faith in December 1844, before the potato blight hit.
4 *The Telegraph*, 21 January 1846.
5 John Kelly, *The Graves are Walking: A History of the Great Irish Famine* (London: Faber & Faber, 2012), p. 85.
6 *Herald*, August 1866.
7 National Archives of Ireland, 7 July 1846 RLFC 3/1/4098.
8 *Herald*, May 1846.
9 Reference taken from Woodham-Smith, *Great Hunger*, p. 93.
10 *The Telegraph* editions of 5 and 19 August 1846.
11 Details of meeting taken from *Freeman's Journal*, 12 October 1846, and Kelly, *Graves*, p. 162.
12 *Freeman's Journal*, 21 October 1846.

13   For a discussion of the role of religious and political ideology in the Great Famine, see Gray, 'Ideology and the Famine', in Cathal Póirtéir (ed.), *The Great Irish Famine* (Dublin: Mercier Press, 1995), pp. 86–103.

14   *Herald*, December 1846 carries the account.

15   Ibid.

16   H. Andrews, *Lion of the West: A biography of John MacHale* (Dublin: Veritas, 2001), p. 136.

17   O'Reilly, *John MacHale*, p. 620.

18   MacConmhara, *Connaught Tribune* interview.

19   National Archives of Ireland, RLFC 3/2/21/33-41 (Mayo).

20   *Herald*, December 1846.

21   Ibid.

Chapter 13

1   *The Telegraph*, 6 January 1847.

2   Statement of schooner mate from Liam Swords (ed.), *In Their Own Words: The Famine in North Connacht, 1845–1849* (Dublin: Columba Press, 1998), p. 171.

3   *The Telegraph*, 21 April 1847.

4   For background to Slievemore Deserted Village see Theresa McDonald, *A Guide to Archaeological Sites on Achill, Achillbeg and the Corraun Peninsula* (Tullamore, Co Offaly: IAS Publications, 2016), p. 67.

5   *Herald*, February 1847.

6   G.E. Bourke's words in visitor book, and subsequent exchanges between him and Edward Nangle, from the *Achill Herald* editions of May and June 1847.

7   Father Michael Gallagher, Achill, to Father Synnott, Archbishop's House, Dublin, 28 January 1848. Dublin Diocese Archives, DDA/AB3/32/4/70.

8   *The Tablet*, 5 June 1847.

9   For a definition and description of 'souperism', see Whelan, 'Edward Nangle and the Achill Mission 1834–1852' in Gillespie and Moran (eds), *A Various County: Essays in Mayo History, 1500–1900* (Westport: Foilseacháin Náisiúnta, 1987), p. 129.

10   National Folklore Collection, MS 1072.

11   The employment numbers appeared in the *Achill Herald* editions of January and February 1847.

12   For a discussion of the Achill Mission employment numbers, see M. Ní Ghiobúin, *Dugort, Achill Island, 1831–1861: The Rise & Fall of a Missionary Community* (Dublin: Irish Academic Press, 2001), p. 49.

13   Anonymous letter writer in the *Liverpool Mercury*, 11 September 1862.

14   *Herald*, May 1847.

15   National Archives, 20 January 1847 RLFC 3/2/21/34.

16   Ibid. February 1847 RLFC 3/2/21/33.
17   *Herald*, September 1847.

Chapter 14

1   Details of Achill visit from James Hack Tuke, *A Visit to Connaught in the Autumn of 1847* (London: Charles Gilpin, 1848).

2   For a discussion of eviction and landlord issues during the Famine, see Donnelly, 'Mass Eviction and the Great Famine: The Clearances Revisited' in Póirtéir (ed.), *The Great Irish Famine* (Dublin: Mercier Press, 1995), pp. 155–73.

3   The Gregory clause's impact is discussed in M. Kelly, *Struggle and Strife on a Mayo Estate 1833–1903* (Dublin: Four Courts Press, 2014), p. 23.

4   *Herald*, September 1847.

5   *Thirteenth Annual Report of the Achill Mission, for the year ended 31 December 1846* (Achill: Achill Mission Press, 1847).

6   Ibid.

7   Account of Asenath Nicholson's latest visit to Achill and to the Achill Mission draws on A. Nicholson, *Annals of the Famine in Ireland [1851]*, ed. Maureen Murphy (Dublin: The Lilliput Press, 1998), pp. 103–7.

8   Details from letter of Robert Savage published in *Mayo Constitution*, 19 October 1847.

9   *Herald*, November 1847.

10   Murphy, *Annals*, p. 94.

11   O'Rourke Murphy, *Compassionate Stranger*, pp. 188–9.

12   Murphy, *Annals*, p. 189.

13   *Herald*, December 1847.

14   Murphy, *Annals*, p. 105.

15   Murphy, *Annals*, pp. 181–2.

16   O'Rourke Murphy, *Compassionate Stranger*, p. 195.

17   *Herald*, December 1847.

Chapter 15

1   This account of Count Strzelecki's work in County Mayo draws on Kinealy, 'A Polish Count in County Mayo. Paul de Strzelecki and the Great Famine', in G. Moran and N. Ó Muraíle (eds), *Mayo – History and Society* (Dublin: Geography Publications, 2014), pp. 415–30.

2   Communications between Edward Nangle and Lord Sligo on this issue in the *Achill Herald* editions for December 1847and January 1848.

3   Westport Union minute books of Board of Guardians for January 1847, National Library, MS 12,607.
4   *Herald*, December 1847.
5   *Herald*, January 1848.
6   *The Telegraph*, 22 September 1847.
7   Kinealy, 'A Polish Count', p. 427.
8   *Herald*, April 1848.
9   *Herald*, August 1848.
10 *Herald*, September 1866.
11 *Fifteenth Annual Report of the Achill Mission for the year ended 31 December 1848* (Achill: Achill Mission Press, 1849).
12 Ibid.
13 Quoted in Woodham-Smith, *Great Hunger*, p. 377.

Chapter 16

1   Detail around Mary and Bridget McNamara and their journey taken from http://mayoorphangirls.weebly.com, accessed 14 December 2017.
2   Details of the guardians' role in the orphan girls' story from Westport Union minute book, 8 September 1849, National Library, MS 12610.
3   *Mayo Constitution*, 28 August 1849.
4   Moran, 'Farewell to Kilkelly, Ireland: Emigration from post-famine Mayo' in Moran and Ó Muraíle (eds), *Mayo – History and Society*, p. 397.
5   The Dugort parish register notes the names of Mary and Bridget McNamara among those who participated in a recantation ceremony in 1844. There is a good possibility that these are the orphan girls who ended up in Westport workhouse.
6   For general information on the Earl Grey scheme and details of the girls' arrival in Australia, see Abbott, 'The Earl Grey Orphan Scheme, 1848–1850, and the Irish Diaspora in Australia' in Kinealy, King and Reilly (eds), *Women and the Great Hunger* (Hamden: Quinnipiac University, 2016), pp. 201–6.
7   http://mayoorphangirls.weebly.com/
8   Accounts of these events appeared in the *Achill Herald* editions of September and December 1849, and in *The Telegraph* on 12 September 1849.
9   Confirmation ceremony detail from *Herald*, September 1849.
10 Ibid.
11 Rev. William McIlwaine (1807–85) described the Achill occasion in *Diary of a Journey from Belfast to the West, and a Visit to Achill in the autumn of 1849* quoted in Seddall, *Edward Nangle*, pp. 176–8. Patrick Comerford has pointed out that the clergyman was responsible for moving Saint George's in Belfast from having an evangelical flavour to being a High Church parish.

Chapter 17

1 *Herald*, July 1850.
2 Scrapbook viewed courtesy of the Nangle family.
3 Details from admission papers to St Patrick's Hospital, Dublin, and North Wales County Asylum, Denbigh, Wales, courtesy of Hilary Tulloch.
4 Grace Warner death certificate courtesy of Hilary Tulloch.

Chapter 18

1 There is an account of John MacHale's Achill visit in *The Telegraph*, 21 September 1851.
2 John MacHale's letter in the *Freeman's Journal*, 9 January 1852.
3 For details of the provisions of the Encumbered Estates Act, see J.C. Brady, 'Legal Developments 1801–79' in W.E. Vaughan (ed.), *A New History of Ireland*, V (Oxford: Oxford University Press, 2009), pp. 456–7.
4 See R.V. Comerford, 'Churchmen, tenants, and independent opposition, 1850–1856', in *New History of Ireland V*, p. 396.
5 *Freeman's Journal*, 9 January 1852.
5 P.J. Joyce, *A Forgotten Part of Ireland* (Tuam: 1910), p. 148.
6 This account draws on material in the *Achill Herald* editions of October and December 1851.
7 *Herald*, April 1852.
8 *Freeman's Journal*, 9 January 1852.
9 *Herald*, January 1852.
10 Occasion reported on in *Freeman's Journal*, 17 August 1852.
11 Joyce, *Forgotten Ireland*, p. 152.
12 *The Telegraph*, 10 November 1852.
13 James Henry letter published in the *Freeman's Journal* on 22 December 1852.
14 Edward Nangle letter to Achill Mission friends appeared in the *Cork Constitution* on 13 November 1850.
15 *Herald*, April 1851.
16 *Herald*, December 1851.

Chapter 19

1 Visits reported on in *Herald*, August 1852.
2 For general information on Alexander Dallas (1791–1869) and his Irish missions, see M. Moffitt, *Soupers & Jumpers: The Protestant Missions in Connemara 1848–1937* (Dublin: Nonsuch Publishing, 2008).

3   See Whelan, 'The Stigma of Souperism' in Póirtéir (ed.), *The Great Irish Famine*, p.145.
4   For details of the arrangements between the Achill Mission and Alexander Dallas, see Ní Ghiobúin, *Dugort* pp. 60–1.
5   A.B. Dallas, *Incidents in The Life and Ministry of the Rev. Alex. R. C. Dallas* (London: James Nisbet & Co., 1872), p. 390.
6   *Herald*, June 1852.
7   Ibid.
8   *Herald,* November 1866.
9   New mast head appeared in *Herald* edition of January 1853.

Chapter 20

1   For an overview of the landlord and tenant situation in the country and in Mayo in the famine and post-famine years, see Donnelly 'Landlords and Tenants' in *New History of Ireland*, V, pp. 340–3.
2   For the impact of the Encumbered Estates Act on landlords in the west, see P.G. Lane, 'The General Impact of the Encumbered Estates Act of 1849 on Counties Galway and Mayo' in *Journal of the Galway History & Archaeological Society*, 1972.
3   An account of the funeral events appeared in the *Mayo Constitution* of 25 January 1853.
4   William Pike defended his actions at the funeral in a letter published in the *Mayo Constitution* on 1 February 1853.
5   *Mayo Constitution*, 8 March 1853.
6   *Herald*, February 1853.
7   An account of the *California* tragedy was carried in the *Mayo Constitution* on 15 November 1853.
8   Letter of James Henry in *The Telegraph* on 16 November 1853.
9   *The Telegraph* edition of 22 March 1854 carried a report of the court case surrounding the *California* incidents.
10   Letter of James Henry in *The Telegraph* on 4 January 1854.
11   See The Banner of the Truth in Ireland, III (Dublin: Curry), 1853, p. 119.
12   Notice appeared in *The Telegraph* on 18 October 1854.
13   *Mayo Constitution*, 19 December 1854.
14   Letter of James Henry in *The Telegraph* on 21 February 1855.
15   *Mayo Constitution*, 6 March 1855.
16   Stories taken from *Folklore Achill*, folklore collected in Achill schools in 1989.
17   Donnelly, 'Landlords and Tenants', p. 340.
18   Letter of James Henry in *The Telegraph* on 2 September 1854.

19 Detail of indenture between the Achill Mission and Murray McGregor Blacker for the sublease of Keem lands from M. Ní Ghiobúin, 'Social conditions', part 2, p. 86.

20 See T. McDonald, 'Booleying in Achill, Achillbeg and Corraun: Survey, excavation and analysis of booley settlements in the civil parish of Achill', unpublished PhD thesis, National University of Ireland Galway, 2014.

21 R.V. Rogers, *Report of a Visit to some of the Scenes of the Labour of the Society for the Irish Church Missions* (1855), p.18.

22 In the case of the main colony site at Slievemore, Edward Nangle acknowledged that it was with 'some difficulty' that possession of the site was secured from the tenants (*Herald*, October 1864) and that goodwill money of £90 had been paid to the tenants (Devon Commission Report, p.432). In the case of the Mweelin lands, a letter from Edward to Sir Richard O'Donnell on 27 April 1845 refers to leases being sought for the Achill Mission developments.

23 *Herald*, March 1866.

24 See M. Ní Ghiobúin, 'Social conditions', part 2, p. 127, where she discusses the Finsheen site: 'When the Achill Mission purchased most of the island in the early 1850s, one of their first acts was to evict the inhabitants of the small village of Finsheen.'

25 Ibid. pp. 113–16, for a discussion of the desertion of the site on the western slopes of Slievemore: 'However, no single cause had been advanced to account for the desertion of Slievemore, but the fact that some descendants of those who belonged to the village still retain title to plots there may indicate a process of gradual evacuation from the late 1830s onwards rather than a single mass departure.' (p. 116)

Chapter 21

1 Patrick Comerford has pointed out that the architectural layout and design of St Thomas' Church is surprisingly 'High Church', given Edward Nangle's evangelicalism. It is a layout that emphasises the liturgical life of the church rather than preaching, an emphasis that is strengthened by having a chancel arch and separate chancel area. This may indicate that Edward Nangle's theology matured later in life.

2 Account of first divine service at St Thomas' Church in *Herald*, March 1855.

3 *Herald*, February 1853 details issues raised around the church endowment.

4 *Mayo Constitution*, 28 August 1855.

5 *Herald*, August 1855.

6 *Herald,* January 1856.

7 Seddall, *Edward Nangle*, p. 215.

8 *Herald*, September 1859.

9   *Herald*, May 1857.
10   *Galway Vindicator*, 17 May 1854.
11   *Herald*, February 1855.
12   A. Dallas, *Incidents in the Life and Ministry of the Rev. Alex. C. Dallas, Dallas* (London: James Nisbet & Co., 1872), p. 406.
13   *Herald*, May 1857.
14   *Herald*, June 1856.
15   For a fuller account of Hector's fishery operations in Achill, see *Herald*, August 1859, and M. Ní Ghiobúin, *Dugort, Achill Island*, pp. 235–8.
16   *Herald*, August 1858.
17   Anonymous writer in *Liverpool Mercury*, 22 July 1862.
18   *Irish Advocate*, July 1875.
19   See D. Bowen, *Souperism: Myth or Reality? A Study of Catholics and Protestants during the Great Famine* (Cork: Cork University Press, 1970), p. 105.

Chapter 22

1   For a full account of the controversy surrounding the respective roles of the Achill Mission trustees and the management committee, see J. Napier and A. Hamilton, *The Case of the Achill Mission estate: Proceedings for the new scheme of management* (Dublin: Hodges Smith, 1864).
2   *Herald*, May 1857.
3   Napier & Hamilton, *The Case of the Achill Mission estate*, p. 32.
4   *Belfast Daily Mercury*, 15 May 1857.
5   An account of visit to Achill by Vere Foster appeared in *Herald*, January 1860.
6   *Herald*, January 1860.
7   A series of letters on the Achill Mission were published in *Liverpool Mercury* newspaper from June to September 1862.
8   See counsel's opinion in appendix to Napier and Hamilton, *Case of the Achill Mission*.
9   Ibid. p. 48.
10   Details of the encounter between the priest and Napier, and the follow-up, in E. Nangle, *The Case of the Achill Mission Estate, plainly stated by Edward Nangle in reply to the Right Hon. Joseph Napier* (Dublin: George Herbert, 1864).
11   *Herald*, November 1866.
12   *Herald*, September 1869.
13   Comerford, *New History*, V, p. 443.
14   *Herald*, September 1869.
15   *Irish Church Advocate*, April 1871.

Chapter 23

1   Advertisement in *Irish Church Advocate*, July 1880.
2   *Irish Church Advocate*, December 1880.
3   See Comerford, *New History*, V, p. 47.
4   *The Church Advocate*, March 1883.
5   *Freeman's Journal*, 8 November 1881.
6   *Irish Times*, 8 November 1881.
7   J. Maguire and J. Quinn (eds), entry on John MacHale in *Dictionary of Irish Biography* (Cambridge: Cambridge University Press, 2009).
8   *Irish Church Advocate*, January 1872.
9   *Irish Church Advocate*, September 1878.
10 Seddall, *Edward Nangle*, p. 349.
11 *The Church Advocate*, October 1883.
12 *Irish Ecclesiastical Gazette*, 15 September 1883.
13 *Irish Ecclesiastical Gazette*, 22 November 1884.
14 *Irish Times*, 3 November 1883.

Epilogue

1   From storyboard at Deserted Village, Achill.
2   National Folklore Collection, MS 1072.
3   'Marking Achill Mission Graves – A Memorial and Healing Service at St Thomas' Church, Dugort on 24 September 2011' (memorial service booklet).

BIBLIOGRAPHY

Alexander, A., *The Ambitions of Jane Franklin, Victorian Lady Adventurer* (Australia: Allen & Unwin, 2013).

Anderson, C., *Historical Sketches of the Ancient Native Irish and their Descendants* (Edinburgh: Oliver & Boyd, 1828).

Anderson, H., *The Life and Letters of Christopher Anderson* (Edinburgh: William P. Kennedy, 1854).

Andrews, H., *Lion of the West – A Biography of John MacHale* (Dublin: Veritas Publications, 2001).

Annual Reports of the Achill Mission for years ending 31 December 1839, 1841, 1842, 1843, 1844, 1846, 1849.

Barrow, J., *A Tour round Ireland through the sea coast counties in the autumn of 1835* (London: John Murray, 1836).

Böll, H., *Irish Journal* (Evanston, Illinois: The Marlboro Press/ Northwestern, 1998).

Bourke, U.J., *The Life and Times of the Most Rev. John MacHale, Archbishop of Tuam* (Dublin: Gill & Son, 1882).

Bowen, D., *Souperism: Myth or Reality? A Study of Catholics and Protestants during the Great Famine* (Cork: Cork University Press, 1970).

Branach, N., 'Edward Nangle and the Achill Island Mission', *History Ireland*, 8, 3 (2000).

Brophy, C.S. and Delay, C. (eds), *Women, Reform & Resistance in Ireland, 1850–1950* (USA: Palgrave Macmillan, 2015).

Byrne, P., 'Women and the Achill Mission Colony', *The Irish Story*, 30 August 2015.

[Central Relief Committee], *Transactions of the Central Relief Committee of the Society of Friends during the Famine in Ireland in 1846 and 1847* (Dublin: Edmund Burke, 1996).

Cherry, J., 'The Maxwell Family of Farnham, County Cavan: An Introduction', *Breifne* (Journal of Breifne Historical Society) 11, 42, pp. 125–47.

Comerford, P., 'Edward Nangle (1799–1883): The Achill Missionary in a New Light', *Cathair na Mart* (Journal of the Westport Historical Society), Part 1, 18 (1999) and Part 2, 19 (1999).

Costello, N., *John MacHale, Archbishop of Tuam* (Dublin: Talbot Press, 1939).

Crawford, G. and Holme, A.R. (eds), *Protestant Millennialism, Evangelicalism and Irish Society 1790–2005* (Basinstoke: Palgrave MacMillan, 2006).

Crowley, J., Smyth, W. J., and Murphy, M. (eds.), *Atlas of the Great Irish Famine* (Cork: Cork University Press, 2012).

Dallas, A.B., *Incidents in The Life and Ministry of the Rev. Alex. R.C. Dallas* (London: James Nisbet & Co., 1872).

Dallas, A.R.C., *The Story of the Irish Church Missions* (London: Nisbet & Co., 1856).

Delaney, E., *The Great Irish Famine – A History in Four Lives* (Dublin: Gill & Macmillan, 2012).

Devon Commission, *Evidence taken before Her Majesty's Commissioners of inquiry into the state of the Law and Practice in respect to the Occupation of Land in Ireland* (Dublin: Alexander Thom, 1845).

Downey, J., 'The Great Irish Famine 1845–1851 – A Brief Overview', *The Irish Story*, October 2016.

Fitzgerald, G., *Irish Primary Education in the Early Nineteenth Century* (Dublin: Royal Irish Academy, 2013).

Fitzpatrick, W., *Achill as it is compared to what it was* (Dublin, 1886).

Foster, R.F., *Modern Ireland, 1600–1972* (London: Allen Lane, 1988).

Gallagher, P., *Unpublished handwritten autobiography of a Scripture-reader educated on Achill*, National Library of Ireland, MS 19846-7.

Gillespie, R. and Moran, G. (eds), *A Various County: Essays in Mayo History, 1500–1900* (Westport: Foilseacháin Náisiúnta, 1987).

Gray, P., *The Irish Famine* (London: Thames and Hudson, 1995).

Greer, J., *The Windings of the Moy with Skreen and Tireragh* (Dublin: Alex Thom & Co., 1924).

Hall, Mr & Mrs S.C. Carter, *Ireland, its Scenery & Character* (London: How & Parsons, 1843).

Hall, Mr & Mrs S.C. Carter, *Handbooks of Ireland: the West and Connemara* (London: Virtue, Hall & Virtue, 1853).

Halpin, N.J. (ed.), *Authentic Report of the Speeches and Proceedings of the Meeting held at Cavan on the 26th January, 1827* (Dublin: Richard Moore Tims, 1827).

Hamrock, I. (ed.), *The Famine in Co. Mayo* (Castlebar: Mayo County Council, 2004).

Hayden, T. (ed.), *Irish Hunger – Personal Reflections on the Legacy of the Famine* (Dublin: Wolfhound Press, 1997).

Hayes, A. and Urquhart, D. (eds), *The Irish Women's History Reader* (London: Routledge, 2001).

Hooper, G., *Travel Writing and Ireland, 1760–1860* (Cork: Cork University Press, 2001).

Inglis, H.P., *Ireland in 1834. A Journey throughout Ireland during the spring, summer and autumn of 1834* (London: Whittaker, 1834).

Jamison, K.R., *An Unquiet Mind* (London: Picador, 2015).

Johnson, J., *Tour in Ireland with Meditations and Reflections* (London: S. Highley, 1844).

Jordan, D.E., *Land and Popular Politics in Ireland: County Mayo from the Plantation to the Land War* (New York: Cambridge University Press, 1994).

Joyce, P.J., *A Forgotten Part of Ireland* (Tuam, 1910).

Keane, M., *Mrs. S. C. Hall: A Literary Biography* (Gerrard's Cross: Colin Smythe, 1997).

Kelly, J., *The Graves are Walking – The History of the Great Irish Famine* (London: Faber & Faber, 2012).

Kelly, M., *Struggle and Strife on a Mayo Estate 1833–1903* (Dublin: Four Courts Press, 2014).

Kinealy, C., *The Great Irish Famine – Impact, Ideology and Rebellion* (Basingstoke: Palgrave, 2002).

Kinealy, C., King, J. and Reilly C. (eds), *Women and the Great Hunger* (Hamden Ct: Quinnipiac University, 2016).

Kingston, B., *Achill Island, The Deserted Village at Slievemore* (Castlebar: Cashin Printing Service, 1990).

Lane, P.G., 'Currane Mountain, Mayo and the 1850s: A Socio-Economic Study', *Cathair na Mart*, 12, 1 (1992).

Lane, P.G., 'The General Impact of the Encumbered Estates Act of 1849 on Counties Galway and Mayo', *Journal of the Galway History & Archaeological Society* (1972).

Larkin, E. (ed.), *Alexis de Tocqueville's Journey in Ireland July–August 1835* (The Catholic University of America Press, 1990).

Ledbetter, G.T., *Privilege & Poverty, The Life & Times of Irish Painter & Naturalist Alexander Williams* (Cork: The Collins Press, 2010).

Luddy, M., *Women and Philanthropy in nineteenth century Ireland* (New York: Cambridge University Press, 1995).

Lyons, F.S.L., *Ireland since the Famine* (London: Weidenfield & Nicolson, 1971).

Lysaght, P., 'Perspectives on Women during the Great Irish Famine from Oral Tradition,' in *Béaloideas*, 64, 5 (1996–7), pp. 63–130.

McCaughey, F.J., *Arva – Sources for a Local History* (Arva Area Development Association, 1998).

McCourt, E., 'The Management of the Farnham Estates during the Nineteenth Century', *Breifne* (Journal of the Breifne Historical Society), No 16 (1973–5), 53

McDonald, T., *Achill Island: Archeology, History, Folklore* (Dublin: IAS Publications, 1997).

McDonald, T., *A Guide to Archaeological Sites on Achill, Achillbeg and the Corraun Peninsula* (Tullamore: IAS Publications, 2016).

McElwee, D. and Baylee, J. (eds), *Authentic Report of Important Discussion held in Castlebar between the Rev. W. B. Stoney and Fr. James Hughes.* (Dublin: William Curry, 1837).

McGuire, J. and Quinn, J. (eds) *Dictionary of Irish Biography* (Cambridge: Cambridge University Press, 2009).

MacHale, T. (ed.), *Sermons and Discourses by the late Most Rev. John MacHale, Archbishop of Tuam* (Dublin: M.H. Gill & Son, 1883).

McNally, K., *Achill* (Devon: David & Charles, 1973).

Maffett, R.S., 'The Achill Press' in *The Irish Book Lover*, 11, 5, (December 1910).

Marlow, J., *Captain Boycott and the Irish* (London: Cox & Wyman Ltd, 1973).

Martineau, H., *Letters from Ireland* (London: John Chapman, 1852).

Maxwell, W.H., *Wild Sports of the West* (Dublin: The Talbot Press, 1833).

Meide and Sikes, 'Manipulating the Maritime Cultural Landscape: Vernacular Boats and Economic Relations on Nineteenth-Century Achill Island, Ireland', *Journal of Maritime Archaeology*, 9, 1 (June 2014), pp. 115–41.

Moffitt, M., *Soupers and Jumpers: The Protestant Missions in Connemara, 1848–1937* (Dublin: Nonsuch Press, 2008).

Moore Institute, NUI Galway: Landed Estates Database.

Moran, G. and Ó Muraíle, N. (eds), *Mayo – History and Society* (Dublin: Geography Publications, 2014).

Murphy, C.C., *Boycott: There are Many Ways to Fight a War* (Dublin: The O'Brien Press, 2012).

Nangle, E., *Rev. Dr MacHale's letter to the Bishop of Exeter dissected in seven letters and the established Church vindicated in seven letters* (Dublin: T.L. White, 1833).

Nangle, E., *The Origin, Progress, and Difficulties of the Achill Mission: As detailed in the minutes of evidence taken before the select committee of the House of Lords, appointed to enquire into the progress and operation of the new plan of education in Ireland, and to report thereupon to the House* (Achill: Achill Mission Press, 1838).

Nangle, E. (ed.), *The Protestant Penny Magazine 1834–1836* (Dublin: Hobertsan & Company, 1838).

Nangle, E., *The Achill Mission and the present state of Protestantism in Ireland: The Statement delivered by the Rev.*

Nangle, E., *Edward Nangle at a meeting of the Protestant Association in Exeter Hall, 28 December, 1838* (London: The Protestant Association, 1839).

Nangle, E., *The Whole Correspondence with Mr S. C. Hall in relation to the hostile notice of the Achill Mission in his book on Ireland* (Achill: Mission Press, 1842).

Nangle, E., *The Case of the Achill Mission Estate, plainly stated by E Nangle in reply to the Right Hon. J Napier* (Dublin: George Herbert, 1864).

Nangle, F.E., *A Short Account of the Nangle Family* (Ardglass: privately published, 1986).

Napier, J. and Hamilton, A., *The Case of the Achill Mission estate: Proceedings for the new scheme of management* (Dublin: Hodges Smith, 1864).

Nicholson, A., *Annals of the Famine in Ireland [1851]*, ed. Maureen Murphy (Dublin: The Lilliput Press, 1998).

Nicholson, A., *Ireland's Welcome to the Stranger*, ed. Maureen Murphy (Dublin: The Lilliput Press, 2002).

Ní Ghiobúin, M., *Dugort, Achill Island, 1831–1861: The Rise & Fall of a Missionary Community* (Dublin: Irish Academic Press, 2001).

Noel, B.W., *Notes of a Short Tour through the Midland Counties of Ireland in the Summer of 1836 with Observations on the Condition of the Peasantry* (London: Nisbet, 1837).

O'Donovan, P.F., *Stanley's Letter: The National School System and Inspectors in Ireland 1831–1922* (Galway: Galway Education Centre, 2017).

O'Reilly, B., *John MacHale, Archbishop of Tuam: Life, Times, and Correspondence* (New York: Fr. Pustet & Co., 1890).

O'Rourke Murphy, M., *Compassionate Stranger: Asenath Nicholson and the Great Irish Famine* (New York: Syracuse University Press, 2015).

O'Sullivan, S., *It's All in Your Head – True Stories of Imaginary Illness* (London: Penguin Random House, 2015).

Otway, C., *A Tour in Connaught* (Dublin: William Curry Junior & Company, 1839).

Póirtéir, C. (ed.), *The Great Irish Famine* (Dublin: Mercier Press, 1995).

Praeger, R.L., *The Way that I went* (Cork: The Collins Press, 1997).

Seddall, H., *Edward Nangle – The Apostle of Achill; A Memoir and A History* (Dublin: Hodges, Figgis & Co., 1884).

Stanford, C.S. (ed.), *Memoir of the late Rev. W. H. Krause* (Dublin: George Herbert, 1854).

Swords, L. (ed.), *In Their Own Words: The Famine in North Connacht, 1845–1849* (Dublin: Columba Press, 1998).

The Achill Missionary Herald and Irish Church Advocate (Dublin: Steam Press, October 1869–July 1874).

The Achill Missionary Herald and Western Witness (Achill: Mission Press, July 1837–September 1869).

The Banner of the Truth in Ireland, monthly publication of the Society of Irish Church Missions (Dublin: Curry, 1853–1854).

The Irish Advocate and Missionary Herald (Dublin, April–December 1875).

The Irish Church Advocate (Dublin, 1876–1879).

The Church Advocate (Dublin, 1879–91).

The Substance of a Speech delivered by Lord Farnham at a meeting held in Cavan on Friday 26 January 1827 for the purpose of promotion of the Reformation in Ireland (Cavan Johnston County Library).

Toolis, K., 'The Prophet in the Wilderness', RTÉ *Sunday Miscellany* (10 May 2015).

Tuke, J.H., *A Memoir* (New York: The Macmillan Company, 1899).

Tuke, J.H., *A Visit to Connaught in the Autumn of 1847* (London: Charles Gilpin, 1848).

Tulloch, H., 'The Family Pictures of Edward Nangle', presentation at Heinrich Böll Memorial Weekend, 2 May 2015.

Vaughan, W.E. (ed.), *A New History Of Ireland, Vol 5: Ireland under the Union,1801–1870* (Oxford: Oxford University Press, 1989).

Waldron, K., *The Archbishops of Tuam 1700–2000* (Tuam: Nordlaw Books, 2008).

Whelan, I., *The Bible War in Ireland* (Dublin: The Lilliput Press, 2005).

Woodham-Smith, C., *The Great Hunger: Ireland 1845-9* (London: Hamish Hamilton, 1962).

Woods, C.J., *Travellers' Accounts as Source Material for Irish Historians* (Dublin: Four Courts Press, 2009).

Newspapers

Connaught Telegraph
Freeman's Journal
Galway Vindicator
Irish Times
Liverpool Mercury
Mayo Constitution
Telegraph
Times

Archives

National Folklore Archives, University College Dublin
O'Donel Papers, National Library of Ireland
Outrage reports (Mayo) and famine files at National Archives of Ireland
Parish Registers and Vestry Books for Dugort, Achill, Representative Church Body Library, Dublin
Relief Commission files, Royal Irish Academy, Dublin
Tuke, G., Diaries 1883-1895, National Library of Ireland
Westport Union minute books and files, National Library of Ireland

Unpublished Theses

Dunn, S.M., 'Little more than a winter home: an historical archaeology of Irish seasonal migration at Slievemore, Achill Island', PhD thesis, Syracuse University, USA, 2008.

Kelley, T.J., 'Trapped between two worlds: Edward Nangle, Achill Island and sectarian competition in Ireland 1800-1862', PhD thesis, Trinity College, Dublin, 2004.

McDonald, T., 'Booleying in Achill, Achillbeg and Corraun: survey, excavation and analysis of booley settlements in the civil parish of Achill', PhD thesis, National University of Ireland Galway, 2014.

Mullowney, P., 'The expansion and decline of the O'Donel Estate, Newport, County Mayo 1785–1852', MA thesis, National University of Ireland Maynooth, 2002.

Ní Ghiobúin, M., 'Social conditions in Achill in the 19th century', PhD thesis, National University of Ireland, Maynooth, 2005.

Thompson, B., 'Footprints on the sand of time: Edward Walter Nangle (1800–1883) and his role in the history of the Achill Island Missionary Colony (1831–1921)', MPhil thesis, University of Wales, 2011.

Zahl, M.J.S., 'The Lion of St Jarlath, John MacHale – Catholic prelate and Irish nationalist', Philosophy thesis, University of Bergen, 2002.

INDEX

Achill Herald 56–8, 67, 72, 74, 96, 103;
Achill Mission, donations and
109; Cashel, removal of stones
157; Catholic confirmation
ceremonies 164–5; criticism of
205–6; death of Matilda Nangle
152; editorship, Nangle and
122–3, 167–8; famine victims,
report on 123; first edition of
56–7; Hall-Nangle
correspondence 79–81; masthead
changes 167, 168; Nicholson,
Asenath 94–5; obituary, Eliza
Nangle 149–50; potato rot,
reasons for 117–18, see also *Achill
Missionary Herald and Western
Witness*
Achill Island 13–14, 15, 18–20, 27, 38,
147; Catholic schools 33, 37, 160,
197; cemetery 152–3; delegation
to Dublin Castle 111; dispensary
services, provision of 177;
evictions 126, 127; housing 38;
islanders 38, 39, 191–2; law and
order, deterioration of 71;
MacHale's visits to 32, 33, 63–4,
69, 159, 185–6, 204; oral history
121, 180, 183; peasant culture and
191; population 122; relief
committee 108–9, 125; salmon
fishery 190; sectarian tensions
and 39, 156–8, 173–5; shipwreck
and 65; storms 27, 66–8; tourism
and 74, 204; winter (1879/80) 201

Achill Mission 11, 22–3, 30; accounts
(1856) 193–4; administration
offices in Dublin 138, 141;
agricultural reclamation and 23,
36, 69, 82, 96, 128, 129; annual
report (1848) 140–1; assaults,
allegations of 27–8; assessment of
73–6, 81; Catholic clergy and 32,
62; Catholics, attitude towards
49–50; colony workers 84;
commercial activities 141;
compassion, lack of 132;
confirmation ceremony 146–8;
conflict within 176–7, 193, 197–8;
conversions and 75, 121; decline
of 187–8, 198, 200, 201–2;
discrimination 85; dispensary 74,
75, 83, 85, 106, 148, 177;
emigration 188; estate
management and 163, 164, 165,
166, 181, 183, 189, 193, 196;
evictions 182, 183; expenditure
75, 141; families and 74–5; famine
relief, conditions for 120–1;
famine response, criticism of
118–19; financial management,
changes in 138; financial pressures
138–9; funds subscribed to 73–4,
75, 81, 140–1, 177–8, 195, 196;
goals/objectives of 35–7, 79, 83,
148; grain shipment and 113;
Great Famine and 84, 85, 90, 106,
107–8, 109–10, 118, 122; hospital
96, 106, 175, 176; hostility

towards 27, 32, 33, 39, 40, 52;
hotel 74, 118; income 140–1, 188,
202–3; infrastructure 30, 74,
79–80, 96, 128, 129, 141;
labourers, payment in food
128–9, 132; Land Act, impact of
202–3; land and employment
offered by 36, 37, 69, 84; land
lease agreements and 166; land
reclamation 20, 22, 23, 36, 69, 82,
83, 128, 129; lands purchased by
161–3, 182–3; literacy and 93, 94,
140; litigation and 197, 198,
199–200; MacHale and 64, 69,
158–9; management committee
138; missionary activities and
194, 199; missionary work,
outsourcing of 164, 165–6, 177–8;
orphanage 76–8, 80; orphans,
expulsion of 77–8, 80; perception
of 31, 210; plan for 20–1; printing
press and 45–6, 56–7; protection
and 32, 62; recantations and 82,
89–90, 108, 121, 143; refinement/
civilised living and 190–1;
reformed priests' asylum 86, 87–8;
relief shops and 132–3; relief work
and 109–10, 113, 122, 141; roles,
conflicting 198; sale of estate 208;
souperism, charge of 119, 121;
stipends, inability to pay 199–200,
201; subletting of lands 162–3,
181, 183; Temporal Affairs
Committee 177; tenants,
treatment of 180–1, 182, 192, 193,
194, 195, 196, 197; trustees 193–4,
196, 202; views on 39–40, 41,
72–3, 92, 94
Achill Mission schools 33, 72–3, 93,
119; children, food and 110,
118–19, 120–1, 128, 133; food

allowances, scantiness of 132;
proselytisation and 120, 133, 159,
160; religious instruction and 119,
133; Sunday school 27;
withdrawal of children from 160
Achill Missionary Herald and Western
Witness 45–6, see also Achill
Herald
Achill Purchase Fund 162
Achill Sound 74, 92, 186, 190; church
consecration 164, 165; Holy
Trinity Church, foundation of
147–8; hotel 130; petty sessions
court 158
Achill Temporal Relief Fund 141
Adams, Isabella 10, 40, 44, 46–7, 48,
59, 124; death of 186, 187; ill
health 177, 186–7; infant school
and 48; obituary 186
Adams, James 10
Adams, Neason 10, 40, 44, 46, 48, 59,
87, 123; Achill Mission hospital
and 175, 176, 177; clothing,
supply of 114, 115, 124; criticism
of 107–8; death of 187; departure
from Achill 187; Dugort
residence, settlement for 187, 194;
famine relief work and 109,
114–15, 124; 'Freize and Brogues'
appeals 115, 124; illness, Eliza
Nangle and 105; Indian meal
distributed by 131; Keel families
and 130–1; medical evidence and
65–6; proselytising texts and
107–8; relief committee treasurer
125; Temporal Affairs Committee
and 177; treasurer, Achill Mission
75–6
Ailt 171, 179, 180
Ailt an Sagart 171
Ailt na mBraintreach 180

Alexander, George 193
Anderson, Christopher 10–11, 14, 15,
    191; *Historical Sketches of the*
    Native Irish 10, 11, 20
Arva, County Cavan 9
Australia 117; emigration schemes
    and 142–3

Baile na hAilte 179
Baker, Revd James 174, 175, 176
Ballina: famine and 12; Nangle and
    Home Mission Society work 22;
    Nangle and MacHale residents in
    24; workhouse 142
Ballycroy 31, 121
Battle of the Stones 156–8
Baylee, Joseph 46–7, 54, 62
Belfast Daily Mercury 194–5
Bell, Mrs (workhouse matron) 142
Bible: Achill Mission converts and 42,
    98; Nangle and 21, 69, 98; Nangle
    family Bible 104–5; Nicholson,
    Asenath and 91
Biddy, Captain 14
bipolar disorder 26, 105–6
Blacker, Murray McGregor 181, 189
Boland, Eavan, 'Famine Roads' 101
booelying (transhumance) 181
Bourke, G.E. 118–19
Boycott, Charles Cunningham 181,
    189, 190
Brassy, Thomas 162
Brett, Henry 98
British Relief Association 136, 137, 138
Bullsmouth 19, 23, 31, 112
Bunnacurry chapel 186
Bunnacurry monastery 160–1, 186;
    building of 156–8; Franciscan
    friars and 160–1
Burke, Catherine 86
Burke, Revd William John 86–7

Cairns, Sir Hugh 194, 196, 197
California, survivors of wreck 176,
    177
Cashel 33, 156–7, 180, 190
Castlebar Board of Guardians 107
Castlebar Courthouse: public debate
    Hughes and Stoney 51–6
Castlebar workhouse 107, 143
Cathaoir an tSolas 172
Catholic Bulletin 208
Catholic Church: converts to
    Protestantism, return of 159;
    Eucharist and 51, 52–3;
    perception of 5;
    transubstantiation and 51, 53,
    54, 56
Catholic clergy: Achill Mission and
    32, 62; 'jumpers' 88; Nangle and
    49; Nangle's views on 159;
    recruited by Nangle 82, 86,
    87–8
Catholic emancipation 5, 167, 200
Catholic nationalism 156
Catholicism: defections from 3, 7, 36,
    40, 56; effects of 5, 7, 73;
    evangelical movement and 4;
    Nangle and 25, 40, 52, 98–9, 140;
    perception of 7, 12, 25, 40
Catholics: conversion to
    Protestantism 3, 7, 36, 40, 56;
    perception of 73
Cavan 3–9; Arva church 9; evangelical
    movement and 3–9; Farnham
    estate schools 5–6; moral
    reformation of the peasantry 5;
    recantations 89
Cavan Association for Promoting the
    Reformation 7
Church of Ireland: disestablishment
    of 199; *Irish Ecclesiastical Gazette*
    and 205–6

coastguards 38; Bullsmouth station
    19, see also Dyer, Commander
    George; Reynolds, Captain
    Francis
Commission of Irish Church
    Temporalities 199
Connaught Telegraph 27–8, 33
Connolly, Revd Michael 33, 39, 43
Corraun 19, 136, 157
Corrymore House, Keem 189
Court of Chancery 197, 198
Croagh Patrick 15, 92, 133
Cruise, Daniel (Resident Magistrate)
    61, 62, 158
Cullen, Paul, Archbishop of Armagh
    156

Dallas, Revd Alexander 165, 188;
    Achill Mission and 165–6; Voice
    from Heaven to Ireland, A 165
Dallas, Anne 165–6
Davis, James 65, 66
de Beaumont, Gustave 16
de Tocqueville, Alexis 16–18, 85
Deansgrange Cemetery 205, 207
Deserted Village 117, 181, 182
Devon Commission 82–5; Nangle's
    evidence 82–5; report 85
dispensary: Achill Island and 177;
    Achill Mission and 74, 75, 83, 85,
    106, 148, 177; discrimination and
    85
Doherty, Margaret 63, see also
    Reynolds, Margaret (née Doherty)
Dooagh 172, 181, 182, 197
Dooega 136, 172
Dookinella 32, 159, 164, 180
Dugort 19, 190; cemetery 209–10;
    hotel 74; inquest 63, 66; mission
    school 33; national school 35;
    parish register 88–9; recantations,

list of 89; St Thomas' Church 182,
    184, 186, 188, 206–7, 208, 209
Dugort Bay: cargo of meal and
    112–13; Nangle's arrival at 22;
    shipwreck at 113
Duncan, Revd Joseph 22–3
Dwyer, Revd James 64, 109
Dyer, Commander George 61, 71, 75

emigration 70, 117, 188; Earl Grey
    scheme 142–3, 144
Encumbered Estates Act (1849)
    155–6, 173, 183
Encumbered Estates Commissioners
    162
Encumbered Estates Courts 161, 178,
    183
Established Church 24–5, 199
Eucharist: Catholicism and 51, 52–3;
    doctrine of 51; Nangle's views on
    53–4; offensive illustration and
    52, 53; reformed church and 51,
    54
evangelical movement 3–8, 20, 165;
    critique of 206
evictions 126, 127–8, 131, 141, 173,
    178–80; Gregory clause and 128,
    141, 173; Pike and 178–80; protest
    ploy 180

famine, west of Ireland and 12–13, 15
Farnham estate, recantations 89
Farnham, John Maxwell-Barry, 5th
    Baron 3, 4–5; conversion of
    tenants 6–7; estate schools and
    5–6; moral agent appointed by
    7–8; moral reform of tenants 5–7
Farnham, Lucy Maxwell-Barry, Lady
    3, 7
Farren, Captain 144, 145
Ferrall, Fergus, Chief Constable 61

Fetherstonhaugh, Sarah 167, *see also*
Nangle, Sarsh (*née*
Fetherstonhaugh)
Finsheen 182
Fishery Bill (1860) 190
flax cultivation 127, 131
folklore 172, 208, 179–80
food: free trade and 111, 112; school
children and 110, 118–19, 120;
shortages 107, 111, 116, 127
Franciscan friars 160–1
Franklin, Lady Jane 30–2, 34; Achill
Island and 39; Achill Mission,
views on 39–40, 41; exploration/
travels and 40–1
Franklin, Sir John 30, 40
free trade 111, 112
Freeman's Journal: Cavan, conversions
and 3; MacHale's death 203;
MacHale's elevation to Tuam
28–9; MacHale's letter to 158;
Reynolds' murder trial 71
Frost, Revd Solomon 87, 88, 98

Gallagher, Revd Michael 120
Galway Vindicator 188
Gardeners' Chronicle 97
Gibbons, Revd 144
Gladstone, William Ewart 198–9, 202,
203
Glendarary House, Achill 189
Grealis, Neal 145
Great Famine: Achill Island and
108–9, 210; Achill Mission and
84, 85, 90, 106, 107–8, 122; burials
and 131; deaths 116; emigration
117; evictions and 126, 127;
'Freize and Brogues' appeals 115,
124; government policies and 111,
112; MacHale and 113–14;
Nangle's reaction to 98, 99, 114,

117–18; potato crop, failure of 97,
98, 110; starvation and 123
Great Famine/Achill Island: famine
relief donation 120; Great Famine
and 108–9, 123
Gregory clause 128, 141, 173, 181–2
Gregory XVI, Pope 24
Grey, Charles (Grey, 2nd Earl) 12;
emigration scheme 142, 143, 144

Hall, Anna Maria and Samuel 72–4,
79; Achill Mission, assessment of
72, 73–8; Achill orphanage and
77–8; *Ireland: Its Scenery and
Character* 73; public disagreement
with Nangle 80–1
Hamilton, George 197
Heanue, Michael 174
Hector, Alexander 189–90
Henry, Revd James 159–60, 173, 175,
190; *California* survivors and 176,
177; Dooagh national school and
197; evictions 178–9; fundraising
and 160; Medical Charities Act
and 177; poor law commissioners
and 177; tenants, Achill Mission
and 180–1
Henry, Lieutenant (emigration agent)
142, 143
Hiland, Bridget 107
Holme, Samuel 162
Holy Trinity Church 147
Home Mission Society 22
Hughes, Revd James 16–17, 29, 51, 64,
71; accusations made by 52;
Nangle's accusations and 71; public
debate with Stoney 52, 54–5

Inishbiggle 19, 121, 141, 151, 182, 190
Ireland: conditions in 12–13, 16,
17–18; potato crop, reliance on

85; poverty, causes of 17–18;
    sectarian tensions in 5, 24
Irish Church Act 198–9, 200; Nangle's
    views on 198–9
Irish Church Advocate 204, 205
Irish Ecclesiastical Gazette 205–6
Irish language 10–11; missionaries
    and 20, 191
Irish Times 203

Jackson, Revd 144
Johnston, Isaac 163
'jumpers' 64, 88, 145

Keel 63, 126; drownings 130–1;
    evictions 126, 127; mission school
    33; national school 136; shipwreck
    65
Keem 162–3, 181, 183, 189
Kildownet 172, 179; burial dispute
    and 173–5; cemetery 174; school
    136
Kinvara, County Clare 86
Krause, William 7–8, 11

land: agitation 173, 182; clearances
    173, 180; leases 20, 82, 83, 163,
    166, 173, 181, 182–3; reclamation
    20, 22, 23, 36, 69, 82, 83, 128, 129;
    system 17, 18
Land Law (Ireland) Act (1881) 202
landlords: evictions and 127–8;
    Gregory clause and 128; tenants
    and 17–18, 84, 85, 126–7; west of
    Ireland and 17–18, 127
Lavelle, Bridget 42–4; deposition
    made by 43–4
Lavelle, Martin 65
Lavelle, Michael 70
Lavelle, Nancy 66, 71
Lavelle, Owen 178

Lavelle, Pat 65, 66, 71
Lieder, Johann 30
Liverpool Mercury 196
Loftus, Revd (Dunmore) 52
London Orphan Institution 70
Longley, Thomas 138
Lowe, Revd Edward 87, 138
Lydney Lass, grain cargo and 113
Lyons, John Patrick, Dean of Killala
    31

McCormack, William 157
McDermott, Bonaventure, OFM 160
McGreal, Mícheál 66
MacHale, John, Archbishop of Tuam
    7, 12, 18, 203–4; Achill Island
    visits 32, 33, 63–4, 69, 185–6;
    Achill Mission and 64, 69, 158–9;
    British perception of 24;
    Bunnacurry chapel and 186;
    Bunnacurry monastery and
    156–8, 186; Bunnacurry property
    purchased by 155, 156;
    confirmation ceremonies and 159,
    164–5; converts to Protestantism
    and 159; death of 203; diocese,
    tour of 29; famine (1830s) and 12;
    government policy, criticism of
    114; Great Famine and 113–14;
    installation as Archbishop 28;
    land purchased on Achill Island
    155–6, 161, 162; Nangle and 24–5,
    49, 64, 115, 158, 186, 204–5;
    national school system and 34, 35;
    Protestantism, views on 24;
    rhetoric 29; temperament 24, 29
McIlwaine, Revd William 148
McMahon, Anita 208
McNamara, Revd George 87–8, 89, 98
McNamara, Mary and Bridget 142,
    143–4, 146

McNamara, Thomas and Honora 143
Malley, Michael 145
Mangan, Bridget 70
Mavis of Dumfries: raid on 116; wheat
    cargo 116
Maxwell, Somerset 193
Maynooth Grant Bill 98; Nangle's
    reaction to 98–9
Maynooth seminary 199
Mayo: famine and starvation 116;
    food shortages 111; starvation
    and 111
Mayo Constitution 13, 175, 179
Medical Charities Act (1851) 177
Monaghan, Revd Malachy 109, 111
Montgomery, Dr 176, 177
Murray, Daniel, Archbishop of Dublin
    120
Mweelin 96, 129, 141, 174, 182;
    infrastructure 165; training
    school 165, 185, 188

Nangle, Catherine 185
Nangle, Edward Neason 48–9
Nangle, Revd Edward 8–9; absences
    from Achill 48, 59, 67, 78, 99,
    103–4, 122, 123; accusations
    made by 145–6, 186; Achill house,
    letting of 202; Achill Island and
    18, 19–20; Achill Island lands and
    161–3; Achill islanders and 62–3;
    allegations made against 194–5,
    196; annual visits to Achill 185,
    189–91; bigotry and 195, 196;
    biography 205, 206; Catholic
    clergy criticised by 137; Catholic
    clergy recruited by 82, 86, 87–8;
    Catholicism and 25, 40, 52, 98–9,
    140; Catholics, attitude towards
    49–50; Christian colony and 11;
    compassion, lack of 206;

confirmations at Dugort 146–8;
    criticism of 120–1, 137, 193,
    205–6; death of 205; departure
    from Achill 167–9; Devon
    Commission and 82–3, 84–5;
    Dublin and 14, 105, 109, 115, 125,
    202; empathy, lack of 47–8, 118,
    169, 206; family background 9;
    famine relief committee,
    exclusion from 125; fundraising
    and 48, 73, 78, 99, 103–4, 122,
    123, 134, 139; funds, Achill
    Mission and 75–7, 120–1; goals of
    Achill Mission 35–7, 148; Halls'
    accusations, response to 79–80;
    headstone 207; Hughes-Stoney
    debate and 52, 55; ill health 9–10,
    26–7, 78, 99, 103–4, 105–6, 115,
    138; illustration, Eucharist and 52,
    53; Indian meal shipment and
    139–40; influences on 11, 20; land
    leased by 20, 96, 128; MacHale
    and 24 5, 49, 64, 115, 158, 186,
    204–5; marriage to Sarah
    Fetherstonhaugh 167; memorial
    plaque 184, 206–7; mission
    schools and 29; moral
    degradation, famine and 141;
    national school system and 34, 35;
    obituaries 205–6; orphanage
    funds and 76–7; orphans,
    treatment of 77–8; perception of
    31–2; printing press and 45–6,
    56–7; Protestant establishment
    and 81, 137, 206; public
    denunciations of 193; publications
    56–7; Reynolds' murder trial and
    70–1; school children, food and
    119; self-reflection and 68, 69;
    Skreen, assignment to 166–7, 187;
    'soul-buyer' 120; souperism,

charge of 119, 121; speaking
engagements 68, 69, 78, 99,
103–4; temperament 9, 14–15, 29,
124, 150; transubstantiation and
56, 58; trustee, Achill Mission and
193–4; verbal fluency and 14–15,
29, 68–9; vision for colony 11, 15,
20, 22, 148, 161–2, 168; Westport
Union meeting and 144–5; wife's
anxieties, attitude towards 47–8,
see also Achill Mission
Nangle, Eliza (*née* Warner) 13–14, 15,
23, 27, 37–8; anxiety and 47–8,
59–60; bookkeeping, Achill
Mission and 76, 150; children 83;
child's illness and 47; death of
149; deaths of infants 31, 49,
58–9, 60, 105; funeral 150–1;
husband's absences 59, 67, 78, 99,
104, 150; ill health and 104, 105;
memorial plaque 184; obituary
149–50; school children, feeding
of 150; visitors, mistrust of 91,
93–4
Nangle family: Bible 104–5; burial
place 31, 149, 152–3; scrapbook
151–2
Nangle, Frances 13, 22, 152
Nangle, George 58, 83, 149, 150, 152,
153, 154
Nangle, Henrietta (Henie) 22, 152
Nangle, Henry 150
Nangle, Matilda (Tilly) 22, 151–2,
153, 154
Nangle, Sarah (*née* Fetherstonhaugh)
167, 185, 201
Nangle, Walter 9
Nangle, William 70, 150
Napier, Joseph 193, 197, 198
National Board of Education 34, 35
national school system 33–4, 37;

MacHale's opposition to 34;
Nangle's opposition to 34;
religious instruction and 33–4
Newport 15, 16, 18, 20, 51; flax
cultivation and 127, 131
Nicholson, Asenath 91–5, 129–34,
191, 206; Achill Mission and
91–5, 132–3; Bible readings and
91; clothing provided by 132; food
distribution and 129; meeting
with the Nangles 91, 93–4;
mission schools food, scantiness
of 132
Night of the Big Wind 67–8
Nottingham (steamer) 13–14, 15
Nugent, James (Justice of the Peace)
61

O'Brien, Revd John 87, 88, 98
O'Donnell, James (schoolmaster) 35
O'Donnell, Sir Richard 17, 125; Achill
Island lands and 161, 162; Cashel
incident and 157; flax cultivation
and 127, 131; land leased to
Nangle 20, 96, 128, 182; lands,
sale of 162, 166
orphans/orphanage: Achill
Mission and 75, 76–8, 80; Earl
Grey emigration scheme and
142–3, 144; expulsion of
orphans 77–8, 80;
proselytising and 76

peasantry: Catholicism and 73;
conditions and 194; moral
reformation of 5, 21; plight of 12;
proselytism and 137
Peel, Sir Robert 82, 98
Pike, William 162, 163, 172, 189;
death of 203; evictions and
178–80; Kildownet burial dispute

and 174–5; Nangle's criticism of
174–5
Plunket, Thomas, Bishop of Tuam:
church consecrations and 164,
165, 185; confirmation
ceremonies and 146–8, 164, 185;
Nangle assigned to Skreen by
166–7
potatoes: blight and 97, 98; crop
failure 110, 111, 141; reliance on
85
printing press 45
proselytism 156, 165, 206; Achill
Mission and 40–1, 42, 49, 76, 108;
Catholic clergy and 137; mission
schools and 120, 133, 159, 160;
peasantry and 137
Protestant Association 68
Protestant converts: burial dispute
and 174; MacHale and 159; public
declarations and 159
Protestant establishment, Nangle and
81, 137, 206
Protestant evangelical movement 4, 5
Protestant Penny Magazine 53
Protestant Reformation 4, 7, 68
Protestantism: conversions to 3, 7, 36,
40, 56, 121–2; inducements to
convert 80; MacHale's views on
24; mission schools and 29;
temporary conversions 121–2,
133
Protestants, perception of 73

Quakers see Society of Friends

recantations: Achill Mission and 82,
89–90, 108, 121, 143; Catholic
clergy and 86, 87
Reynolds family 70
Reynolds, Francis 70

Reynolds, Captain Francis 27, 32;
attack and 65; death of 61, 62, 66;
exhumation 61, 62, 67; House of
Lords Select Committee and
62–3; inquest into death 61–2, 63,
65–6; reinterment 68; shipwreck
and 65; trial of murder accused
70–1
Reynolds, Margaret (née Doherty)
38–9, 69–70; death of husband 61,
62, 63, 65, 66
Routh, Sir Randolph 111, 112, 125
Russell, Lord John 113, 114

St Thomas' Church, Dugort 182,
184–5, 186, 188, 208; cemetery
209–10; Nangle memorial plaque
184, 206–7
Savage, Robert 74, 92, 125, 130, 132,
145
Savage, Susan 92, 132
schools: national schools 35, 36, 37,
137, 197, see also Achill Mission
schools
second reformation 4, 5
sectarian tensions 5, 24; Achill Island
and 39
Seddall, Henry 205, 206
Seymour, Revd Charles 138, 139
Sheridan, John P. 153
shipwrecks 113; California 176;
coastguard and 38, 65; protection
of cargo 65; William & George
64–5
Skreen, County Sligo 166–7, 187
Slievemore 19–20, 182, 209;
depopulation of 181; Deserted
Village 117, 181, 182
Slievemore Hotel 153
Sligo, John George Browne, 3rd
Marquis of 17, 137, 162;

confrontation with Nangle 137; famine relief and 136

Society of Friends 126, 130, 131–2

Society for Irish Church Missions 165, 166, 177–8, 185; withdrawal from Achill Mission 188, 195

souperism 121–2; Achill Mission and 119, 121; Nangle and 119, 121

Stanley, Edward, Chief Secretary 33

Stoney, Revd William Baker 15, 16, 17, 22, 51, 148; public debate with Hughes 52, 54–5

Strzelecki, Paul Edmund de, Count 136–7, 138, 141

Synod of Thurles 156

Tablet, The 120

Telegraph, The: Adams, criticism of 107–8; evictions, Pike and 178; Nangle's illness 103–4; Night of the Big Wind 67; potato crop failure 97–8, 110; starvation 107, 111, 116

tenants: Achill Mission and 180–1, 182, 192, 193, 194, 195–6, 197; landlords and 17–18, 84, 85, 126–7; 'three Fs' and 202

Times, The 83–4, 110

tithes 199

tourism 74, 204

transubstantiation: Catholic Church and 51, 53, 54, 56; Nangle's views on 56, 58

Tuam 26, 188, 203

Tuke, James Hack 126–7, 131

Vesey, Molly 92, 132

Warner, Grace 22, 23, 31, 32, 59, 150; Achill, return to 153–4; care of nephew George 153; death of 153

Warner, Patience 23

west of Ireland: conditions in 12–13; famine (1830s) and 12–13, 15, 17; landlords and 17, 127

Westport 136–7; deaths 116; relief committee 112

Westport Union 116, 127, 136–7, 138; accusations made by Nangle 145–6; board meeting at 144–5; emigration scheme and 142, 143; Protestant inmates, treatment of 144–6

Wilde, William 97

William & George (brig) 64–5

Wilson, John 195

workhouses: Ballina 142; Castlebar 107, 143; emigration schemes and 142–3, *see also* Westport Union